No Godforsaken Place

T&T Clark Studies in Social Ethics, Ethnography, and Theologies

Over the last half century, there have been numerous calls for Christian theology and ethics to take human experience seriously—to delve into particular economic, socio-political, racial-ethnic, and cultural contexts from which theological and moral imagination arises. Yet actual theologies that draw upon descriptive-rich, qualitative methods—methods that place such particularity at the center of inquiry and performance—are few and scattered. **T&T Clark Studies in Social Ethics, Ethnography, and Theologies** is a monograph series that addresses this gap in the literature by providing a publishing home for timely ethnographically driven theological and ethical investigations of an expansive array of pressing social issues, ranging from armed conflict to racism to health care inequities to sexuality/gender and discrimination to the marginalization of persons with disabilities. The scope of the series projects, taken together, is at once global and intensely local, with the central organizing conviction that ethnography provides not only information to plug into a theology, but a valid and vibrant way of *doing* theology.

No Godforsaken Place

Prison Chaplaincy, Karl Barth, and Practicing Life in Prison

Sarah C. Jobe

LONDON • NEW YORK • OXFORD • NEW DELHI • SYDNEY

T&T CLARK

Bloomsbury Publishing Plc, 50 Bedford Square, London, WC1B 3DP, UK
Bloomsbury Publishing Inc, 1359 Broadway, New York, NY 10018, USA
Bloomsbury Publishing Ireland, 29 Earlsfort Terrace, Dublin 2, D02 AY28, Ireland

BLOOMSBURY, T&T CLARK and the T&T Clark logo are trademarks
of Bloomsbury Publishing Plc

First published in Great Britain 2026

Copyright © Sarah C. Jobe, 2026

Sarah C. Jobe has asserted her right under the Copyright, Designs and
Patents Act, 1988, to be identified as Author of this work.

For legal purposes the Acknowledgments on p. ix constitute an
extension of this copyright page.

Cover Design © Susannah Conner
Cover image: Barbwire stock photo © manfredxy / iStock

All rights reserved. No part of this publication may be: i) reproduced or transmitted in any form, electronic or mechanical, including photocopying, recording or by means of any information storage or retrieval system without prior permission in writing from the publishers; or ii) used or reproduced in any way for the training, development or operation of artificial intelligence (AI) technologies, including generative AI technologies. The rights holders expressly reserve this publication from the text and data mining exception as per Article 4(3) of the Digital Single Market Directive (EU) 2019/790.

Bloomsbury Publishing Plc does not have any control over, or responsibility for, any third-party websites referred to or in this book. All internet addresses given in this book were correct at the time of going to press. The author and publisher regret any inconvenience caused if addresses have changed or sites have ceased to exist, but can accept no responsibility for any such changes.

A catalogue record for this book is available from the British Library.

Library of Congress Cataloging-in-Publication Data
Names: Jobe, Sarah, 1981- author
Title: No godforsaken place : prison chaplaincy, Karl Barth, and practicing life in prison / Sarah C. Jobe.
Description: 1. | London ; New York : T&T Clark, 2025. | Series: T&T Clark studies in social ethics, ethnography and theologies | Includes bibliographical references and index. | Summary: "How is it possible to inhabit the atonement? How do we enact Jesus' prior act of reconciling the world to God? What does it mean to live and die with Christ the salvation of the cosmos in our own bodies and lives today? In the tradition of theological ethnography, this work brings together theological and biblical reflection with data from a two-year, collaborative ethnography on current and former prison chaplains"–Provided by publisher.
Identifiers: LCCN 2025020168 | ISBN 9780567719492 hardback | ISBN 9780567719485 paperback | ISBN 9780567719515 pdf | ISBN 9780567719508 epub
Subjects: LCSH: Barth, Karl, 1886-1968 | Atonement | Reconciliation–Religious aspects–Christianity | Prison chaplains | Prisoners–Religious life
Classification: LCC BX4827.B3 J58 2025
LC record available at https://lccn.loc.gov/2025020168

ISBN:		
	HB:	978-0-5677-1949-2
	PB:	978-0-5677-1948-5
	ePDF:	978-0-5677-1951-5
	eBook:	978-0-5677-1950-8

Series: T&T Clark Studies in Social Ethics, Ethnography and Theologies

Typeset by Integra Software Services Pvt. Ltd.
Printed and bound in Great Britain

For product safety related questions contact productsafety@bloomsbury.com.

To find out more about our authors and books visit www.bloomsbury.com
and sign up for our newsletters.

*In memory
of all who have lived, worked, died, and persisted at
the North Carolina Correctional Institution for Women*

CONTENTS

Acknowledgments ix

Prelude   Inhabiting Salvation 1
    Living and Dying with Jesus in Prison

1 Into the Witness Box 5
    Methods and Motivation for Writing

2 The Crisis of Presence 43
    Incarnating God in Prison

3 Risking Atonement 73
    Reconciling Race, Rank, and Religion

4 Counting the Cost 107
    Being Made Sin for the Sake of Salvation

Interlude   The Crucifixion and 58 Other Carceral Deaths 143

5 Recollecting Death 159
    Dying with Jesus in Prison

6 Inhabiting the Resurrection 173
    The Work of Life after Death

Postlude   A Practical Soteriology   207
  Penal Atonement in Prison

Works Cited 220
Index of Subjects, Authors, and Biblical Texts 229
Index of Stories and Transcripts 234

ACKNOWLEDGMENTS

First and foremost, I would like to thank the twenty prison chaplains who were brave to go on record about what they have witnessed in America's prisons. I have experienced your stories as a heavy gift, and I am honored to have been trusted to hold and tell them. To those who read each word with me as I wrote—Jerusha Neal, Eugene Rogers, and Douglas Campbell—I have been shaped by your creativity and care as much as this work has. Thank you for encouraging me to write what I needed to write in the style that the data demanded. Because of your flexible mentorship and belief in me, I know theology to be freedom and collecting stories of death to be the work of life. Thank you to Shelly Rambo, Warren Kinghorn, Todd Whitmore, and AnneMarie Mingo for the example of your own interdisciplinary scholarship and the support you gave to this work; publication would not have been possible without you. Susannah Long Conner got this book (and me) over the finish line with the usual amount of joy, wit, and excellence! Finally, these stories and the world in which it was possible for me to hold them would not exist without the circle of women who comprised my life during the course of this project—Naomi and Fay Schwankl-Jobe, Lauren Winner, Casey Stanton, and Anathea Portier-Young—you have been life in death for me.

This book was made possible through the generosity of institutions. I am indebted to Duke University Divinity School for years of supporting my education, my scholarship, and my vocation in prison education. I also wish to acknowledge grant support from the Louisville Institute and from P.E.O. International. Finally, I wish to thank the thousands of incarcerated women who have allowed me to be their chaplain. I have learned how to practice persistent life in the face of prison death from you.

Prelude

Inhabiting Salvation:

Living and Dying with Jesus in Prison

How can that which has happened once, even if it did happen for us, be recognized to-day as having happened for us, seeing it does not happen to-day? Or, to put it another way, how can that which happened once have happened for us when we who live to-day were not there and could not experience it ourselves? Or, to put it yet another way, how can we to-day exist as those for whom it happened when it happened once and not to-day? The only answer which it seems we can give is the profoundly ambiguous and unsettling one that it can do so only as we accept it from others, from the tradition of the Church and ultimately from the biblical witnesses; that it is, in fact, the case that "Jesus Christ for us" is valid to-day, and is relevant to us, only as we accept what is told to us as true in this sense. But how can we hold to be true what we have not seen and cannot attest to be true? Especially a truth which is so decisive for ourselves as that of the then being and activity of Jesus Christ for us to-day and in our place?
—KARL BARTH, *CHURCH DOGMATICS IV/1*, 287

This is a book about life-in-death work, what the Christian tradition has often called salvation or atonement. What is the connection between what

Jesus did in first-century Judea and the cosmic and social order of life today? Or put differently, how can the scandal that the Son of God became the Prodigal Son—or that the Judge became a Judged One—be anything but strange, not to mention life-giving or life-sustaining?[1] Whether it is the question of time and history or the question of God's radical otherness, Karl Barth names that there is a wide chasm between the work of Jesus Christ and the ones for whom Jesus Christ acted. This book seeks to stand in that chasm and answer, in granular ethnographic description:

> *How is it possible to inhabit the atonement? How do we enact Jesus' prior act of reconciling the world to God? What does it mean to live and die with Christ the salvation of the cosmos in our own bodies and lives today?*

Barth struggles to answer these questions, though he continues to ask them all the way through volume four of *Church Dogmatics,* what he titles, "The Doctrine of Reconciliation" or, alternately translated, the Doctrine of Atonement.[2] Yet, even as he struggles in his dogmatics to bridge the gulf between Jesus' arrest, trial, execution, and life today, Barth begins a ministry of preaching and pastoral care inside of Basel Prison that he will continue for the entire ten years that it takes him to write his Doctrine of Reconciliation. The chapel at Basel Prison becomes his most consistent place to preach in the decade in which he writes his doctrine of atonement.[3] As he writes volume after volume detailing the saving work of Christ, Barth moves in and out of prison.[4] When Barth can no longer visit the prison due

---

[1] Karl Barth, *Church Dogmatics* IV/1, trans. G.W. Bromiley (Edinburgh: T&T Clark, 1956), 289.

[2] Barth names the entirety of Volume IV of *Church Dogmatics* "The Doctrine of Reconciliation." In the standard English translation, Bromiley translates *Versöhnung* as both "reconciliation" and "atonement" depending on the context, but in Barth's original text, there was no distinction. For a note from the translator, see the introduction to the volume in *CD* IV/1, vii.

[3] There are two volumes containing Barth's sermons at Basel Prison, originally collected and typeset by the men incarcerated at that prison. The sermons are dated and arranged in chronological order, allowing the reader to correlate Barth's prison preaching to his work in *Church Dogmatics.* See Karl Barth, *Call for God: New Sermons from Basel Prison* (London: SCM Press LTD, 1967) and Karl Barth, *Deliverance to the Captives* (Eugene: Wipf & Stock Publishers, 1978). One also gets the sense in Barth's personal correspondence during this time period that his friends and colleagues understand him to have a close connection to Basel Prison. For example, in personal correspondence with Ernst Wolf in 1961, he says simply, "I'll be preaching in the usual place" and presumes his friend will know that he refers to the prison. See Karl Barth, *Letters: 1961–1968,* ed. Jurgen Fangmeier and Hinrich Stoevesandt, trans. Geoffrey A. Bromiley (Grand Rapids: William B. Eerdmans Publishing Company, 1981), 16.

[4] Christiane Tietz, *Karl Barth: A Life in Conflict* (Oxford: Oxford University Press, 2021), 344.

to his declining health, incarcerated people used their home leave passes to visit him instead.[5]

Attention to the passion of Jesus Christ directs one toward prisons because the drama of salvation happens inside the story of his arrest, trial, conviction, death sentence, execution, and release from carceral death through the resurrection. Because prisons continue to be places steeped in both social and physical death, prisons press the question of why and how the person and work of Christ make any real difference in life today.[6] The carceral is the original site of Jesus' saving work, and the continuation of carceral spaces (and the death inherent to them) presses the efficacy of Christ's work to its logical breaking point. Barth seems to know this. On the same page where he asks the above questions, he quotes Angelius Silesius' *Cherubinishcher Wandersmann* as another way to name the question at stake:

> Were Christ a thousand times to Bethlehem come,
> And yet not born in thee, 'twould spell thy doom.
> Golgotha's cross, it cannot save from sin,
> Except for thee that cross be raised within.
> I say, it helps thee not that Christ is risen,
> If thou thyself art still in death's dark prison.[7]

I say, it helps thee not that Christ is risen, if thou thyself art still in death's dark prison. Golgotha, the site of one person's state-sponsored execution, has no innate power to save from sin, particularly if one is still trapped in the clutches of state-sponsored death.

What does Jesus' life after death in state custody have to do with life and death in state custody today? What does it matter if Jesus risked arrest, was executed, and was released from state custody through the resurrection for people who are still in prison—as incarcerated people or as prison staff—today? And what do those carceral lives, deaths, and freedoms mean for the whole of the cosmos? This book seeks to answer those questions from prison: the same site from which both Jesus and Barth sought to answer them. And I have sought to answer them using the same methods as both Barth and Jesus: by bringing myself in and out of prison to bear witness to carceral life and death in myself, in incarcerated people, in prison chaplains, and in other prison staff. I will embark on what Barth says above is the "profoundly ambiguous and unsettling" act of depending on the witness of

---

[5]Martin Schwartz, "Karl Barth in der Strafanstalt," *Kirchenblatt für die reformierte Schweiz* 125 (1969): 210–13. Available at http://barthresearch.org/barth/cgi-bin/resultaat.cgi?searchid=21339&taal=Eng&zoekmet=wildiid&zoeknaar=artikel&searchvalue=17962.
[6]Joshua Price, *Prisons and Social Death* (New Brunswick: Rutgers University Press, 2015).
[7]Angelus Silesius, *Angelus Silesius, Cherubinischer Wandersmann*. Vol. 135 (M. Niemeyer, 1895), 61–3. As translated in *CD* IV/1, 287.

other people through ethnographic research, the witness of the church in theologians like Barth who have come before me, and the biblical witness to the story of Jesus to try to work out *how can we to-day exist as those for whom* Jesus was arrested, tried, convicted, sentenced, executed, and freed.[8]

Sarah Jobe, Durham, All Souls Day 2022
Revised on Saint Peter in Chains Day 2024

---

[8] Or, as Barth phrases the question again in this same section: "How are we going to apprehend Jesus Christ, or rather, how are we going to apprehend ourselves in relation to Him, ourselves as those for whom that has taken place which has taken place in him?" (*CD* IV/1, 289–90).

1

Into the Witness Box:

Methods and Motivation for Writing

> *The essence of their vocation is that God makes them His witnesses ... their calling means that ... God summons them into the witness-box as those who know.*
> —KARL BARTH, *CHURCH DOGMATICS* IV/3.2, 575–6

I wrote in black sharpie in the center of the paper, "Sgt. Wilson committed suicide on Memorial Day 2022."[1] A yard of white butcher paper lay on the floor in front of me. I wrote again, "He resuscitated a woman who overdosed the week before."

I had spent the week listening to officers on his shift talk about his baritone voice, quick laughter, and timeliness in arriving each dusk to relieve dayshift. Just two days prior, his wife had hugged my neck against a backdrop of officers in dress uniform at his formal Department of Public Safety funeral. State and national flags hung above the altar of the country church, and the Color Guard performed their choreography. His memorial was saturated by his work at the prison, but there was no mention of the drug epidemic

---

[1] All names of prison staff, prison chaplains, and incarcerated people in this study have been changed. In some instances, the genders and locations of people and their prisons have also been changed. Additionally, dates of major incidents have sometimes been changed. At the same time, the original language of chaplains has been retained in direct citations as closely as possible. For instance, in the quote above, I wrote "committed suicide." While I now use the phrase, "died by suicide," in my own professional practice, I report the way the page read.

sweeping the prison during the funeral. No one said that his shift was under investigation. No one mentioned that one of his officers had been dismissed that week. No one speculated that perhaps incarcerated people and prison staff were using at higher rates to deal with the impact of two and a half years of Covid lockdowns, Covid deaths, and wave after wave of disease. The nursing staff from his previous post sat together. The officers from his current shift sat together. The prison administration all sat in front, and I sat in the back with the chaplain whom I was training to replace me. We honored Sgt. Wilson as a leader among us. We did not name that prison might have hastened his death.[2]

I was sitting on the floor of my home office. I wrote again, "Tara, overdose, died with her unborn son." I wrote, "Wendi, kicked to death." I paused. I thought about one of the chaplains in this study and her description of what happened when she left prison chaplaincy after more than a decade of work inside.

Chaplain Love:

> You're mediating a lot, and it's just coming at you.
> And you're having to ...
> I think that what happened was
> there's,
> there was a backlog of grief.
> That really was not unleashed fully ... until I left.
> Tremendous grief that I carried.
> About that place and,
> seeing what,
> what you see every day.
>
> Yeah.
>
> I ...

---

[2] There is substantial research documenting the health impacts of prisons on the people working inside of them. See M.A. Cooperstein, "Correction officers: The forgotten police force," *Pennsylvania Psychology Quarterly* 61, no. 5 (2001): 7–23; National Institute of Justice, Justice Department. "Correctional Officer Safety and Wellness Literature Synthesis," *Government. Justice Department*, December 31, 2016. https://www.govinfo.gov/app/details/GOVPUB-J28-PURL-gpo84572; Steven J. Stack and Olga Tsoudis, "Suicide risk among correctional officers: A logistic regression analysis," *Archives of Suicide research* 3, no. 3 (1997): 183–6; Peter Finn, "Correctional officer stress-a cause for concern and additional help," *Federal Probation* 62 (1998): 65; Gaylene S. Armstrong and Marie L. Griffin, "Does the job matter? Comparing correlates of stress among treatment and correctional staff in prisons," *Journal of Criminal Justice* 32, no. 6 (2004): 577–92; Caitlin Finney, Erene Stergiopoulos, Jennifer Hensel, Sarah Bonato, and Carolyn S. Dewa, "Organizational stressors associated with job stress and burnout in correctional officers: A systematic review," *BMC Public Health* 13 (2013): 1–13.

tell you the truth, I don't even know fully how to talk about it.

I think it's …
We …
we don't talk about it so much.
We didn't talk about it too much as chaplains, I can tell you that, in our chaplain meetings.³

*There was a backlog of grief that was not fully unleashed until I left.*⁴ My throat constricted. I had served as a prison educator for fourteen years and as a prison chaplain for eleven. I had just finished my last shift before nine months of extended leave in which I hoped to write this book and heal from what I had witnessed while working in prison during the Covid-19 pandemic. I wrote in quick succession:

"LaTasha died of COVID."
"Linda's bloody eyes as she gave me the owl."
"Barbara's daughter kidnapped."
"Lauren's daughter kidnapped."
"That dead 4yo girl, Cassie's."
"Jocelyn drugged for 2 years, always waking to men on top of her."
"The woman who died of cancer with her unset broken arm."
"That lovely Wiccan woman, overdosed. Her boyfriend killed a man the day I met her."
"The dismembered body on the street in front of the prison. Women's memories of their dead sons during that lockdown."

My list stretched on, and in fifteen minutes I had filled the yard of paper before me. Prison chaplaincy is death work.

Many forms of chaplaincy involve death work. In their introduction to chaplaincy, Naomi Paget and Janet McCormack note that chaplains serving

---

³Interview with the author on March 12, 2021.
⁴Throughout this text, I will lift a phrase from a cited interview transcript and repeat the phrase in italics before going on to explain the phrase further. This mode of writing is meant to replicate the interview process, inviting the reader into the texture of ethnographic interviewing. I was taught tactics for collaborative ethnographic interviewing by Glenn Hinson, Associate Professor of Anthropology at the University of North Carolina, Chapel Hill. One interview tactic is to simply repeat back to one's conversation partner something that the person has just said. The repetition reflects a person's wisdom back to them, honoring that the words are worthy of repetition and attention. More often than not, a person will explain what they mean by the phrase without being asked directly to elaborate. Even if the person does not elaborate, the repetition creates a reflective silence, helping to make the interview feel more like a conversation and less like an interrogation. By replicating the method here in the written text, I am both indicating to the reader what in the transcript most caught my attention and inviting the reader into the conversational practices that were foundational in collecting the transcripts presented here.

in a variety of institutions from hospitals to the military make "death notifications" as part of their official job responsibilities, delivering the news of a loved one's death to their family members in person whenever possible.[5] Alongside this basic task of death notification, chaplains from universities to businesses are often sought in moments of crisis that involve death—terminal illness, death of a loved one, suicide, shootings, and the aftermath of natural disasters.[6] In her book on hospital chaplaincy, Wendy Cadge notes that in every interview she conducted with ICU staff and chaplains, death was one of the most common topics even though she did not ask a single direct question about death.[7] Hospital chaplains were "naming death, facilitating conversations about death, and accompanying patients and families through the process."[8] They "work with dead bodies, facilitate trips to the morgue, lead memorial services and other institution-wide death rituals (which never include dead bodies), and act as memory-keepers for families and staff alike."[9] Ronit Stahl's account of the entanglement of the United States government with matters of faith through the development of military chaplaincy opens with a story about combat death and the botched offering of a Catholic memorial for a Jewish soldier.[10] The legal, political, and multi-faith issues that make up military chaplaincy happen against a backdrop of combat, corpses, and "death with dignity" protocols that attempt to honor a soldier's life and remains.

Prison chaplains engage death work in ways that are both commensurate with their peers in other sectors and specific to the prison context. A primary function of chaplains in the bureaucracy of prisons is to notify incarcerated people of the death of their loved ones and (ad)minister the process of incarcerated people attending private viewings or funerals when permitted. Prison chaplains routinely serve as grief counselors in the aftermath of those notifications. In this study, chaplains describe breaking prison policy to hold the hands of incarcerated people as they die in prison hospital wings. In a process called "death watch," they walk with people condemned to execution in the month after their death warrants have been signed, even sitting in the death chamber when invited or mandated. Chaplains describe being first responders to the murders, suicides, and life-threatening assaults of both incarcerated people and prison staff. My interviews for this study were riddled with horror: an incarcerated person committing suicide by

---

[5] Naomi K. Paget and Janet R. McCormack, *The Work of the Chaplain* (Valley Forge: Judson Press, 2006), 25.
[6] Ibid., 31.
[7] Wendy Cadge, *Paging God: Religion in the Halls of Medicine* (Chicago: University of Chicago Press, 2012), 173.
[8] Ibid., 174.
[9] Ibid.
[10] Ronit Y. Stahl, *Enlisting Faith: How the Military Chaplaincy Shaped Religion and State in Modern America* (Cambridge: Harvard University Press, 2017), 1–5.

jumping over the railing of a five-story pod; being a first responder to the stabbing of a fellow staff member; praying at the edge of a room through an unsuccessful CPR attempt on an incarcerated man; and officiating memorial services for fellow prison staff who have committed suicide.

Between these stories of physical death are more mundane stories of the daily experiences that hasten death. One person served 4,500 incarcerated people as the only chaplain of his facility for a year and a half during Covid. Most every chaplain in this study referenced the hyper-vigilance that gets written into one's nervous system when one is trained to scan every room, find exits and allies, and identify possible weapons—a bodily habituation that cannot be turned off after shift. These sorts of stressors to the central nervous system, alongside the actual threat of bodily harm, explain why corrections workers, according to the US Department of Justice, "are at higher risk of suicide, substance abuse, and divorce, while their mortality rate is the second highest of any occupation."[11] The life expectancy of people working in prison has been reported as fifty-nine years, compared to the US average of 78.8 years.[12] People working in prison have a suicide rate 39 percent higher than any other occupation.[13] Prison chaplaincy is not just death work; it is work that hastens the death of the chaplain.

One of the chaplains in this study worked for almost thirty years at a prison housing a men's death row. After accompanying forty-two men on death watch and witnessing nineteen executions, including one botched execution, he decided he needed a break. He told me the story of attempting to train his replacement, Deacon Joe.

Chaplain Harald:

It was a week and a half before Christmas.
And a warrant came down for a fella that Deacon Joe had started doing spiritual advising for.
And it was the Wednesday before Christmas that the warrant came down.

---

[11]J. Lee, R. Henning, and M. Cherniack, "Correction workers' burnout and outcomes: A Bayesian network approach," *International Journal of Environmental Research and Public Health* 16, no. 2 (2019): 282.

[12]Jennifer C. Buden, Alicia G. Dugan, Sara Namazi, Tania B. Huedo-Medina, Martin G. Cherniack, and Pouran D. Faghri, "Work characteristics as predictors of correctional supervisors' health outcomes," *Journal of Occupational and Environmental Medicine/American College of Occupational and Environmental Medicine* 58, no. 9 (2016): e325; Albert Deamicis, "A real tragedy: Suicide by correctional officer," *American Jails* 30, no. 1 (2016): 26–30; Sabrina Tavernise, "White Americans are dying younger as drug and alcohol abuse rises," *New York Times*, April 20, 2016, A11.

[13]DeAmicis, "A real tragedy: Suicide by correctional officer," 26.

The night before Christmas Eve that year, Friday night, he went home.
I'd seen him that day.
His granddaughter, first grandchild, had been born that morning.

And the last thing he did before he went to sleep, was he sent in his email to the prison, to the Warden, requesting a death watch appointment, his first death watch appointment, with this fella for the Wednesday after Christmas. So he's gotta start deathwatch even before New Year's, because the warrant was signed for the first or second week of January.

Deacon Joe had been through one execution.
He'd done it. He knew what was involved.
And I'd stayed very close with him while he went through that.

That night at about 2am, he sent in his email requesting his first deathwatch appointment with this fella …
for the Wednesday after Christmas.
He went to sleep in his Nascar pajamas.

Number 42.

> *(laughs, teary)*

The guys at the prison *loved* him.
They always thought I was kind of an alien, but they loved Deacon Joe.

> *(long pause)*

And …

He died of a heart attack in his sleep …

> *(knocks his hand against the table, holding back tears)*

Between 3 and 3:30 in the morning …

A widow maker.

> *(pause)*

That was the stress of sending in that request to start a death watch over again with another man.

Because he really cared about the guys.

My experience is, the death row ministry, what makes it effective is when the guys realize you really care about them. They're not a notch on your belt. They're not something to hang on your trophy case. They're there, and you are there to be with them and share as much as you can their circumstances so that you can accompany them. Because you love and care about them as a person.

But then when you watch them be killed ....

    (long pause)

there's no words to describe it.

There's no words to describe.

You realize the depth of the horror of needlessly taking a human life. Whatever the reason or justification is, it's needless. These men have not killed or harmed anybody since they've been in prison, some of them for thirty years. And they're not going anywhere! We can keep them where they are and let them live out their lives.

And ...

Joe died of a heart attack.[14]

You are there to be with them and share as much as you can their circumstances so that you can accompany them. Deacon Joe went into

---

[14]Interview with the author on May 6, 2021. The reader will notice that while I sometimes transcribe interviews into traditional block text, I often use an ethnopoetic form in which the words appear more like poetry than prose on the page. Line breaks indicate natural breaths and small pauses. Ellipses indicate longer pauses. Skipped lines indicate even longer pauses. At some times my conversation partners remained silent for long enough that their silence has been indicated in italics and parentheses. Italics and parentheses are also used to indicate other affective gestures and actions (laughing, crying, shaking one's head). Ethnopoetics was developed to better capture the rhythms and repetitions of oral communication as they are translated onto the written page. I have found ethnopoetics particularly appropriate to transcribing traumatic or distressing narratives. In telling distressing stories, speech breaks apart, repetition can heighten to a stutter, and fragments replace sentences as a person tries to bring to speech experiences that defy easy or linear sense-making. Because so many of the stories in this text are distressing in nature, ethnopoetics emerged as the dominant form of transcription. For more on ethnopoetics and transcribing traumatic texts see Maria Grazia Guido, "Trauma-Narrative Analysis at the Level of Text Structure," in *English as a Lingua Franca in Migrants' Trauma Narratives* (London: Palgrave Macmillan, 2018), 85–111; Robert Moore, "Reinventing ethnopoetics," *Journal of Folklore Research: An International Journal of Folklore and Ethnomusicology* 50, no. 1–3 (2013): 13–39; Ida Tolgensbakk, "'More or less word for word' Barbro Klein and transcription as analytical craft," *Western Folklore* 79, no. 4 (2020): 453–68.

prison to enact what is widely termed a "ministry of presence" in chaplaincy literature. While a "ministry of presence" is straightforwardly what it sounds like, it also eludes a specific, shared definition. In *A Ministry of Presence: Chaplaincy, Spiritual Care, and the Law,* Winnifred Sullivan devotes an entire chapter to defining the phrase, but she begins with a vignette of a prison chaplain responding to an incarcerated person's affirmation that it was "cool" that the warden employed a chaplain to "keep us from freaking out." The chaplain responded, "I'm not really here to keep you from freaking out, I'm here to be with you while you freak out."[15] A ministry of presence is fundamentally about *being with*. Sullivan notes that the phrase is malleable enough to apply to the work of chaplains from any faith tradition and accommodates the interfaith mandate of prison chaplaincy to provide religious services to people of any or no faith tradition as a protection of incarcerated people's First Amendment Right to the free exercise of religion. Even so, Sullivan claims the phrase has roots in the incarnation of Jesus Christ.[16] The Christian God is *Emmanuel,* God with us. In enacting a ministry of presence, chaplains follow God's example in drawing near and being present with people in the flesh. One of the chaplains in this study explained, "The role of the chaplain is to do what supports life, what supports health. It is to be visible, to be present, to show the population, whether it's prisoner or staff, that there is no godforsaken place. There is always a representative of the Holy, even in the midst of unholy things."[17]

The role of the chaplain is to do what supports life. Prison chaplains did not describe their work to me as death work. They talked about doing work that supports life, health, and transformation inside institutions purposed toward the confinement and control of human persons. They told me about founding higher education programs in partnership with local universities. They described running religious services calendars filled with Christian worship, Islamic Jumah prayer, Buddhist meditation, and Wiccan rituals. They talked about hosting concerts, forming debate clubs, and running trauma-recovery groups. They told me about the power of one-on-one conversations, even if those had to occur through grates, food slots, and the cracks in concrete and steel doors. They talked about death as an interruption (though they admitted it is an interruption that occurs every shift). They named carceral death as needless, a horror, and an injustice, when they could name it at all. Sometimes they would simply shake their heads and say that they do not have words for what they have seen. They would tell me stories in which they were clearly at risk of bodily harm—in riots, breaking up fights, receiving death threats—and then insist that they

---

[15]Winnifred Fallers Sullivan, *A Ministry of Presence: Chaplaincy, Spiritual Care, and the Law* (Chicago: University of Chicago Press, 2014), xii.
[16]Ibid., 13, 174–85.
[17]Interview with the author on September 27, 2021.

do not feel at risk in the prison. Which is all to say, Deacon Joe did not go into prison to die or even to do death work. He went into prison to do life work. In attempting to do life work in prison, Deacon Joe came face to face with the death of incarcerated people, and he both risked and hastened his own death for the sake of being present with someone facing execution by the state.

This is a book about life-in-death work. I will also say life-in-the-face-of-death work, life-after-death work, or wake work.[18] When I say any of these, I mean what is often in the Christian tradition called salvation or atonement. Salvation is a capacious word; it means many things to many people. Like "ministry of presence," the term "salvation" resists an easy, shared definition. Based on the work of Karl Barth and the chaplains in this study, I offer a working definition of salvation as the revelation and enactment of the truth that there is no God-forsaken place and no God-forsaken person.[19] In addition to "salvation," Barth will call the truth that Jesus has vacated conditions of godforsakeness "reconciliation" or "atonement." Salvation, reconciliation, and atonement will be used synonymously in this text, as they are often used synonymously in the theology of Karl Barth.

Yet even as I offer a working definition of the term, I want to note that neither the Bible nor Barth offers a definition of salvation. When it comes to salvation, Christians are not given a definition; they are given the person and work of Jesus Christ. This book tries to lean into the truth that salvation comes not as a propositional statement but in the embodied witness of Jesus' life, death, and life after death. How do the life, arrest, trial, conviction, execution, and release of Jesus Christ enact the salvation of the cosmos, and how does that one carceral life-in-death link up with life in the face of death today? I am using prisons as a case study in soteriology because the carceral was the site of Jesus' original enactment of salvation. I am exploring how salvation happens by attending to the granular details of carceral lives and deaths because of the biblical witness that salvation came packaged in the granular details of one such life. In the pages that follow, I will try to write the prison deaths and the myriad prison experiences that hasten death into the life, death, and life-after-death of Jesus Christ, but if I valorize the deaths of prison staff and incarcerated people (including Jesus) in doing so, I have written the deaths wrongly. That is not how they were told to me. This is not a book about choosing death; it is a book about facing it, challenging it, experiencing it, and living on the other side of it. This book was not always about that.

---

[18]Christina Sharpe, *In the Wake: On Blackness and Being* (Durham: Duke University Press, 2016), 1–24.

[19]Karl Barth resists offering a definition of salvation, but the idea that Jesus comes to be "with us" and "for us" in a way that eradicates the possibility of godforsakeness even at the point of death is at the heart of his doctrine of atonement. As a starting point, the reader might begin with attention to *CD* IV/1, 185, 215, 239, & 306.

From Complicity to Death Work: The Story of This Book

I have spent my career with one foot in prisons and one foot in the academy. I was the founding director of Duke Divinity School's prison education program in which Duke students and professors go into local prisons for classes with incarcerated people. After two years of serving as a prison educator, I took a part-time chaplaincy position at one of the state prisons in which we offered classes. Prior to writing this book, I served as a chaplain of a women's minimum-custody work-release prison for twelve years alongside my work co-directing Duke Divinity School's Prison Studies Program. As I moved back and forth each week between prison and academy, I heard each critique the other, and I observed that chaplains are marginal in both the academy's narration of mass incarceration and the prison administration's plans for how to operate a prison. Yet prison chaplains have been part of the paid staff of prison administrations since at least 1807 when Newgate Prison in New York hired the Rev. John Stanford for $250 per annum.[20] Jennifer Graber documents the responsibility of Quakers, Baptists, and Presbyterians in envisioning and building America's first prisons in Pennsylvania and New York, noting the key role of chaplains in making public sense of punitive theories and practices as they developed.[21] In *Religion and the Development of the American Penal System,* Andrew Skotnicki argues that chaplains specifically were foundational in shaping the penal methodologies that still inform American prisons today.[22] In my own experience, I knew the power of prison chaplains to shape the culture of the institution, and yet prison chaplains routinely disappear in the formal discourse of both prisons and academy.

While chaplains do not show up in most scholarship on prisons, when chaplains do show up, they tend to do so in brief mentions that confirm their support of and complicity with the prison industrial complex.[23] Michel

---

[20]Jennifer Graber, *The Furnace of Affliction: Prisons and Religion in Antebellum America* (Chapel Hill: University of North Carolina, 2011), 45–56.
[21]Ibid., 15–102.
[22]Andrew Skotnicki, *Religion and the Development of the American Penal System* (Lanham: University Press of America, 2000), 5.
[23]For example, prison chaplains are not mentioned at all in Michelle Alexander's *The New Jim Crow*, Ruth Wilson Gilmore's *Golden Gulag*, Beth Richie's *Arrested Justice*, Sarah Haley's *No Mercy Here*, Elizabeth Hinton's *From the War on Poverty to the War on Crime*, Angela Davis' *Are Prisons Obsolete?*, Dan Berger's *Captive Nation*, or Mogul, Ritchie, and Whitlock's *Queer (In)Justice*. Even in scholarship specifically on Christian religion in prison, the following books either mention prison chaplains not at all or in passing as administrators of the system: James Logan's *Good Punishment*, Tanya Erzen's *God in Captivity*, and Amy Levad's *Redeeming a Prison Society*.

Foucault introduces chaplains early in *Discipline and Punish* on a list of prison administrators who "reassure (the public) that the body and pain are not the ultimate objects of (the prison's) punitive action" but then only mentions chaplains once again in passing.[24] In his influential *Just Mercy: A Story of Justice and Redemption,* Bryan Stevenson mentions only one prison chaplain who was convicted of raping incarcerated women at the Julia Tutwiler Prison for Women in Alabama.[25] In *Blood in the Water: The Attica Uprising of 1971 and Its Legacy,* Heather Ann Thompson mentions chaplains three times, and they are always on the side of prison administration rather than on the side of the incarcerated men demanding humane treatment. David Oshinsky's work on the convict lease system remains sparse but more diverse in its treatment of prison chaplains. Three mentions include one in which a chaplain serves as a record-keeper documenting emancipated slaves, one in which a chaplain shares publicly about the brutal torture and murder of an incarcerated man, and one in which a chaplain publicly supports the convict lease system comparing it to his own farm work growing up.[26]

Prison chaplains are admittedly complicated characters. The first time I felt seen and well-described as a prison chaplain was reading Joshua Dubler's *Down in the Chapel: Religious Life in an American Prison*. Dubler was invited into Pennsylvania's Graterford Prison to observe and participate in the life of the prison chapel as an ethnographer. I was five years into prison work when his book came out, and I read the following passage:

> The chaplains are in a bind. Because they are trained in a caring profession, they are predisposed to distinguish themselves from the administration's custody-based approach, in which prisoners alternatively appear as dangerous criminals or as tedious babies, requiring in either case the identical regimen of callous discipline. While the chaplain's aspiration to treat prisoners as men is generally quite practicable, a conspiracy of factors nonetheless reinforces the prison's dehumanizing operating logic ... Periodically burned and, before long, burned out, the chaplains come to deflect, to indulge in gallows humor, and to adopt as a default condition a posture of sardonic remove, which in a roundabout way brings them into proper alignment with—as Father Gorski puts it—"the World of No!"[27]

---

[24] Michel Foucault, *Discipline and Punish: The Birth of Prisons*, trans. Alan Sheridan (New York: Vintage Books, 1977), 11. Parentheses added.
[25] Bryan Stevenson, *Just Mercy: A Story of Justice and Redemption* (New York: Spiegel and Grau, 2014), 238.
[26] David M. Oshinksy, *Worse than Death: Parchman Farm and the Ordeal of Jim Crow Justice* (New York: Free Press Paperbacks, 1997), 15, 62, 225.
[27] Joshua Dubler, *Religious Life in an American Prison* (New York: Farrar, Strauss, and Giroux, 2013), 61.

I underlined every word. I was deeply enmeshed in the prison's "World of No," and I was trying every day to speak God's "Yes" into it. But Dubler was right. I could see myself being shaped by the prison's culture of No as much as, or perhaps more than, I was shaping it in return. Dubler named the complexity of my situation, but by the end of the book, Dubler would argue that while chaplains and chapel religion do transform incarcerated people, they simply transform "convicts into prisoners," i.e., "those with the embodied know-how to survive prison."[28] Dubler argued that chaplains ultimately support the prison industrial complex by offering human beings the skills they need to accommodate themselves to life in prison, skills that are in direct tension with the bodily postures and practices that might confront, challenge, or critique prisons.[29]

I knew that at one level Dubler was right, but I also knew that accommodating people to prison was not all that was happening in my ministry. Seven years later, still serving as a prison chaplain and prison educator, I pre-ordered Dubler's next book, *Break Every Yoke: Religion, Justice, and the Abolition of Prisons,* written with Vincent Lloyd. It landed on my porch in the early days of the Covid-19 pandemic. Staring down the barrel of what every prison worker and incarcerated person knew would be a catastrophic sweep of a deadly and contagious disease through the tight quarters of prison, I was more convinced than ever that prisons were doing more harm than good. I settled in to read what I hoped would be a history of chaplains' participation in Christian abolitionist movements, however spotty and unsuccessful, looking for models that might fuel my own work behind bars. Shortly into Chapter 1, they tell the story of Austin Reed, a Black seventeen-year-old incarcerated at Auburn Prison in New York in 1840.[30] Dubler and Lloyd recount a chaplain visiting Reed after he is whipped forty times with a cat-o-nine-tails for speaking to another incarcerated person. Their analysis of this encounter between the incarcerated Reed and his chaplain is worth reading in full both because of the impact it had on me and because it is characteristic of—though more pointed than—the way I have routinely experienced people in the academy talking about those who work in prisons. Dubler and Lloyd write:

> Reed's testimonial would seem to be a strong brief in defense of religion as a place of opposition within the carceral state. Amid darkness, the chaplain is a light; amid suffering, the chaplain is a lifeline. Though of the system in body, the chaplain is decidedly not of the system in spirit. Or so it would appear on the face of it. In Reed's account, the chaplain is

---

[28]Ibid., 309.
[29]Ibid., 273.
[30]Joshua Dubler and Vincent W. Lloyd, *Break Every Yoke: Religion, Justice, and the Abolition of Prisons* (Oxford: Oxford University Press, 2020), 36–7.

a healer, but he is also an agent of torment. This is not so merely because he hangs his hat beside that of Reed's torturer, but also, quite simply, because as often as he arrives, he departs, and once he has left, the prison is no better than it was prior to his arrival. Even as he experiences his relief, Reed understands its fleeting character: "How lonesome, sad, and pensive I'd feel again when he was gone."

It is tempting to see religious healing as the antidote to prison suffering, and, at times to a life-saving degree, for those in captivity, it is. Assessed systematically, however, the temptation doesn't withstand scrutiny. In theory and in practice, the religious healing the chaplain provides belongs squarely to the prison system that is the cause of Reed's suffering. Whether in making this claim we are reading with the grain of Reed's testimony or against it, we are uncertain, but the judgment stands in either case. In effect, the torturer and the chaplain administer their services in complement.[31]

In effect, the torturer and the chaplain administer their services in complement. My face flushed. I shut the book. I knew they were in some sense right. I also knew, from my own daily experience, that complicity is not the whole story. Complicity is simply the price of admission.

Prison chaplains inhabit a set of tensions. The academy often names the tension between complicity and access. Mass incarceration, as practiced in America, involves comparatively harsh and historically novel rates of incarceration that are concentrated among men with either low levels of education or from historically marginalized groups.[32] A chaplain is complicit in this biased carceral system as one who follows and administers its policies, most often in a paid capacity, and yet the chaplain's status as a prison employee is what grants the chaplain access to both incarcerated people and locations inside the prison not permitted to religious volunteers, prison educators, or researchers. Chaplains also inhabit tensions between the pastoral and custody sides of the job, debating how and when to carry radios and pepper spray, if and when to write up incarcerated people, and how to mediate disputes and control violence when they are the person in charge of a space or program. They often find themselves standing between incarcerated people, prison administrators, and corrections officers, attempting to offer enough solidarity with each group to be a safe resource while not so much solidarity with any one group that they are perceived as

---

[31]Ibid., 37.
[32]E. Ann Carson, PhD and Rich Kluckow, DSW. Correctional Populations in the United States, 2021—Statistical Tables. February 2023. NCJ 305542. Bureau of Justice Statistics: Washington, DC; Alexander F. Roehrkasse and Christopher Wildeman, "Lifetime risk of imprisonment in the United States remains high and starkly unequal," *Science Advances* 8, no. 48 (2022): eabo3395.

a threat to the people in the other categories. They are ordained or endorsed in their specific faith traditions as a requirement of the role, and yet they follow a mandate to offer religious services and care to incarcerated people of any or no faith tradition.[33] Regardless of their own racial identity or the dominant racial identity of their particular facility, they are often the only minister in a prison, offering care across racial divisions complicated by both gang affiliations and racialized religious identities. They attempt to offer trauma healing in an environment in which trauma is ongoing, a task that trauma theorists generally conclude is impossible.[34]

When I started this project, my aim was simple: I wanted to bring the complexity of prison chaplaincy into the academic conversation around prisons and name how chaplains are navigating the tensions inherent to their work. Even more basically, I wanted to gather a broad-based set of data describing the work. I have found only one nationwide, qualitative study of prison chaplains which was conducted by the Pew Center in 2012.[35] The study gathers valuable demographic data, but because it was a survey, it is unable to shed light on the ways that chaplains are negotiating the daily tensions at the heart of the work. Federal prison chaplains were not included in that study. When I attempted to receive approval of my research from the Federal Bureau of Prisons, I learned that the Federal Bureau of Prisons Research Review Board had refused to approve the Pew Center study. The lack of data on the field of prison chaplaincy cannot be credited to academic oversight or bias alone. Prisons are hard to get into, and prison employees are acculturated not to speak about their work. Prison chaplains sign confidentiality statements and follow policies that prohibit certain sorts of data sharing. As importantly, chaplains are embedded in chains of command that encourage employees to put as little on the record as possible in order to protect themselves against future lawsuits. The process of gathering even basic data in such a culture is not simple.

Chaplains Bearing Witness in This Study

I developed the protocols for this study by asking myself, "What would it take for me to share my experience as a prison chaplain on record?" I had spent more than a decade turning down every request I had received to go on record about working in a prison because I never felt that the studies were set up in such a way as to truly protect my identity given the types of things

---

[33]For the fullest treatment of how the First Amendment right to free exercise of religion has been interpreted inside of American prisons, see Winnifred Fallers Sullivan, *Prison Religion: Faith-Based Reform and the Constitution* (Princeton: Princeton University Press, 2009).
[34]Judith Herman, *Trauma and Recovery: The Aftermath of Violence—From Domestic Abuse to Political Terror* (New York: Basic Books, 1992), 155–74.
[35]"Religion in Prisons—A 50 State Survey of Prison Chaplains." Pew Research Center, March 2, 2012. https://www.pewresearch.org/religion/2012/03/22/prison-chaplains-exec/.

I have witnessed. I possess fifteen years of information that my superiors and state government officials would not want shared, and I assumed my peers possess the same. As a researcher, I knew that I needed an exact record of a person's words because the stories would be traumatic and copious, thus not conducive to accurate notetaking, but as a chaplain, I knew that a video recording that linked me to my stories would be unacceptable to me. While the interviews were conducted on Zoom, I settled for only recording audio files. In the age of voice recognition software, even the existence of an audio file felt risky to me. How could a chaplain be assured that such a file would not be found online? I petitioned for my data to be stored on Duke University's Protected Research Data Network. This network comes with processes that make data analysis more cumbersome, but storage on this system comes with added protections for the data. I knew that an exact written transcript of any conversation would contain individuals' names and the names of the institutions at which they worked. As a chaplain, I would not feel comfortable with such a transcript existing. I agreed that the only transcripts that would be saved would be transcripts that had been stripped, by me, line by line, of any identifying information.

I also knew that if I felt safe enough to share what I have witnessed in America's prisons honestly, if such stories were published, there was a good chance that some state or individual actor would see the potential for legal action and try to compel a researcher to disclose the identity of the speaker. I learned that the National Institutes of Health has a mechanism by which to legally protect research subjects. If a study is protected by an NIH Certificate of Confidentiality, the researcher is legally prohibited from revealing the names of study participants. Even government entities or a lawsuit cannot compel the researcher to reveal the names of participants. I applied for a CoC and was denied because the NIH concluded that the study was unrelated to health outcomes. I appealed. The NIH granted this research a Certificate of Confidentiality, and I began to feel that I could ask my peers to share their stories in a safe and protected way.

The final legal protection was acknowledging that my dual roles as researcher and actively serving prison chaplain meant that there were some stories that I would have a duty to report irrespective of the above protections. I consulted a lawyer. It was determined that because I was not a chaplain *to* my research subjects, I did not have a duty to report suicidal ideation. However, North Carolina is a mandatory reporting state for child abuse, so any stories told to me about active and ongoing child abuse would have to be reported. As a chaplain, my duty to report unreported cases of rape or sexual assault from any time in any state, federal, or local facility under the Prison Rape Elimination Act trumped the above confidentiality protections.[36] My Consent Form stated these limitations clearly. It is

---

[36] "Prison Rape Elimination Act (PREA)—An Overview." Bureau of Justice Assistance. Accessed on January 27, 2023. https://bja.ojp.gov/program/prea/overview.

perhaps then no surprise that stories of sexual assault in prison are notably absent from this study, though I know from my professional experience that chaplains routinely hear them.

In addition to study design and legal protections, there were many small ways that I tried to build a safe space for violent and sacred stories to be shared.[37] Because these interviews were conducted during Covid, Duke University's Institutional Review Board required they be done on Zoom rather than in person, but I knew that eye contact, open body postures, and postural mirroring build empathy between listener and speaker and create the sense of trust needed for vulnerability.[38] I set up my camera in my basement home office where no one could hear me, and I positioned myself so that my participants could see more of my body. I opened my palms for their hardest stories. I nodded and gave nonverbal affirmations. I had to choose between looking at my screen to best see their faces and looking at the little red light of the computer's video camera to give them the experience of me looking directly at them. Both people in a virtual interview cannot simultaneously have the experience of making eye-contact with one another. I mostly chose to look directly at the little red light, giving my study participants the visual experience of being fully witnessed. I left every interview with a headache, and I was gifted 662 single-spaced pages of de-identified data about what twenty prison chaplains have witnessed behind bars in the past four decades.

For this study, I conversed for three years with thirty-eight current and former prison chaplains serving in state systems, federal prisons, and a large county system that houses people both pre and post sentencing. Of the twenty chaplains who decided to go on record, I have interviewed men and women who have served as chaplains at men's facilities, women's facilities, co-ed facilities, and on transgender-specific prison wings. These prisons range from minimum to maximum custody. Most are adult facilities, but some chaplains also served at juvenile facilities and adult prisons that contain children who are sixteen or seventeen years old. Many of the chaplains in this study served in multiple different facilities in their careers, some even switching state systems or having experience in both state and federal systems. The chaplains in this study have served in North Carolina, Illinois, Georgia, New Jersey, Missouri, Pennsylvania, California, Massachusetts, Florida, Delaware, Minnesota, Iowa, and Oregon.

---

[37]The interviews were semi-structured to provide plenty of space to respond to the comfort level of the chaplain who was being interviewed and omit questions or reroute as appropriate. Most of the interviews lasted a full two hours, but I offered a break for stretching, tea or water, and other bodily needs at the hour mark.

[38]On the role of eye-contact and postural mirroring in the neuropsychology of empathy, see Babette Rothschild with Marjorie L. Rand, *Help for the Helper: The Psychophysiology of Compassion Fatigue and Vicarious Trauma* (New York: W.W. Norton and Company, 2006), 35–86.

I have interviewed primarily state-funded chaplains but also volunteer chaplains and community-funded chaplains. The majority are what I would call "facility" chaplains who serve the entire population of a prison including both staff and residents, but a few participants in this study were denomination-specific chaplains who primarily provide services for incarcerated people of their specific faith-group.[39] I have interviewed chaplains who left the profession after two to ten years and chaplains who retired after twenty to thirty-five years. At the outer edge, I interviewed one chaplain who is still serving at forty-four years. Their denominations are weighted toward a variety of Baptists (which is also the national trend), but include Presbyterian, Methodist, Episcopalian, Pentecostal, Evangelical Free Bible Convention, Unitarian Universalist, and Catholic. While I did not ask direct questions about participants' race, sex, sexual orientation, or criminal history, chaplains self-disclosed the following. The chaplains are racially diverse, self-identifying as Black, white, Asian, Native American, Innuit, and Pakistani. Chaplains self-identified as both queer and straight, as well as married, partnered, divorced, and single. A few chaplains shared that they have criminal records themselves, others shared that they have family who are incarcerated, and others came to prison ministry with no personal experience of the prison system.

Surprisingly Absent: Analyses of Disparate Impact by Race, Gender, and Religious Diversity

As important as who is represented in this study, is what is not. The academy has been diligent in naming the anti-Black bias in America's arrest and sentencing practices and the wider negative impacts of that bias on communities of color who are not incarcerated.[40] That work has contributed to sentencing reforms that have reduced incarceration rates overall and narrowed the gap in white and Black rates of incarceration, though rates

---

[39]There is a significant structural difference in these categories of prison chaplain, the roles that they play in the institution, and the degree to which they feel responsible for or aligned with prison policy and other prison staff. My data set and style of data collection are not large enough to draw out those distinctions based on the data collected in this study. For more on distinctive types of chaplaincy inside of institutions and the differences in ideology and practice produced by those distinctions, see Margaret Whipp, "Embedding Chaplaincy: Integrity and Presence," in *A Christian Theology of Chaplaincy*, ed. John Caperon, Andrew Todd, and James Walters (London: Jessica Kingsley Publishers, 2018), 101–18.

[40]Donald Braman, *Doing Time on the Outside: Incarceration and Family Life in Urban America* (Ann Arbor: University of Michigan Press, 2007); Reuben Jonathan Miller, *Halfway Home: Race, Punishment, and the Afterlife of Mass Incarceration* (Boston: Little, Brown, 2021); Sara Wakefield and Christopher Wildeman, *Children of the Prison Boom: Mass Incarceration and the Future of American Inequality* (Oxford: Oxford University Press, 2013); Bruce Western, *Punishment and Inequality in America* (New York: Russell Sage Foundation, 2006).

seem to be rising again since 2022.[41] When one names the disproportionate rates of incarceration for various racial subgroups, one is primarily noting the widespread and unjust disparate impact of incarceration on wider Black and brown communities that live mostly outside of prisons. This, however, is a study on what happens internally to prisons, specifically the religious and spiritual life that chaplains facilitate.

The racial dynamics inside of prisons—particularly after 2010—are different and less-named than the racism of policing and sentencing rates. In federal prisons, the majority of incarcerated people are white. As of July 2024, federal prisons are roughly 57 percent white and 39 percent Black.[42] State prisons vary widely. Just considering some of the states where chaplains in this study work, Oregon's state prisons house a majority white population, New Jersey majority Black, and California majority Hispanic.[43] The small sample size of this study combined with the wide variety of racial make-ups in the various prisons represented here means that it is beyond the scope of this study to make representative claims about the way that race impacts religious life inside America's prisons. However, Chapter 3 of this book tries to name the ways that a racially and religiously diverse-by-force carceral community navigates life together. The results do not contradict the dominant narrative in the academy about the anti-Black racism built into America's prison system, but they highlight the different racial dynamics that happen once people are inside. Chaplains and incarcerated people are both fighting against and succumbing to a variety of systemic forces, including racial divisions, in their religious practices and chapel programs. I hope that these stories nuance and complexify our understanding of the role of race in the religious practices within America's prisons.

The reader will also notice that there is little analysis about the way that the gender of a given prison or the gender of a given chaplain impacts any given story being shared. I have worked in a women's prison for fifteen years, and I went into this study expecting to hear radically different stories from men's prisons versus women's prisons. I expected differences in narratives from chaplains working in facilities of their same gender identity

---

[41] Junsoo Lee, Paul Pecorino, and Anne-Charlotte Souto, "A comparison of the female and male racial disparities in imprisonment," *Journal of Economics, Race, and Policy* 6, no. 2 (2023): 102–25; Magnus Lofstrom, Brandon Martin, and Steven Raphael, "Effect of sentencing reform on racial and ethnic disparities in involvement with the criminal justice system: The case of California's proposition 47," *Criminology & Public Policy* 19, no. 4 (2020): 1165–207; Samuel L. Myers, Jr., William J. Sabol, and Man Xu. *The Determinants of Declining Racial Disparities in Female Incarceration Rates, 2000–2015*. Available at: https://www.prisonpolicy.org/scans/thedeterminantsofdecliningracialdisparities.pdf, 2018.

[42] The Federal Bureau of Prisons maintains publicly accessible data on the racial makeup of federal prisons that is updated weekly. The statistics above were accessed on July 6, 2024 at https://www.bop.gov/about/statistics/statistics_inmate_race.jsp

[43] The Prison Policy Initiative maintains updated state-by-state data. The above were accessed on July 6, 2024 at https://www.prisonpolicy.org/profiles/

versus chaplains working in facilities dominated by a gender different than their own. While those threads were there, I was overwhelmed by the way that narratives of complicity and access, navigating a chain of command, direct witness of violence, the impacts of mundane prison trauma on the body, the routinization of fight, flight, freeze and tend/befriend responses, and the dogged insistence that life can be cultivated in the face of and after death remained consistent across gender, custody level, and race—of both chaplains and their particular prisons. I have named throughout the text the racial or gender identity of a chaplain and/or their facility when it seemed germane to understanding the particular story being shared, but I have chosen to focus the book on the themes that arose consistently across categories, and importantly, I did not have to cut data to enact that focus. The transcripts of chaplains in this study had many more commonalities than differences, even across categories like gender, in which I was primed to see differences.

Finally, this book describes an interfaith profession, but it does so from an explicitly Christian theological perspective. Nineteen of the twenty chaplains who went on record in this study are Christian. There is another book to be written that includes prison chaplains from a variety of faith traditions—a comprehensive history, ethics, and practices of prison chaplaincy. There was a point early in this study when I thought this would be that book. But 85 percent of prison chaplains serving in the United States are Christian.[44] Chaplains in this study were naming that their Christian seminaries had not trained them for either the realities of prisons or the profession of chaplaincy. They took Clinical Pastoral Education (CPE) for their chaplaincy-specific training, but that training occurred almost universally in hospitals.[45] Honoring the fact that most chaplaincy is interfaith work, CPE teaches tactics for pastoral care and metaphors for theorizing the work that are largely not faith-specific. CPE thus offers chaplaincy training that is neither specific to prisons nor specific to the Christian faith. But while they are not being trained in how to do it, ordained Christian clergy serving as prison chaplains are still resourcing their interfaith pastoral work from within their own Christian commitments. Prison chaplains are doing that faith-specific sense-making alone, in the field, while facing both primary and secondary trauma exposure. I realized early in this study that as a practical theologian in the Christian tradition with a data set from primarily Christian clergy, I could offer a Christian theology of prison chaplaincy that would be a needed

---

[44]"Religion in Prisons—A 50 State Survey of Prison Chaplains."
[45]For insightful overviews of Clinical Pastoral Education, see Simon J. Craddock Lee, "In a secular spirit: Strategies of clinical pastoral education," *Health Care Analysis* 10 (2002): 339–56; Bonnie J. Miller-McLemore, "Revisiting the living human web: Theological education and the role of clinical pastoral education," *Journal of Pastoral Care & Counseling* 62, no. 1–2 (2008): 3–18; Homer L. Jernigan, "Clinical pastoral education: Reflections on the past and future of a movement," *Journal of Pastoral Care & Counseling* 56, no. 4 (2002): 377–92.

faith-specific resource for how to do the interfaith work of chaplaincy. As I listened to more and more stories of carceral death in these interviews, while witnessing a growing number of Covid-related prison deaths at my job, I also realized that *I* needed an account from within my Christian tradition of how life might persist in the face of and after these accumulating prison deaths. I needed life-after-death, which is to say, I needed saving.

The Ethnographer as a Witness

While this protocol might sound like a semi-structured interview process, this study is a collaborative ethnography as described by Luke Eric Lassiter in *The Chicago Guide to Collaborative Ethnography* and as taught to me by Lassiter's teacher Glenn D. Hinson, to whom the *Chicago Guide* is dedicated.[46] Ethnography is founded on the principle of participant-observation in which the researcher does not simply observe, document, collect, and interpret data about a community or practice but actively participates in the community or phenomenon being studied. The ethnographer learns about the subject being studied through embodied experience, *being with* the people and places she seeks to understand. Hence, ethnography is the method appropriate when a researcher is seeking to understand the depth and complexity of a subject, rather than trying to prove causation or to gather a large representative data set.[47] Because ethnographic data is always received and processed through the body of the ethnographer, there is an inherent limit to how much data can be collected in this way. The body of the ethnographer is both research tool and research limit. The method of participant-observation can only be used where the ethnographer's body is permitted to be.

It is harder to get into prison than one might think. *The Palgrave Handbook of Prison Ethnography* treats access to prisons as the fundamental hurdle to be overcome in the art of prison ethnography.[48] As one reads more deeply, one sees that some studies are being classified as ethnographies even though researchers were only granted a week of access to a prison as an observer. How does one really *participate* in the life of a prison as a non-incarcerated researcher who is on site for a week? These articles are filled with advice on critically assessing one's own subject position, acknowledging outsider status, and owning privilege, but when I read them as a person who has been arrested, jailed, and strip searched, as a person who has stood before a court and pled guilty to crimes, as a person who has served a year on federal

---

[46]Luke Eric Lassiter, *The Chicago Guide to Collaborative Ethnography* (Chicago: The University of Chicago Press, 2005), i.
[47]John W. Creswell and J. David Creswell, *Research Design: Qualitative, Quantitative, and Mixed Methods Approaches, Fifth Edition* (London: Sage Publications, 2018), 134.
[48]Deborah H. Drake, Rod Earle, and Jennifer Sloan, eds., *The Palgrave Handbook of Prison Ethnography* (New York: Palgrave Macmillan, 2015).

probation, has a criminal record, and has subsequently worked for fourteen years inside a prison, this genre of scholarship seems to hold more wisdom on being an outsider to prisons than on prisons themselves. There are some notable exceptions. In *Newjack: Guarding Sing Sing,* Ted Conover enrolls in a two-week officer training course after being denied access to observing one as a journalist.[49] After taking the course, he decides to spend a year serving as a corrections officer in order to learn about the profession from the inside out. In *Reading Is My Window: Books and the Art of Reading in Women's Prisons,* author Megan Sweeney is first exposed to prisons as a social worker and then undergoes the training to become a prison volunteer. She embeds her study of reading practices in prison in a few years of offering book studies and volunteer GED instruction inside women's prisons.[50] Her prison exposure is limited to the times and spaces allotted to her work as a volunteer prison educator, but because she dedicated herself to years of such exposure, she is able to create a detailed and nuanced account of intellectual life behind bars.

Of course, one way to observe and participate in prisons is as an incarcerated person. It is not surprising that some of the most well-known writing on prisons comes from scholar-activists who did time themselves. Authors like Angela Davis, George Jackson, Martin Luther King, Jr., Nelson Mandela, Malcolm X, Daniel Berrigan, and Dorothy Day all theorize jails and prisons as those who were imprisoned within them, sometimes for crimes directly related to their work for racial and economic justice. More recent and less known are formerly incarcerated writers like Shaka Senghor, Wilbert Rideau, Susan Burton, or Piper Kerman, whose prison memoir *Orange Is the New Black* was popularized as a Netflix series.[51] These scholars, activists, and writers became participant-observers of prisons by force. They then turned their experiences of the brutality and mundane degradations of prisons toward social change by writing and theorizing what they experienced. Most of these writers waited until after their release to write and publish, both because of the fear of retribution they might have experienced if they told the truth of prison while still incarcerated and because many prison systems have explicit policies prohibiting incarcerated people from publishing.

Perhaps the earliest example of prison ethnography occurred in 1913 when members of the New York State Prison Reform Commission Thomas Mott Osborne, Madeline Z. Doty, and Elizabeth Watson intentionally subjected themselves to incarceration in the New York State prison system to provide an eyewitness account of prisons for the sake of prison

---

[49]Ted Conover, *Newjack: Guarding Sing Sing* (New York: Vintage Books, 2000).
[50]Megan Sweeney, *Reading Is My Window: Books and the Art of Reading in Women's Prisons* (Chapel Hill: University of North Carolina Press, 2010), 9–17.
[51]Piper Kerman, *Orange Is the New Black: My Year in a Women's Prison* (New York: Spiegel and Grau, 2016).

reform.⁵² Bronislaw Malinowski is widely touted as one of the earliest anthropologists developing the method of participant-observation, but Malinowski was embedded in the Trobriand Islands at the same time as Osborne, Doty, and Watson were embedded in New York's prisons.⁵³ Osborne chose to be embedded into the New York State Prison at Auburn with some staff and administrators knowing his true identity. He therefore experienced some of the truth of prison life, but he was afforded privileges—like having paper and pencil to document his experience—not granted to the other incarcerated men. Osborne had arranged for his week of voluntary incarceration to be publicized in both the *New York Times* and *New York Journal* throughout the week it occurred, which proved to be impactful activist-scholarship that spurred on prison reforms but also created a certain set of protections around Osborne as more and more people in the prison learned his true identity throughout the week. Of notable contrast is that Doty and Watson chose to have none of the facility-level staff know of their true identities or the voluntary nature of their incarcerations. They thus experienced a fuller, harsher prison reality, and unlike Osborne, made it only three days before cutting the experiment short and being pulled out of prison.⁵⁴

The final way to serve as a regular participant and observer in prisons is to work in and for them. This ethnography falls in the category of practitioner-observation, and I join scholar-practitioners who write and reflect on their own professions with the structure and intentionality that characterize an academic study.⁵⁵ I intentionally chose to keep working as a prison chaplain as I embarked on this study in order to engage in a reflexive process in which I could look for the dynamics that were being named in my interviews in my own practice as a prison chaplain. I also wanted the opportunity to keep conversing about what I was learning with the incarcerated women who had formed me as a chaplain. I served as a prison chaplain during the conception, data collection, and data analysis phases of this study. I also engaged in participant-observation by making myself the first participant in the interview protocol described above. I wanted to know what my conversation partners would be experiencing in the interview process, and I wanted to be able to include some of my own experience within the anonymized and protected container that I had created. I also wanted a record of my own answers to my interview questions before collecting any

---

⁵²Rebecca M. McLennan, *The Crisis of Imprisonment: Protest, Politics, and the Making of the American Penal State, 1776–1941* (Cambridge: Cambridge University Press, 2008), 319–40.
⁵³David J. Rothman, *Conscience and Convenience: The Asylum and Its Alternatives in Progressive America* (Boston: Little Brown, 1980), 119.
⁵⁴Madeline Z. Doty, *Society's Misfits* (New York: Century Co, 1916).
⁵⁵Lilian Ayete-Nyampong, "Changing Hats: Transitioning between Practitioner and Researcher Roles," in *The Palgrave Handbook of Prison Ethnography*, ed. Deborah H. Drake, Rod Earle, and Jennifer Sloan (New York: Palgrave Macmillan, 2015), 307–25.

other data as a way to reflect back on both possible bias in my analysis and possible movement in my own understanding throughout the course of the study.

In some important ways, I failed to uphold the rigors of participant-observation as a practicing chaplain. Part of the ethnographic method is to keep an active journal recording one's observations in the field. While I have kept a journal, I began this study attempting to journal during and immediately after my shifts as a chaplain. It lasted one week. By the end of the first shift, I had a laundry list of mundane prison happenings that all of a sudden seemed like injustices. I had refused a woman a phone call to her child because it did not rise to the standard of "death or serious illness" by which my facility decides whether a staff person can provide an incarcerated person with a phone call. I had offered prayer and pastoral care to a woman whose home was being repossessed because she could not pay the taxes while incarcerated. I had not offered to help her find a lawyer because it was prohibited as "undue familiarity," a catch-all policy that keeps staff and incarcerated people from forming close, mutually beneficial relationships. I realized quickly that whatever goods I may or may not achieve as a prison chaplain, I am able to function in the role each shift by suspending a certain level of detailed ethical reflection. Jamie Bennett, who served as both a prison manager and prison researcher, named a similar dynamic. He writes:

> When I had entered prisons as a professional, I rather idealistically felt that this was an opportunity to engage with issues of social justice, but by the end of my research, my perspective had shifted and instead I saw myself engaged in a messy set of compromises and challenges regarding values and beliefs, getting my hands dirty in a social field of struggle.[56]

I was compromised as a chaplain, and my ethnographic process had to adapt to accommodate me. My role as an embedded participant-observer revealed my compromised position and exacerbated the impact of that compromise on my own psyche, and yet that participant-observation remained the bedrock of my exploration of the field of prison chaplaincy.

While prison ethnographers with no pre-existing relationships to prison write about the difficulty of "getting in," Bennett wrote about the importance of "getting out" of prison for practitioner-observers to gain the critical distance necessary to make sense of one's experience inside.[57] While I ultimately heeded his wisdom and took nine months of extended leave from my job in order to write, I stayed embedded in prison for most of this study

---

[56]Jamie Bennett, "Insider Ethnography or the Tale of the Prison Governor's New Clothes," in *The Palgrave Handbook of Prison Ethnography*, ed. Deborah H. Drake, Rod Earle, and Jennifer Sloan (New York: Palgrave Macmillan, 2015), 289–306.
[57]Ibid., 294.

because of the collaborative commitments of collaborative ethnography. In collaborative ethnography, the ethnographer is committed to testing her sense-making by offering it back to the community she is studying to test for resonance and fit. While I knew that I could continue in conversation with the twenty chaplains who went on record for this study, I also knew that once I left the prison, I would not easily be able to communicate with the incarcerated people who have formed my understanding of what prison chaplaincy is.[58] Throughout the course of this study, I have engaged in conversations with my Chaplain Clerks and other incarcerated women who regularly participate in chapel life about what I am learning from chaplains.

During my last shift, I sat in the storage closet that serves as both the Chaplaincy Library and Chaplain Clerk's Office. I told my (incarcerated) clerk Shirlye about the latest updates on the dissertation. I told her I was starting to think about salvation as life-in-death work, and she nodded emphatically saying, "That's right. That's what we do." I prayed over the ministry she would have in the prison during the nine months I was gone, and she prayed for me to write what I needed to write and come back to them. We both knew that prison policy meant we would not communicate for the entirety of the nine months I was on leave. When we finished praying, she said, "You know, I'd like to read it when you're done." "You have to read it," I said, "How else will I know what I've gotten wrong or right?"

The moment was important to me and representative of how I interact with women inside, but I would be lying if I suggested that I left prison to write, bathed in the prayers of my incarcerated co-worker, because it was a responsible research decision. I left prison because my body and mind were breaking. I said before that ethnography uses the body of the interpreter as the tool to gather, receive, and process data. This limits what can be learned to where the body of the ethnographer is permitted to be. I could engage in collaborative ethnography because of my role as a prison chaplain, but my body still served as a limit in the amount of data it could process. As it turns out, there is a limit to how much violence, death, disease, and carceral mundane one body can receive and metabolize on any given day.

I began listening to chaplains in recorded conversations in January of 2021. I immediately and concurrently began processing their transcripts, scrubbing them line by line of identifiable data. At that time, my prison had been living under Covid conditions for ten months. This meant that in addition to the normal degradations of prison life, women had not seen

---

[58]In most state systems, prison staff are prohibited from being in contact with people incarcerated in that system via letter or personal visitation. Some systems have exceptions whereby an employee at one prison can be in contact with an incarcerated person in a different prison, particularly if the person incarcerated at the other facility is a family member. For instance, I have been permitted to be on the personal visitation list of personal friends incarcerated at other North Carolina prisons than the one at which I work, but I would not be able to be on a personal visitation list of anyone at the prison at which I work.

their children or family members for ten months, they had spent months confined to their beds for as many as 21–24 hours each day, and we had experienced the fear, hospitalizations, and deaths of the first full wave of the disease hitting our facility. I would conduct an interview or transcribe a set of stories and then go work a shift in a place where social distancing was laughable and the prison-issued masks hung around women's chins because they had been sewn to fit men's faces.[59]

Sometimes it would take me only a few days of work to finish transcribing an interview, but I noticed that particular types of stories slowed me down. When chaplains named "officer suicides" as the hardest part of the job, I felt nauseous. I could transcribe only a few paragraphs, sometimes only a few lines, about the reality that both incarcerated people and prison staff sometimes choose death over prison before I had to stop listening. Detailed descriptions of murders, bodily attacks, and executions would end my ability to transcribe more in a given day. It is not particularly surprising that death would slow me down. Metabolizing violence is hard work.[60] Metabolizing violence—in either physical or narrative form—means receiving it, dissipating the energy of it (ideally without returning it), making sense of it, and maybe even transforming it into its parts, i.e., waste that can be properly disposed of and energy that can be used to feed. I have found that metabolizing violence works like metabolizing food, medicine, or poison; it takes time, sleep, water, exercise, sweat and tears, and a regeneration of the body that has metabolized violence in order to be able to do it again.

What surprised me, however, was that I was also slowed down by descriptions of the mundane aspects of prison. One chaplain told a story of being yelled at by another staff person for using the wrong bathroom. I thought about a time I had been mistaken for an incarcerated woman and yelled at for walking across a prison yard. I had to shut my computer. One chaplain talked about having a goal of looking into the eyes of all 1,600 men incarcerated in his facility each week. He was spending his time making rounds to each cell door because Covid lockdowns meant that men could not come to the chapel. I was doing the same at my prison, and I could barely interact with 130 people each week. I could not pick up that interview transcript for three weeks. The mundane overwhelm of prisons was as hard to metabolize as the overt stories of prison death.

When I could not bear to attend to the transcripts of other chaplains, I would simply go to work as a chaplain myself. I oscillated throughout each work week between hearing the stories of other chaplains and serving

---

[59]Women make up between 7 and 10 percent of carceral populations in most states. Their gender-specific needs are often lost in wider prison planning.

[60]I am indebted to Luke Bretherton for introducing me to the metaphor of "metabolizing violence" and for his help thinking through the use of the term within carceral contexts. For his wider use of the metaphor, see Luke Bretherton, *A Primer in Christian Ethics: Christ and the Struggle to Live Well* (Cambridge: Cambridge University Press, 2023).

as one. By July 2021, seven months into this process, I was exhausted. I gave myself a month off from research, but I continued to serve as a prison chaplain under Covid's restrictive conditions. In early August 2021, I told myself I would ease back into research by reading Eyal Press' *Dirty Work: Essential Jobs and the Hidden Toll of Inequality in America*. Press describes the way that American society outsources our dirty work like drone strikes, slaughterhouse work, and maintaining prisons, to workers who have little freedom to choose other professions and few resources to cope with the mental, physical, and moral impacts of the shadow sides of the political, economic, and legal systems on which we all depend. In a laundry list of stories about the impact of prisons on corrections officers, I read the following:

> There was a CO from New England I'll call Johnny Nevins (he did not want his real name used) who went home one day, drank an entire bottle of whiskey, posted a video on Facebook saying goodbye to his family, and then pointed a loaded gun at his head. The cartridge jammed when he pulled the trigger, and Nevins had since launched a support group to help troubled CO's avoid going down a similar path.[61]

Looking back, one could have read this story as a success and an inspiration. That is not how I read it. At the time, Press' description of this death plan sounded attractive: a bottle of Jack, one bullet, and the simple promise that I would never see a person in a cage again.

I did not pick up these transcripts or a book about prisons for eleven months after that. Instead, I dove headlong into the theology of Karl Barth and the story of Jesus Christ. In retrospect, I think my body was keeping me alive. I would not pick up these transcripts again until I was out of prison myself. I could not metabolize the sounds, smells, and stories of my own prison during Covid and metabolize the stories of twenty of my peers and their prisons at the same time. My conscious mind did not know that I could no longer engage as a participant-observer, but some part of me did. I could choose to stay with my congregation of incarcerated women and prison staff, or I could choose to stay present to the testimonies of twenty prison chaplains. Though I could not have articulated that I was making a choice at the time, I chose to shelve other chaplains' stories so that I could stay with my congregation for one more year. In that year, we were all moved (with two days' notice) from our minimum custody work camp to a maximum custody prison due to state-wide staffing shortages. We experienced a second and third prison-wide sweep of Covid that made

---

[61]Eyal Press, *Dirty Work: Essential Jobs and the Hidden Toll of Inequality in America* (New York: Farrar, Straus and Giroux, 2021), 60.

for another season of intensive 24-hour-a-day lockdowns and more deaths. I contracted Covid twice and pneumonia from the impacts of Covid three times. A drug epidemic grew in direct correlation to these lockdowns, and ultimately overdoses and overdose deaths would begin to rise, bringing us to the story at the beginning of this chapter.

I was not just an eyewitness to the illness and death of incarcerated people and prison staff during this study. I have felt in my body the hypervigilance, nightmares, and insomnia that chaplains in this study describe. I have felt the shock, horror, and allure of prison death as it kept coming at me in both narrative and physical forms. At the same time, I felt enlivened enough by my work with incarcerated people that I could not imagine trading in life with them for the possibility of better health outcomes. My choice to stay in prison both as a career and for the majority of this study was partially about finding joy, meaning, and purpose, but I also stayed out of guilt, duty, and a sense of call. I spent more than a decade feeling I could not choose a life without the stressors of prison because my incarcerated congregants could not choose such a life. In the end, I left prison for a season anyway. I acted to preserve my own life and mind—and the possibility of the creation of this book—by taking nine months of extended leave from my job as a prison chaplain. I could not be a participant and an observer of prison chaplaincy simultaneously for the whole of this project. My own body could not metabolize that much violence.

Karl Barth and the Incarcerated Christ

When I dove headlong into the story of Jesus and the theology of Karl Barth in August 2021, I found two witnesses who were much more involved in prisons than I had previously understood them to be. While Barth is widely acclaimed as one of the most influential theologians of the twentieth century, he may not seem an obvious conversation partner for someone struggling with prison death. At the time, I turned to Barth because I needed to remember how to say God's "Yes" to the prison's "World of No," and saying "Yes" to humans is one way that Barth describes God's saving work in Jesus Christ.[62] I felt like I was drowning, and I had always loved that Barth uses the metaphor of being snatched from an abyss to describe God's

---

[62] Karl Barth introduces the rhetoric of God's "Yes" and "No" to the world in the first pages of his first major published work. See Karl Barth, *The Epistle to the Romans*, trans. Edwyn C. Hoskyns (London: Oxford University Press, 1933), 38. While his dialectic theology changes over time, this particular dialectic remains a feature of his theology, even to the end of *Church Dogmatics* IV.3.2. See for example Karl Barth, *Church Dogmatics IV.3.2: The Doctrine of Reconciliation*, ed. G.W. Bromiley and T.F. Torrance (Edinburgh: T&T Clark, 1962), 797–801.

saving work, from his first published words to his last.[63] I had also noticed that Barth uses language from the criminal justice system to describe the person and work of Christ: Judge, Witness, and the Judge Judged in our place. My turn to Barth was no more intentional than the hunch that those threads might help me tie together God and prisons and that I needed to tie them together in order to stay alive.

However, Barth has made it into this book as a constant conversation partner because I realized in re-reading Barth during this study that he is a carceral theologian. Karl Barth is a person with a criminal record and a person who has spent significant time behind bars as both a prison preacher and as a volunteer prison chaplain at Strafanstalt Schällenmätteli, also called Basel Prison, in Basel, Switzerland. In April 1934, Barth was detained by the Nazi government and put through a three-hour interrogation by the Gestapo.[64] At that time, Barth was released from custody without formal charges.[65] That began a year of interactions with German police and courts that ended in June 1935 when Barth was ultimately found guilty of charges against the state, fined a fifth of his annual salary, and dismissed from his teaching post by the Minister of Cultural Affairs.[66] Twenty years later, in August 1954, Barth agreed to the invitation of Chaplain Martin Schwartz to preach one sermon at Basel Prison. It was the start of a ten-year ministry of preaching, teaching, and pastoral care behind bars.[67]

Perhaps the reader is wondering if parallels can rightly be made between Barth's experience of German and Swiss carceral contexts and present-day American prisons? Swiss and German prisons of the 1930s–60s have at least as many dissimilarities as similarities to American prisons of the 1960s–2020s. Rates of incarceration, sentence length, conditions of confinement, and the disproportionate impact of mass incarceration on communities of color in the United States have no correlation to how incarceration is practiced in Germany or Switzerland. After visiting the first of three American prisons in 1962, Barth himself acknowledges the differences:

> I am interested in prisons. Sometimes I preach to prisoners. I, therefore, asked for permission to visit an American prison. I will not give you its

---

[63] For some examples, see Barth, *The Epistle to the Romans*, 46–9, 91, 110, 240–1, 253–5. While the image of the abyss appears throughout *CD IV*, it is notably in the final passage of *CD IV.4*, the last partial volume of *Church Dogmatics* published posthumously. See Karl Barth, *Church Dogmatics* IV/4, trans. G.W. Bromiley (Edinburgh: T&T Clark, 1969), 211–13.
[64] Keith L. Johnson, *The Essential Karl Barth: A Reader and Commentary* (Grand Rapids: Baker Academic, 2019), 9.
[65] Ibid., 261–2.
[66] Eberhard Busch, *Karl Barth: His Life from Letters and Autobiographical Texts*, trans. John Bowden (Eugene: Wipf & Stock Publishers, 1976), 242–5. This history will be taken up in detail in Chapter 3.
[67] For an overview of Barth's ministry at Basel Prison see Martin Schwartz, "Karl Barth in der Strafanstalt."

name. It was called a "cell-house." But they were not even cells; they were cages. Tiny cages for two human beings, without a view, without a bath, without floor space. It was a terrible shock for me to see these conditions. Prisons in Switzerland are a paradise compared to this. These small cages were, for me, the sight of Dante's Inferno on Earth.[68]

At the same time, two of the carceral moments in Barth's own life occurred within national aberrations in carceral practices that made the Swiss and German contexts more similar to the American context than usual. First, Barth begins writing about prisons in his earliest published work *The Epistle to the Romans*. It seemed odd to me because he had not yet had experiences of arrest or imprisonment himself, and it will be thirty years before he begins his own ministry behind bars. We have no record of Barth engaging local prisons or jails as an early-career pastor in Safenwil, probably at least in part because of the relative scarcity of prisons there. When Barth names the social context of his commentary on Romans, he asks the reader to remember instead that the book was written inside of his experience of the First World War. What he does not say explicitly is that Switzerland's major role in that war was to become a country-sized prison for prisoners of war from the surrounding nations.

During the First World War, Switzerland held some 68,000 prisoners of war, not including deserters, war resisters, and civilian internees who were also incarcerated there at the time.[69] In 1918, Switzerland had a population of 3.8 million people. For perspective, prior to the 2020 drops in incarceration levels, North Carolina had a population of 10 million people and some 35,000–40,000 incarcerated people. During the First World War, Switzerland was more heavily saturated with prisons and prisoners than most American states at the height of mass incarceration. As a pastor in Safenwil, Barth was within a one-hour drive of five different internment camps. Serving on home guard patrol, which Barth did, was less about looking for enemy combatants and more about watching for escaped prisoners. Additionally, Barth's own experience of multiple arrests, charges, trials, appeals, verdicts, and sentencing happened in a moment in which Germany's normal policing and carceral rates were radically accelerated toward the end of racial control, rendering the German carceral context of Barth's justice-involvement more like the American context of mass incarceration than it normally is.

These experiences—i.e., Barth being a person who has patrolled for escaped prisoners, has a criminal record himself, and has served as a prison

---

[68] Jessica DeCou, "The First Community: Barth's American Prison Tour," in *Karl Barth and the Making of Evangelical Theology: A Fifty-Year Perspective*, ed. Clifford B. Anderson and Bruce L. McCormack (Grand Rapids: William B. Eerdmans, 2015), 71.
[69] Susan Barton, *Internment in Switzerland during the First World War* (London: Bloomsbury Academic, 2019), 9.

chaplain—seem to impact his understanding of who Jesus is: first, as a tried and convicted person, and later, as the prisoner who sets prisoners free. Throughout this book, I will show how Barth's primary descriptions of Jesus mirror and develop alongside his own specific experiences of the criminal justice system. In the twenty years after his own arrest, trial, and conviction, when Barth reads the Gospels, he is drawn to the fact that, "what these chapters bring before us is an arrest, a hearing and prosecution in various courts, a torturing, and then an execution and burial."[70] Rather than stressing Jesus' innocence in this court drama, Barth leans into the ways that Jesus looks like and is treated like anyone else who undergoes these experiences. Barth writes that Jesus "was sought out and arrested as a malefactor ... accused as a blasphemer ... and agitator."[71] He says that Jesus, "is not dying a hero's death, but the death of a criminal."[72] Jesus' arrest, trial, and conviction are not incidental to Barth's narration of salvation; rather, judicial and carceral terms become the nouns used to describe Jesus and the verbs for what he does in and for the world. Barth's Doctrine of Reconciliation centers around the concept of Jesus as a righteous judge who, for all his righteous actions, is unthinkably arrested, tried, found guilty, and sentenced to death—the Judge Judged in our place.[73]

As Barth moves in his own life from being a judged and convicted person into his experience as a preacher and volunteer prison chaplain at Basel Prison, his depiction of Jesus as a judged and convicted person becomes more explicitly an image of Jesus as an incarcerated person. In Barth's sermons to the men incarcerated at Basel Prison, Jesus looks more and more like an incarcerated man. Barth preaches that Jesus was "a prisoner, a convict,

---

[70]Barth, *CD* IV/1, 226.
[71]Ibid., 239.
[72]Ibid., 226–7. I have retained Bromiley's translation above, but it is worth noting that Barth does not use the word *Kriminell* here, or by my accounting, ever in *Church Dogmatics* or in his sermons to the men at Basel Prison. Similarly, he does not use the terms *Straftäter*, "offender" or *Rechtsbrecher*, "law breaker." He uses the term *Insassen*, "inmates," rarely—twice in sermons to men at Basel Prison in which he is listing various subject positions in prisons (warden, officers, inmates, etc.). Barth seems to avoid using language like the English terms "criminal," "inmate," and "offender." He opts for terms like *Gefangenen*, "prisoner," or simply "those in prison." When the biblical text uses it, he uses *Übeltäter*, translated something like wrong-doer or malefactor. In the case above, the German grammar does not require a noun where Bromiley has supplied "criminal" in English. The German reads, "*Und die dann—erst recht unfreiwillig!—mit ihm gekreuzigt werden, sind (Mr. 15, 27 f.) die beiden Räuber, deren Gemeinschaft mit ihm nur eben zeigt, daß, was ihm widerfährt, nicht einmal so etwas wie ein Heldentod ist, sondern—«Er wurde unter die Übeltäter gezählt»*." Karl Barth, *Die Kirchliche Dogmatik* IV/1 (Zollikon: Evangelischer Verlag, 1953), 251.
[73]Barth, *CD* IV/1, 211–82.

sentenced to death."⁷⁴ Three years into his preaching at Basel Prison, on Good Friday 1957, Barth preaches a sermon called "Die Übeltäter mit ihm," translated and published in English as "The Criminals With Him."⁷⁵ In this sermon, Barth boldly proclaims that "the first certain, indissoluble and indestructible Christian community" is that of Jesus and the two criminals crucified with him.⁷⁶ He claims that these two "criminals" have an intimacy with Jesus because of shared experience.⁷⁷ He says,

---

⁷⁴Barth, *Deliverance to the Captives*, 30. The German text reads, "*Indem ich nämlich an eure Stelle trete: an die Stelle, die euch zukommt—indem ich selbst werde, was ihr seid (nicht nur Einige von euch, sondern ihr Menschen alle!): ein Verurteilter, ein Gefangener, ein Sträfling, der den Tod erleiden muß.*" Karl Barth, "Ich lebe, und ihr werdet leben, Johannes 14,19 (1955)," in *Predigten 1954–1967, Gesamtausgabe*, ed. Hinrich Stoevesandt (Zurich, Zurich Canton: Theologischer Verlag, 1979), 23–30.

⁷⁵Karl Barth, "The Criminals with Him," in *Deliverance to the Captives* (Eugene: Wipf & Stock Publishers, 1979), 75–84. As noted above, "criminals" is perhaps not the best translation of *Übeltäter*. Barth is pulling this term directly from Luke 23:33, and it means "wrongdoers." For the German see Karl Barth, "Die Übeltäter mit ihm, Lukas 23,33 (1957)," in *Predigten 1954–1967, Gesamtausgabe*, ed. Hinrich Stoevesandt (Zurich, Zurich Canton: Theologischer Verlag, 1979), 84–93.

⁷⁶Barth, *Deliverance to the Captives*, 77.

⁷⁷The nouns that one uses for people with criminal records matter. The reader will notice that I predominantly use language like "incarcerated person," but that I retain language like "criminal, inmate, convict, and offender" when either dominant English translations of Barth or the chaplains in this study have used those terms. I then sometimes retain one of those terms in my analysis of that particular material. The word "criminal" is a loaded term, taking a single act in which a person violated the law and rendering that moment into an identity. Calling someone a "criminal" is a label that comes with a set of assumptions about a person's character and history, what society can expect of such a person, and what confinements and even violences society can do to such a person with impunity. I have worked with incarcerated people as an educator and chaplain for fifteen years. I have a criminal record myself. In my work, rejecting the language of "criminal, felon, and convict" is an important way to restore humanity and dignity to human beings who have been systematically denied it. People who have been called "criminals" are actively asking to be called "justice-involved, formerly incarcerated, or system-impacted" people instead. While that is my preferred practice, Barth and the chaplains in this study take seriously the degrading nature of prisons, and language about incarcerated people is a part of the degradation. When Barth uses language of criminality, he seems to know that it operates in a shaming register, and he applies the terms to Jesus in ways that challenge the shaming work of the terms as they come to live in the identity of Christ. Similarly, some of the chaplains in this study were self-reflexive about their use of the terms "inmate" and "offender," but they also acknowledged that changing language without changing the structures of prisons does nothing to humanize carceral conditions. Many chaplains are mandated to call incarcerated people "offenders" or "inmates" in their official writing and language at the prison. One chaplain shared how his prison system had recently mandated that incarcerated people no longer be called inmates, as it was de-humanizing, but rather be called "Adults in Custody" which had been shortened to "AIC's." He sardonically notes in the interview that calling a person an AIC neither humanizes nor changes the material conditions of prisons. Erasing the terms that are actually used for incarcerated people from this book would erase the reader's experience of the tenor and texture of prison speech, the speech to which chaplains and incarcerated people are exposed every day. I have chosen to retain the language of criminal, inmate, and offender as it appears in the texts and cultures of prisons, while prioritizing person-first language when

No one before and no one afterwards has witnessed so directly and so closely God's act of reconciliation, God's glory and the redemption of the world, as these two thieves ... These two companions were evidently and undeniably criminals, evil people, god-less people, unjust people. And (Jesus), like them, was condemned and crucified as a lawbreaker, a criminal. All three were under the same verdict.[78]

The more time that Barth spends in prison, the more he sees Jesus as an incarcerated person, and the salvation of the cosmos happening in an execution chamber. He says that by being executed alongside Jesus, these two men are eyewitnesses of God's act of reconciling the world. Even more shockingly, Barth says in this sermon that because they died with him, they will live with him (which he grounds in Rom. 6:8). Finally, he says that the rest of us can do nothing but get in line behind the criminals if we ever want to get close to Christ.

Barth's incarcerated Christ does not stay inside the walls of Basel Prison; rather, his carceral theology shows up in *Church Dogmatics* from this point forward. Barth preaches his sermon about a criminal Christ and a Christian community that begins at Golgotha in 1957, and then he works for the next two years to write *CD* IV/3.1.[79] This is the volume of *Church Dogmatics* in which Jesus is called the man of Gethsemane and Golgotha, the Victor of Gethsemane and Golgotha, and the Afflicted of Gethsemane and Golgotha. Gethsemane is the site of Jesus' arrest, and Golgotha is the site of his execution. The carceral has become embedded in Barth's primary descriptors of who Jesus is. This is the volume in which Jesus is described as "alien," "foreign," and "strange," precisely as Jesus starts showing up in places where people are routinely called alien, foreign, and strange.[80] This is the volume of *Church Dogmatics* in which Barth starts talking about prison explicitly. In the section titled "The True Witness," he writes that Jesus is "present here today among us in all our confusion, aberration and abandonment, before all our locked prison doors, at all our sick-beds and gravesides."[81]

---

writing in my own voice. For one example of a language guide created by and in conversation with formerly incarcerated scholars, see the Underground Scholars Language Guide, an initiative of the University of California, Berkeley. Available at: https://undergroundscholars. berkeley.edu/blog/2019/3/6/language-guide-for-communicating-about-those-involved-in-the-carceral-system.
[78]Ibid., 81.
[79]For dating see Barth, *Deliverance to the Captives*, 75 and Karl Barth, *Church Dogmatics* IV/3.1, trans. G.W. Bromiley (Edinburgh: T&T Clark, 1961), xiii.
[80]Sarah Jobe, "The monstrosity of god made flesh," *Journal of Reformed Theology* 13 (2019): 238–56. The German for "alien, foreign, and strange" is most often *fremde*. See for example *KD* IV/1, 235–6.
[81]Barth, *CD* IV/3.1, 395.

The Incarcerated Christ and the Sacrament of Christ's Presence in Prison

The more I read Barth, the more I could see the Incarcerated Christ that he articulates in both Scripture and the witness of the chaplains in this study. Chaplains repeatedly referenced Matthew 25 in which Jesus says, "While I was in prison, you came to visit me" (Mt. 25:36). One chaplain described seeing Jesus in incarcerated people as a surprise:

Father Michael:

> I kind of went into it with this feeling of dread and apprehension, but as soon as I walked in the prison, as soon as I closed the door behind me, I actually wasn't uncomfortable, and I had a very, very intense beautiful experience that first couple days there where I really felt like I was meeting the, meeting Jesus, and at least seeing the face of Christ in the men and women that are at this prison.[82]

Chaplains also described seeing Jesus in incarcerated people as a mandate, inspiration, and foundation for conceiving of the work.

Chaplain King:

> Chaplaincy is one of the most rewarding ministry opportunities that can be afforded to you. You have access to the entire institution. You have access into lives that have been broken, lives that have been rejected by society, but yet Jesus said, "I was in prison and you visited me." We're told in the book of Hebrews to remember those in prison, as if you were there yourself. And so God is at work in places where there seems to be more darkness than light.
>
> And I would say: be led by God's Spirit because God is always ministering to those who are on the margins of life. He's closest to those who have the broken hearts. He is in solidarity with the least of these.
>
> And so if you're looking to be famous, or you're looking to have your ego stroked, *(laughing)* chaplaincy is not for you. Hospital chaplaincy, prison chaplaincy, no! No form of chaplaincy … because chaplains are in the trenches. Chaplains care. And we care not just for people of our own faith group. We are to care for *all* of God's creations.

---

[82] Interview with the author on April 16, 2021.

> And we are to minister to them as if Jesus himself were physically present, and he is!
> He's present in you.[83]

We are to minister to them as if Jesus himself were physically present, and he is! When I first heard these readings of Matthew 25, I understood them to be operating at something of a metaphorical level. "Seeing Jesus in prison" is a justification for why chaplains keep going into prisons even when it is hard. It is also a statement about the fundamental dignity and worth of incarcerated people as bearers of the image of Christ. I did not understand that chaplains might be making a sacramental or ontological claim about the real presence of Christ in prisons. But chaplains kept saying that it was worth risking death to stay in the compromised ethical position of working in a prison because they got to see Jesus in incarcerated people, and I began to wonder if they were doing more than speaking in metaphor. I now understand chaplains to be naming a foundational mystery at the heart of the Gospel: Jesus came to set the captives free, but in doing so, he becomes a captive himself. What Jesus does for others, he does first in his own body. Salvation history happens in prison.

When Jesus stands up to preach his first recorded sermon at the synagogue in Nazareth as narrated in Lk. 4:14-30, he chooses a passage from Isa. 61:1-2 to ground his public ministry. Jesus says, "The Spirit of the Lord is upon me, because he has anointed me to bring good news to the poor. He has sent me to proclaim release to the captives, and recovery of sight to the blind, to set free those who are oppressed, and to proclaim the year of the Lord's favor" (Lk. 4:18-19). When Jesus looks out at his home people and tells them he was called to alleviate poverty, to heal the sick, and to let people out of prisons, his home people try to push him off a cliff (Lk. 4:29). Jesus passes miraculously through the crowd, but from that point on in Luke's Gospel, Jesus is home-less. He also goes about doing what he said he was called to do. He does give sight to the blind (Jn 9:1-6). He does enact a redistribution of wealth (Lk. 19:1-10). He heals and frees people from their demons (Mk 5:1-20, Lk. 8:26-40). But Jesus does not abolish prisons. He does not even free a single incarcerated person. Rather, he becomes one himself.

As Jesus goes about this prophetic life-work as a homeless man of an occupied ethnicity in an occupied country, he starts experiencing more and more death threats and run-ins with the law. In John's Gospel alone, crowds try to stone Jesus twice (8:59, 10:31). He is seen as a public nuisance. Authorities meet to discuss legal and politically advantageous ways to kill

---

[83]Interview with the author on January 15, 2021.

him four times.[84] Governing authorities attempt to arrest him three times before they ultimately succeed (7:32, 11:57, 18:36). Jesus is arrested, tried on charges of sedition, found guilty, given a death sentence, and executed. The man who said he came to proclaim freedom for the prisoners becomes one himself. I have known the story since before I could read it, but I had never named it that way. I was not taught to say that Christians worship a Savior who was a repeat offender, a public nuisance, or as Jens Soering puts it, "A Convict Christ."[85] Yet it is from prison, from the site of carceral death, that Jesus enacts the salvation of the cosmos. Jesus is resurrected from state-sponsored execution. This thing he says he was called to do—liberty to the captives—he does in his own body first, and it only happens once the state has done its worst to him. Jesus is not only the Judge who is judged in our place. He is the Prisoner who sets us free. God's ultimate revelation to the world that life will persist in the face of and even after death is enacted at the site of the carceral.

Life-in-Death Work: A Practical Soteriology

After processing all of this material, I realized that I had made a mistake. Chaplains are not bringing God's "Yes" to the prison's "World of No" any more than they are bringing Jesus to prison. In Barth, God's Yes and God's No are always housed together in the body of Jesus Christ. Jesus does not just speak God's Yes and God's No to the world (though he does do that). Rather, Jesus *is* God's Yes and God's No to the world. Salvation happens when horror and holiness, life and death, God's Yes and God's No, are held together in the body of Jesus Christ. Salvation happens not by simply getting these realities together in one body—reconciling them in Christ—but precisely as Jesus then takes his body to zones of social abandonment where others are holding horror and holiness together within themselves as well.[86] In Barth's later works, after he had spent time in prison, Jesus is not snatching people from an abyss. Rather, Jesus is jumping into the heart of the abyss with us and experiencing all the impacts of life in the abyss, even to the point of death. What chaplains call a ministry of presence, Barth calls the person and work of Christ.

While Jesus holds a primary and foundational role in enacting that salvific work, Barth says that each person is called to become a witness both in saying what one has seen of who Jesus is, and in following Jesus' example—"to be like Him, to copy or repeat His revealing and proclaiming,

---

[84]See The Gospel of John chapters 5, 7, 8, and 12.
[85]Jens Soering, *The Convict Christ: What the Gospel Says about Criminal Justice* (Maryknoll: Orbis Books, 2006).
[86]I am borrowing the term "zones of social abandonment" from João Biehl, *Vita: Life in a Zone of Social Abandonment* (Berkeley: University of California Press, 2005).

to approximate to Him as His representatives."[87] Even Barth, with his firm distinctions between God and human beings, can say, "the Christian really is where Christ is and Christ where the Christian is."[88] Barth says this after he has spent significant time in prison, and I see him joining the ranks of the prison chaplains in this study in their sacramental reading of Matthew 25 in which the real presence of Christ is available in people behind bars. Furthermore, Barth ties the embodiment of the real presence of Christ to the work of salvation, asking in this same passage, "How could they be His witnesses if Christ did not disclose and impart to them Himself and the fulness of salvation enclosed and actualized in Him?"[89] I will argue that salvation is enacted, made efficacious, and materialized when one is willing to hold God's Yes and God's No together in one's body and journey to the same sites of social abandonment to which Jesus journeyed until one is so impacted by death that one needs the salvation one enacts. This is a book about inhabiting Christ and coming alongside Christ in other people. This is a book about living and dying the salvation of the cosmos, a practical soteriology.

Chaplains say they are following Jesus' example in his person-by-person healing ministry. They also say they are going to prison to visit a Jesus that they see in incarcerated people. Chaplains never say they are going into prison to die or to be like Jesus in his death. But Jesus, like Deacon Joe, also does not articulate his ministry as death work. Jesus comes to *be with* people and to do the prophetic life-work that he grounds in Isaiah 61. But like all life-work, Jesus' life-work threatens the powers of death, drawing him so close to those powers that he ultimately bears the full weight of them in his own execution. I see chaplains following the arc of Jesus' life: following Jesus in his ministry of presence, embodying the way that Jesus' life-work threatens social divisions and death-dealing authorities, receiving the same death-threats that Jesus received and bearing the impact of that in their bodies, standing with Jesus and others in carceral death, and participating in Jesus' resurrected life-after-death, sometimes while still in prison and sometimes having been freed from it.

The architecture of this book follows that storyline—the arc of Jesus' incarnation, prophetic ministry, arrest, death, and resurrection—what I take and confess to be the arc of salvation. That salvific scaffolding is then filled up with the narratives of chaplains—historically, from within this study, and from my own professional experiences. The words of chaplains become the eyewitness accounts to life-in-death work, i.e., to the texture of salvation. Barth serves as a conversation partner throughout, helping to make sense of both prison chaplain narratives and the narrative arc of salvation because he

---

[87]Barth, *CD* IV/3.2, 607. See also *CD* IV/3.2, 575–6.
[88]Ibid., 651.
[89]Ibid.

enters the witness box as one who knows both the incarcerated Christ and the work of prison chaplaincy himself.

Chapters Two and Three work together to give a foundational overview of the work of prison chaplaincy. Chapter 2 shows the way that chaplains are inhabiting the logic of the incarnation in their "ministry of presence" in prisons. I seek to push the "ministry of presence" literature beyond easy affirmations that chaplains are Christ-like in their willingness to go and be with people where they are. While this may be true, a chaplain will, in this process, inevitably witness practices and structures that stand against the way of God, and the chaplain will have few ways to change those systemic patterns. Barth describes the incarnation as a *krisis;* and this chapter names how a ministry of presence in prison both happens amid the mundane and acute crises that make up prison life, and how the chaplain is thrown into crisis as she witnesses injustice and must decide what, if anything, she can effectively do with her eyewitness account. As chaplains sit with people who have been sentenced by a judge to be removed from society through incarceration, "just being with" becomes a radical political act. Chapter 3 pushes beyond the understanding of a ministry of presence as individual pastoral care to name the ways chaplains face systemic divisions—wicked problems—in the creation of chapel programming. I suggest that chaplains are inhabiting the doctrine of atonement, or reconciliation, as they work to create religious programs that are diverse, authentic, and free and that many referred to as a glimpse of the kingdom of God. Even as they create these spaces of life and freedom in prison chapels, divisions of race, religion, and carceral status threaten to disrupt the community being created. This chapter describes how chaplains are both using their authority and risking themselves to stand against wicked problems and reconcile divisions, an approach that looks strikingly like what Barth describes as Jesus' approach to atonement: the Judge becoming judged in our place.

As chaplains inhabit both the incarnation and Christ's reconciling work in prison, they—like Christ—come up repeatedly against powers and authorities, and they bear in their bodies the impacts of those mundane stressors and sometimes violent encounters. Chapter 4 "counts the cost" of inhabiting salvation by naming the ways that chaplains are risking death for life work—telling stories about lawsuits, death threats, and the "slow violences" of prison that hasten death. More often than creating heroes, risking death accommodates chaplains to prisons, jades, and callouses, and creates hypervigilance and PTSD. This chapter uses concepts of "being made sin" and becoming "sin-sick" to take seriously the mental, physical, and spiritual impacts of journeying daily into a place that is barreling toward death. Chapter 4 is followed by an Interlude: seven stories of carceral death in which fifty-nine people die. Like the deaths it describes, the Interlude stands as a rupture in this text. Chapter 5 does not seek to make sense of these and other carceral deaths; rather, the chapter simply places these carceral deaths alongside the carceral death of Jesus Christ in a "dying alongside" that Barth calls the first Christian community. In three attempts to describe how carceral death might possibly participate in the economy of salvation, this chapter tries to let horror and holiness sit together, as they do in both prison and the body of Jesus Christ.

In both Christian theology and prison, carceral death is not the end of the story. Chapter 6 turns to life-after-death work, asking what it means to inhabit the resurrection in the wake of carceral death when the tomb is not empty. Borrowing a term from Christina Sharpe, the chapter describes the practices of chaplains after death as "wake work" and explains how these practices are the site from which to see the mundane miracles of persistent life. The chapter names the ways in which both chaplains and incarcerated people are inhabiting Christ's resurrection as a triumph over and freedom from state-sponsored confinement and execution, while naming how it often seems that death and prison are winning. The chapter concludes with the ways that chaplains are dreaming the resurrection when it is not there to see, a restored dreamscape that empowers chaplains to simultaneously refuse, and refuse to leave, prison. The book concludes with a Postlude that attempts to make explicit the theological claims in the eyewitness accounts that have filled this arc of salvation. The Postlude takes up what it means to live our soteriology. The chapter offers soteriological models that retain the pieces and vocabulary of various atonement theories while rearranging them in such a way as to bear witness to the truth that while carceral death is always the site of the salvation of the cosmos, carceral death is never an acceptable end, goal, or even weigh station in the arc of salvation, for chaplains, for incarcerated people, for prison workers, or—even and perhaps especially—for Jesus Christ himself.

2

The Crisis of Presence:

Incarnating God in Prison

> *To believe in Jesus is the most hazardous of all hazards.*
> —KARL BARTH, *THE EPISTLE TO THE ROMANS*, 99

> *So what does it mean to embody the Good News?*
> —CHAPLAIN LEVINE, INTERVIEW ON APRIL 5, 2021

What is the work of prison chaplaincy? What does it look like, and what impact does it have—for better or worse—on the chaplain, on incarcerated people, and on the prison facility as a whole? In her book *A Ministry of Presence: Chaplaincy, Spiritual Care, and the Law*, Winnifred Fallers Sullivan explains how chaplains have been established as legal and necessary government employees in institutions like hospitals, prisons, and the military even though the Constitution mandates a separation of church and state.[1] In brief, chaplains have been established as the administrators of an institutionalized person's First Amendment Right to free exercise of religion. Chaplains do this in two ways: by offering non-specific "spiritual care" to people of any or no faith tradition and by providing faith-specific religious services for any religious group recognized by that state or federal prison system. In *Fear No Evil: A Guide for Prison Chaplaincy*, Aaron W. Mobley explains how the constitutional right to free exercise of religion was interpreted for prisons by the Religious Land Use and Institutionalized

---

[1] Sullivan, *A Ministry of Presence*, 139–72. For the ways in which religious freedom has been legislated for private prisons and religious volunteers in prisons see Sullivan, *Prison Religion*.

Persons Act (RLUIPA), passed by Congress in 2000.[2] RLUIPA is then interpreted through the policies of any given state or federal prison system to guide the practice of chaplains. The chaplains in this study referenced RLUIPA frequently. They understood a major part of their job to be protecting the religious freedom of incarcerated people. While offering non-specific spiritual care and faith-specific religious services are a legal mandate for prison chaplains, the chaplains in this study have a robust theological and political understanding of how and why they offer these services that goes well beyond fulfillment of the law.

Theologically, prison chaplains often described their spiritual care work as a ministry of presence.[3] While they conduct a laundry list of religious services, volunteer management, educational services, death notifications, pastoral care, and paperwork on any given shift, they frame those "doings" within a theory of ministry that is primarily about "being with" people inside of prisons. "Just show up," Chaplain Floating told his trainee, "90% of the job is just being there." Similarly, before Barth answers "why" or "to what effect" God became human, he asks "how" or "in what way" God becomes human.[4] A dominant way of describing "how or in what way" chaplains are in prison is "a ministry of presence." When chaplains use the phrase, they are describing the non-specific spiritual care that they offer to people of any or no faith tradition, but they are also describing a way of being with people that they understand to be modeled on the incarnational nature of the Christian God as that God draws close to the people of Israel and takes on flesh in Jesus Christ.

The idea that a ministry of presence is rooted in the incarnation is not new. It is a dominant theme in pastoral theology.[5] Robert Hubbard concludes his article "Chaplaincy: Incarnation in Action," with the claim that "one thing chaplains do is present to people God-with-skin. They are an incarnation of God's presence and work in the world, visible with eyes to see, ears to listen, a voice to speak, and hands to touch."[6] In this article, Hubbard shows how it is characteristic of God in both the Old and New Testaments to "desire

---

[2]Aaron W. Mobley, *Fear No Evil: A Guide for Prison Chaplaincy* (Manchester: Aaron W. Mobley, 2017), 83–102.
[3]Kevin Adams, "Defining and operationalizing chaplain presence: A review," *Journal of Religion and Health* 58, no. 4 (2019): 1246–58.
[4]Barth, *CD* IV/1, 184.
[5]See for examples see Janet Stokes, "Ministry of presence and presence of the spirit in pastoral visitation," *Journal of Pastoral Care* 53, no. 2 (1999): 191–9; Joel A. Jueckstock and Klye J. Vlach, "Claiming a substantive view of presence: The significance of the pastor's self," *The Covenant Quarterly* 73, no. 3–4 (2015): 30–9; Stephen T. Hall, "A working theology of prison ministry," *Journal of Pastoral Care & Counseling* 58, no. 3 (2004): 169–78; Joe E. Pennel Jr., *The Gift of Presence: A Guide to Helping Those Who Suffer* (Nashville: Abingdon Press, 2010).
[6]Robert L. Hubbard Jr., "Chaplaincy: Incarnation in Action," *The Covenant Quarterly* 73, no. 3–4 (2015): 13.

proximity" to God's people.[7] God actively seeks to live among God's people in the Tabernacle and Temple, through the bodies of the prophets, in the appearances of the Angel of the Lord, and in the incarnation of God in Jesus Christ. In this literature, a ministry of presence brings calm in a storm and a non-anxious presence in the face of anxiety. When practicing a ministry of presence, the chaplain brings her body into crisis situations in a way that is grounded, empathetic, and nonjudgmental. In this way, a ministry of presence is an answer to crisis. While this is true, a ministry of presence *in prison* presses into view the way in which presence provokes as many crises as it solves. As chaplains sit with people who have been sentenced by a judge to be removed from society through incarceration, "just being with" becomes a radical political act that creates tension between chaplains and other prison staff. Furthermore, a ministry of presence throws the chaplain into crisis as she witnesses injustice and must decide what, if anything, she can effectively do with her eyewitness account (often not much).

While this is not usually how a ministry of presence is described—as a radical political act that creates crisis—this is precisely how Karl Barth understands the incarnation. This chapter will detail how Barth understands the incarnation of Christ to create crisis by revealing the way of God in this world. Christians see this way of God, see that it is utterly against the ways of this world, and are yet mostly powerless to enact the way of God in its fullness. The incarnation, by revealing God's way in the world, immediately throws Christians under judgment as they try and fail to enact that way. Barth describes Jesus as bringing God's Yes wrapped up in God's No. The most faithful posture in the face of God's No is a willingness to accept culpability and stand under the judgment of God. This sounds like bad news. Barth calls it the "impossible possibility" of Christian ministry.[8] But while standing under judgment can create fatalism and despair, it can also habituate chaplains in a sort of world-weary wisdom and resigned bravery in which they are willing to risk judgment in the violation of prison policy when they perceive that the real presence of Christ is at stake.

Ministry of Presence and the Incarnation of Christ

Chaplain Mav was describing "intense listening" to incarcerated men as one of his primary job responsibilities, and I asked if he had a theology to frame that ministry of presence work. Chap Mav did not miss a beat:

---

[7]Ibid., 5.
[8]While this chapter will focus on the use of the phrase "impossible possibility" in Barth's *The Epistle to the Romans*, I am also informed on this point by Karl Barth, "The Word of God and the Task of the Ministry," in *The Word of God and the Word of Man*, trans. Douglas Horton (New York: Harper Torchbooks, 1957), 183–217.

I believe in the Christ made flesh, John Chapter 1, Word made flesh. Your intimacy with the Word should lead to your ability to incarnate the Word in your own life. You want to look at an image of Christ? Look at the face of the person who helps you as Christ would: that's your image for the day.[9]

I believe in the Christ made flesh, John Chapter 1. Chap Mav places his ministry of active listening inside a theology of the incarnation. In Jesus Christ, Christians profess that creation is met by a Creator who is "in flesh," the Latin root for the word "incarnation." The Gospel of Matthew, citing the prophet Isaiah, calls this God-in-flesh Emmanuel, from the Hebrew *'immanu-El*, with-us-God (Isa. 7:14, Mt. 1:23). God takes on flesh to be with God's people in the act of incarnation as described by Jn 1:1-18, but Jesus extends this incarnational logic into the texture of his ministry as well. Jesus enacts a mobile ministry of presence, continuing to meet people where they are. The Gospels present Jesus as out on the road, in the marketplace, outside of the Temple, in people's homes, walking and talking with people where he finds them. Jesus does not seem to expect people to come to him. In the geography of salvation, Jesus is fundamentally presented as "on the move" or even on the run, meeting people outside of the structures of organized religion at least as often as he meets them inside of those structures.[10]

This is one way in which chaplains are different from local church pastors. Pastors work within the institution of the local church in which much of the choreography involves parishioners coming to church to encounter God, pastor, and community.[11] Chaplains, however, are sent out to do the work of the church primarily outside of its walls. At a macro level, chaplains are sent as ordained ministers into secular institutions (hospitals, universities, prisons, the military, etc.). Prison chaplains have been sent by their ordaining bodies to enact their ministries inside of prisons. But just as with Jesus and the incarnation, the incarnational logic does not stop once a chaplain gets onto the prison grounds. Prison chaplains go to where the people are *inside of* a prison complex as well. Chaplains hold a unique role among other caregiving prison staff in that "only the chaplain is sent into the setting of the

---

[9] Interview with the author on January 25, 2021.
[10] I am borrowing the term "on the run" from Alice Goffman, *On the Run* (Chicago: University of Chicago Press, 2014). In an ethnography of an over-policed neighborhood in Philadelphia, Goffman describes the way that policing can create not just moments of flight but a lifestyle of being "on the run" for men in over-policed neighborhoods. I see these same dynamics at work in the Gospel narratives in which Jesus is presented as itinerate, not simply for missional reasons but because he has repeated run-ins with authorities.
[11] This is not to undercut the role of missions and the ways in which churches work outside their doors, but simply to note a difference in primary location and a distinction in basic choreography.

prisoner, in many contexts being allowed to sit alone in the cell."[12] Sundt, Dammer, and Cullen also note this dynamic, explaining, "chaplains are the only members of the prison work group, other than correctional officers, who regularly have contact with inmates in the tier area," i.e., the areas where prisoners live in cells, pods, and dorms.[13]

Christian prison chaplains are "on the move" not simply because Jesus gives an example of mobile ministry, but because many prisons do not permit incarcerated people the mobility that would enable them to come to the chaplain or Chapel. Father Michael, who served in maximum security men's prisons in two different states during his career, described simply finding the people who had requested his presence and negotiating how he could communicate with them as the first and foundational task of each day.

Father Michael:

> You go in there and find out where you need to meet them (incarcerated men). In the mainline section, they could open the cell door, and we could talk. Or they could come out of their cell for that matter. We could go sit down somewhere and talk in the yard. But in the Death Row unit, it was high security, and they were always behind a barrier, so almost always behind the cell wall. Now the cells were kind of this wire mesh. It wasn't like a solid door, so it was relatively easy to talk through that without any obstruction. The sound, the hearing ... sometimes with the solid doors, it can get hard to hear, and then you have other noises in the background.[14]

Father Michael's description represents a major theme of this study. Every chaplain in this study talked about going from cell to cell to offer conversation, a rolled-up newsletter, a Communion wafer, or simple eye contact through bars, through mesh wire, and through food slots in metal doors. One chaplain described being permitted to meet with men for one-on-one pastoral care in an empty bathroom shower because the shower spaces were always monitored by security staff while the tier hallways were not. Two chaplains described meeting in "cramped closets," and many referenced walking lap after lap with residents "on the yard." Like Jesus, the choreography of prison chaplaincy is about being on the move, meeting people where they are in cells, on tiers, in the yard, in hallways, in dayrooms, and even in shower stalls.

---

[12]Kevin Hargaden, "Prison chaplaincy in the age of Covid-19," *Theology* 123, no. 5 (2020): 339.
[13]Jody L. Sundt, Harry R. Dammer, and Francis T. Cullen, "The role of the prison chaplain in rehabilitation," *Journal of Offender Rehabilitation* 35 (2002): 60–1.
[14]Interview with the author on April 16, 2021.

Though Christ-like, this mobility did not always feel holy. Chaplain Tyrone lamented, "I wish I could spend more time actually dealing with issues a little bit more closely. A lot of times I just kind of feel like I'm constantly on the move." He describes his ministerial mobility as a by-product of being only one of two chaplains serving 3,000 incarcerated men during the Covid-19 pandemic, a time period in which incarcerated people were confined to their cells and bed areas even more than usual, forcing chaplains to go cell-to-cell to see incarcerated people if they were to see them at all.[15] Father Michael, described above, said he could do this cell-to-cell work for about an hour before needing to take a break. He would balance that work with time in the chapel "hanging out" with the incarcerated men serving as Chaplain Clerks. This unstructured fellowship in the open space of the Chapel "kind of balanced out the heaviness of just talking to people in these tiny little cramped cells. You know, just the environment itself is oppressive."[16]

While the oppressive environment of the prison limits how long a chaplain can be physically present to the sites within the prison where that oppression is most palpable, there was also a way in which it was precisely because the environment was oppressive that chaplains understood their presence to have an impact. At a very basic level, chaplains named that both officers and residents change their behavior in the presence of a chaplain. Officers might begin to yell and then cut themselves off, apologizing to the chaplain, rather than to the person being berated. An officer or resident would launch a string of curse words at another person, see the chaplain, apologize, and quickly change tone. Chaplain Love explained with a laugh, "I would say that a lot of the officers would not say things in front of me, which is another reason to be present!"[17] Chaplain Moise described the positive behavioral change that happens in front of the chaplain saying,

> You are God's representative as the chaplain, and when people see you, whether you like it or not, they see God. So you can have whatever theology you want to have about that. You can try to get away from it, or you can try to live into it. But whatever you want to think about it, you are God's person there.[18]

In an environment in which abusive communication patterns such as yelling and cursing are normalized, the simple presence of a person representing God can prompt voluntary suspension of those abusive behaviors, even if just momentarily.

---

[15]Interview with the author on March 15, 2021.
[16]Interview with the author on April 16, 2021.
[17]Interview with the author on March 12, 2021.
[18]Interview with the author on January 1, 2021.

A Ministry of Presence as Crisis Intervention

Conflict de-escalation and crisis intervention were routinely named as what chaplains were doing with their bodies in a ministry of presence in prison. The quote at the beginning of this chapter was pulled from a wider discussion about the fundamental activities of prison chaplains. Chaplain Levine asks rhetorically, "What does it mean to embody the Good News and carry the Good News in a way that people can experience?" He answers himself by saying, "being present, active listening, restorative justice, and conflict transformation."[19] Walking around a prison just "being present" will bring the chaplain repeatedly into conflicts, and the chaplain's simple presence will not always be enough to de-escalate those conflicts. Chaplains also used conflict de-escalation tactics that they learned intuitively on the job or explicitly in non-violence trainings. They described using their body-postures and the tone and volume of their voices to communicate non-threat. They talked about intentionally using grounding practices before, during, and after their shifts to steady their central nervous systems, so that people with dysregulated nervous systems could regulate off of them.[20] They talked about being called intentionally by custody staff to intervene when an incarcerated person was yelling, hyperventilating, in an active panic attack, enraged, threatening others, or sobbing. They also named that if one routinely makes rounds in a prison, one will simply come upon those situations, often in the minutes before a fight erupts. They talked about the power of using a calm, quiet, firm tone of voice to ask an incarcerated person, "What is wrong?" showing the person that their needs and concerns matter, at least to the chaplain in that moment, in a wider system in which it is hard to get concerns heard and needs met. When the people around a chaplain go loud, the chaplain goes quiet. When a person clenches their fists to fight, a chaplain opens her palms. These are basic non-violent crisis intervention and de-escalation tactics. They are also how Jesus acts in the face of conflict.

In Jn 8:1-11, a group of people invested in "the law" drags a woman in front of Jesus and makes her stand between them (8:3). They explain that she was caught in the act of adultery and that the law says she should be stoned. Jesus does not answer. He bends down and begins to move the dirt

---

[19] Interview with the author on April 23, 2021.
[20] For more on the intentional use of co-regulation in therapeutic relationships, see Mark Sossin and Jan Charone-Sossin, "Embedding: Co-regulation within therapeutic process: Lessons from development: Response to 'Co-regulated interactions: Implications for psychotherapy: Paper by Stanley Greenspan,'" *Journal of Infant, Child, and Adolescent Psychotherapy* 6, no. 3 (2007): 259–79; Patricia Gerbarg, Richard Brown, Chris Streeter, Martin Katzman, and Monica Vermani, "Breath practices for survivor and caregiver stress, depression, and post-traumatic stress disorder: Connection, co-regulation, compassion," *OBM Integrative and Complementary Medicine* 4, no. 3 (2019): 1–31.

around with his finger. They keep arguing. Jesus stands up only to say one line: "If any of you is without sin, let him be the first to throw a stone at her," and then he bends back down again. Jesus makes himself small, calm, and quiet in the face of accusatory speech that seems poised at the edge of physical violence. His response dissipates the energy of the crisis, and the text says that the crowd walks away one person at a time, the older people leaving the fight first (8:9). In this text, a woman is saved from a violent death at the hands of an angry crowd.[21] Jesus enacts her salvation in the form of crisis response and de-escalation.

Chaplain Dismas calls this conflict intervention style "acting in the opposite spirit," and he told me a story about the way that it works even when the person in front of him is legitimately mad at him. Chaplain Dismas is a big, loud guy who loves motorcycles and seemed like the type of person who is both the life of a party and quick to throw a punch in a bar fight. Within the first minute of meeting him, he told me that he had a prison number and that he had been a gun-runner and drug-dealer before his conversion and career in prison chaplaincy. Yet when faced with the eruptions of anger that typify prison life, Chaplain Dismas does not rely on his size, the strength of his voice, or his congeniality. Instead, he acts "in the opposite spirit" of the anger that is being levied at him. He told me this story.

Chaplain Dismas:

> One of my techniques is to act in the opposite spirit. I kind of learned this early on.
>
> So I'm walking down what we call Main Ave., which is one of the tunnels, and an inmate comes up and starts screaming at the top of his lungs. You know, just, I mean he's going to murder me right there. That's what it looks like to anybody around us.
>
> And he's in my face. He is screaming. He's saying, "you know, you took me off of that class list! Who do you think you are? What's going on? I need to get back into that thing!"
>
> And ...
>
> > *(pauses, takes a breath)*
>
> I learned how to respond to that. I kind of made it up in my head. It's like, whoa what is correct here? And it hit me.

---

[21] Jens Soering reads this story explicitly as Jesus interrupting a death penalty trial. See Soering, *The Convict Christ*, 24–30.

After he was completely done with everything, I said, "Okay. You know what? Let's do this: I'm going to write this down. Give me your number. Give me your name. Give me the program. I'm going to find out. I'm going to get to the bottom of this."

Now I become his lawyer.

After I'm done, I look at him and say, "So, how are you doing, man?"

And all of a sudden, I'll see the real guy.

That other thing was some kind of emotional outburst attached to what he was looking at, but it wasn't really him. So, by acting in the opposite spirit, I could draw him back out. And then we move on from there.

And then I would actually go make this happen, you know. Even if I made the decision to pull him out of that program, I would now make a decision to put him back in. And now I've got one of these crazy, wild, bipolar, dangerous guys as my best friend who is going to spread the word that chap's okay.[22]

Chaplain Dismas received yelling without responding in kind. He let the person before him yell at him until he "was completely done." He shows with his words and actions that he is interested in the legitimate concern of the person in front of him by taking out his notepad, asking questions, and writing down what he needs to know. He "becomes the lawyer," the advocate, comforter, and friend of the person before him. He offers a safe container for the person to share about himself. Chaplain Dismas allows himself to be convicted by the encounter, and the "real person" can be seen and heard as the anger dissipates.

At one level, this is a story about tactics that any chaplain could use to de-escalate conflict. The story also reverberates with the work traditionally assigned to the Holy Spirit, our Advocate, Comforter, and Friend. The word for Spirit in Hebrew is *ruach,* and it can be translated as wind, breath, or spirit. As noted in the transcript above, I watched Chaplain Dismas invite a big breath into his body to calm himself after the memory of the altercation. After inviting breath to settle him, Chaplain Dismas becomes the incarcerated man's advocate. In these stories of crisis intervention, there are often hints of something more metaphysical at work than simply the de-escalation tactics being deployed by the chaplain. Breath ushers in Spirit, and de-escalation tactics become a site to know oneself, God, and neighbor anew.

---

[22]Interview with the author on July 1, 2021.

The Chaplain as the Real Presence of Christ?

I mentioned before that Robert Hubbard concludes his article "Chaplaincy: Incarnation in Action," with the claim that "one thing chaplains do is present to people God-with-skin. They are an incarnation of God's presence and work in the world, visible with eyes to see, ears to listen, a voice to speak, and hands to touch."[23] Hubbard claims that Christian chaplains are following the example of their God when they "*get out there* where the people are," but he presses a ministry of presence beyond divine mimicry when he says that chaplains *present God-with-skin* to the people that they encounter.[24] Hubbard is not alone in this claim that chaplains somehow embody God, present God, or act as the presence of God as they go about their work. Sonny Guild says that chaplains "mediate God's presence."[25] Scott Jablonksi writes that a ministry of presence "means that we, as the Church's ministers, intentionally make ourselves present to people as best we can so as to prolong the Lord's incarnation into their lives ... We have been marked by his presence in a special way at our ordination and now are able to act *in persona Christi.*"[26] Similarly, Kevin Hargaden writes that prison chaplains serve "as a walking sacrament."[27]

Chap Lin, one of the chaplains in this study who served for over twenty years in men's federal facilities, seemed to have this incarnational theology embedded in her understanding of prison chaplaincy. She explains that the role of chaplains is to be a "representative of the Holy," showing by their presence with both staff and residents that there is "no God-forsaken place."

Chap Lin:

> So I guess the ...
> What I think is the role of the chaplain
> is to do what supports life,
> what supports health,
> what is,
> is to be visible,
> is to be present.
> To show the population, whether it's prisoner or staff, that
> there is no godforsaken place.
> There is always a representative of the Holy

---

[23] Hubbard, "Chaplaincy in Action," 13.
[24] Ibid., 10. Italics original.
[25] Sonny Guild, "The Ministry of Presence: A biblical view," *Leaven* 2, no. 2 (1992): 7.
[26] Scott Jablonksi, "Making Christ present: Ministry of Presence calls us to bring God to the lives of others," *The Priest* (December 2018), 14–15.
[27] Hargaden, "Prison chaplaincy in the age of Covid-19," 338.

> even in the midst of unholy things.
> God would never turn God's back.
> I mean, maybe biblically God turns God's back,
> but we don't want that to …
> to be … *(laughs)*
> Yeah …
> they feel abandoned enough already!
> Yeah …
> But at least there's a presence,
> whether it looks effective or not effective,
> at least God is there with them.[28]

Chaplains *show the population, whether it's prisoner or staff, that there is no godforsaken place. There is always a representative of the Holy, even in the midst of unholy things.* Chap Lin's presence in the prison means it is not a godforsaken place because she, as a representative of the divine, actually makes God present there in some real way. Chaplain Dismas is not simply *an* advocate, but somehow *the* Advocate as he comforts, befriends, and meets the needs of the man in the tunnel. This claim—that chaplains are the embodied presence of God, a "walking sacrament" to use Hargaden's phrase—falls apart as much as it holds together. In the tradition of negative dialectics, the claim seems to ache for a partner phrase: "The Chaplain is the presence of Christ, and the Chaplain is not the presence of Christ." As soon as Father Michael says, "we represented the Light in a dark place," he quickly amends himself to add, "I wasn't the light, but I was there to witness to the light. You know Christ is already there in that place."[29] Hargaden does something of the same in his article where he calls chaplains "walking sacraments" by being careful to then say that the chaplain's presence is grounded in a pre-existing presence of God that is at work in the prison with or without the chaplain.[30]

Can a prison chaplain, or anyone for that matter, be the "real presence" of Christ, in the fullness of that phrase? If the prison chaplain "is the presence of Christ," what about the Christ who claims to appear in incarcerated people (Mt. 25:36)? What about the Christ who is both cosmically, wholly other and the Christ who was his own distinct, historical person? Are chaplains super-ceding either that Christ or the Christ in incarcerated people when their very presence indicates that there is no godforsaken place? In some ways, the entirety of this book will circle around these questions. As important as they are, I want to suggest that Chap Lin's words show a more immediate problem with the idea that prison chaplains can mediate

---

[28] Interview with the author on January 6, 2021.
[29] Interview with the author on April 16, 2021.
[30] Hargaden, "Prison chaplaincy in the age of Covid-19," 343.

the presence of God in prison, which is that the very nature of prisons—and chaplains as duty-bound employees within them—compromises the chaplain's ability to represent the God who "sets the captives free"[31] or offers "life abundant"[32] in practical ways on every single shift.

As quickly as Chap Lin affirms that the prison is not a godforsaken place, she nervously acknowledges that sometimes God does turn God's back on people in the Bible. Of course, divine abandonment is not what the chaplain wants to portray, she adds, since people in prison have been "abandoned enough already." Before sharing the above words, Chap Lin had told me about an incarcerated person being kicked to death, a staff person being stabbed in the neck by an incarcerated person, and her own experience of an altercation with an incarcerated man. Her description of prisons as "godforsaken" resonates, as does her honest admission that sometimes the presence of the chaplain does not seem effective in ushering in the presence of God in the realities of carceral death that she has witnessed. A chaplain offers a ministry of presence in the face of prison crises, but prison also throws the chaplain's ministry of presence into crisis.

A Ministry of Presence in Crisis

The following reflection is from Chaplain Love, a woman who served in a men's closed-custody prison, on the role of the chaplain during prison crises.

Sarah Jobe:

> I'm interested in these moments when prison chaplaincy kind of tips from just the mundane stressors and violence levels of prison to something more like disaster chaplaincy—so major fights, lockdowns, escapes, riots, death of staff, or death of residents. For those of us currently serving, COVID. What is it like to minister in those moments? What does the ministry look like in those moments when the facility is in crisis?

Chaplain Love:

> What I saw ... what I what I felt called to do was to go to those housing units when the SWAT teams—they didn't call them SWAT teams. What did they call them? They were the teams that were activated from other institutions, and the officers would come together, and they had special training, and they would come into the institution, and they would go through every, every man's cell looking for weapons.

---

[31] Isaiah 61:1-3, Luke 4:17-21.
[32] John 10:10.

There'd been some kind of outbreak,
and they are looking for drugs or looking for other,
other signs,
that things could,
could be used, after some incident had happened.

I, but I would go down and stand in the housing unit.

Next to

usually the

the

the officer in charge.
And the, you know, maybe a lieutenant or sergeant
and just stand there.
And I
wanted
the inmates to know
as they were,
as you know,
they were stripped down to their underwear
and had to stand handcuffed
outside of their door, cell door,
while officers would go in
and dismantle everything.
They had to carry their mattresses out of the cell,
and take them through a metal detector.
And some of the men were so old that couldn't do that themselves,
and it was painful to watch
that happening,
and so all I knew to do
was to be present
and it didn't
it, you know,
it didn't seem like …

of course, I wanted to do something.

But.

I felt like,

I felt like that was important.

(long pause)

To say, "I see what's going on."

to at least bear witness

to this terrible thing
that's happening.

So …

I did that
a lot of different times in disaster situations
where things would be on lock down,
and I would go where I could go.

Even in lockdown, you know, I could go to solitary confinement, as that was always a lock down situation.

And I could go to the, I could go to the offices of staff, and I,

you know, so I could make my,
I could make my presence known.

But …

You know, like that … the story I told at the very beginning was about the terrible disaster of one, one inmate slashing the neck of another, of another inmate, and you know that when the codes are called, Medical leaps to attention, and officers who are able are there. But chaplains are not expected.

But I would do the best I could to be present.

(Huge sigh. Long pause)

But I sure did feel sometimes …

You know we were called non-essential staff.

We *are* called non-essential staff! *(laughs)*

And I felt that!

You know I wanted to be essential. I wanted to be able to wrap up a wound. I wanted to be able to stop the conflict. I don't know … I just

... but in those kind of disaster situations, the best I knew to do was to be present and to bear witness.³³

I felt like it was important to say, "I see what's going on," to at least bear witness to this terrible thing that's happening. If a chaplain puts her body in the places that Jesus says he will be in—in the presence of people who are hungry, thirsty, strangers, naked, sick, and incarcerated—she will have no choice but to witness the conditions that are making them hungry, thirsty, unwelcome, naked, sick, and incarcerated. The chaplain will become an eyewitness to the major injustices of this world, and the chaplain will have to decide what to do with that eyewitness testimony.

In the story above, Chaplain Love is caught between two important truths. At one level, "just bearing witness" to people undergoing traumatic experience has been proven to mitigate the ongoing impacts of trauma on those experiencing it. Peter Levine explains that the witness needs to be "empathetic" to have a positive impact on the health outcomes of those undergoing trauma.³⁴ The empathetic witness is most impactful when directly present in the moment of trauma, though they can also have a positive impact during later healing stages as well.³⁵ Importantly, the witness need not be able to change the conditions of trauma in order to have a positive impact; the mere presence of an empathetic witness communicating that the person's experience is seen and that the person is not alone can mitigate against the impacts of traumatic exposure.³⁶ Chaplain Love's intuition that it was important for incarcerated people to see her seeing them as they were stripped, handcuffed, and marched through a metal detector carrying their mattresses is correct ... *if* they perceive her to be an empathetic witness.

Chaplain Love also laments the possibility that her presence did not make a difference. She did not intervene or attempt to stop the Prison Emergency Response Team (PERT). She did not bind up a wound. She was labeled as and experienced herself as "non-essential." From a critical perspective, the way in which she stands beside the Officer in Charge could even be perceived by some incarcerated people as a show of support for the prison, its leadership, and subsequently its current methods of maintaining safety and security. By that reading, this story is another example of Dubler and Lloyd's assessment that, in prison, the chaplain hangs her hat beside the torturer.³⁷ If Chaplain Love were perceived to be on the side of the institution in the story above, her presence would cease to have a mitigating impact on the degradation of incarcerated people.

---

[33] Interview with the author on March 12, 2021.
[34] Peter A. Levine, *In an Unspoken Voice: How the Body Releases Trauma and Restores Goodness* (Berkeley: North Atlantic Books, 2010), xii, 215–21.
[35] Herman, *Trauma and Recovery*, 133–54.
[36] Levine, *In an Unspoken Voice*, 3–9, 97–132.
[37] Dubler and Lloyd, *Break Every Yoke*, 37.

I said in Chapter 1 that chaplains rarely compare themselves directly to Jesus, though they are quick to say that they see Jesus in incarcerated people. The few occasions in which chaplains directly compared their ministries to the ministry of Christ seem to be in these moments when they feel overwhelmed by the reality of prisons and their inability to change those realities. Chaplain Love was one of the chaplains who made such a comparison.

Chaplain Love:

> I've always wanted to do something really big for God. And I want to dismantle the prison industrial complex. And I want to end mass incarceration. And yet what I did was to traffic in small stories and small encounters that didn't feel like I was dismantling the prison system. And certainly for people who are in the social justice world that I traffic in quite a bit, I never did enough. All I had were these tiny stories.

Sarah Jobe:

> Mmmm ...

Chaplain Love:

> But ....we have only tiny stories from Jesus! *(both laugh)*

Sarah Jobe:

> That's a good point. *(still laughing)* That's true.

Chaplain Love:

> And he did not dismantle the Roman Empire, although it needed to be dismantled. And he was with this leper, and this bent-over woman, and this blind person, and you know ... just these tiny little stories.
>
> And we can extrapolate and make it into some beautiful, strong, social justice work of the blindness of the prison system, and things like that, but it started with an encounter. It started with those small moments.
>
> And I had to, you know there were days I wanted to go to the administrator and bring my list of how oppressive this was, and what was wrong with all these things.
>
> And there were times I got, I had my say.

But I had to be very careful, because I could be so easily dismissed as Chaplain and fired. So I had to weigh that.

How do you walk within the policies and keep being there? When some of them were terrible policies! And it would go against everything I believed.

How do I walk within that,
and ... and ... seek,
seek to say what,
you know, that
that right now I feel called to still be with,
with people here.

And I can't do that if I'm ... if I get fired.

It's hard. It's a hard balance though.[38]

Prison policies and practices throw the chaplain's ministry of presence into crisis. Chaplain Love witnesses things that are "wrong," "oppressive," and "go against everything I believe." She says that there are some times when "I had my say," but she is clear that she risks being fired if she appears critical of the institution too often. She names a bind that all the chaplains in this study named: being present in prison means bearing witness to legally sanctioned injustices, but speaking out against every one of those legal and approved injustices would compromise the chaplain's ability to continue to be present in the institution. Are chaplains "just being present" because it is pastoral best practice, or are chaplains "just being present" because they cannot figure out anything else to do in the face of a massive system rolling over people like a Prison Emergency Response Team? Are chaplains enacting the real presence of Christ, or is the idea that they are modeling themselves after the one-person-at-a-time ministry of Christ simply a panacea that makes life-work in the face of carceral death bearable? *It's hard. It's a hard balance.*

Karl Barth and the *Krisis* of the Incarnation

Karl Barth was serving as a local church pastor of a Reformed congregation in Safenwil, Switzerland, when the First World War broke out on August 1, 1914.[39] Many people from his town were called up to serve as guards

---

[38]Interview with the author on March 12, 2021.
[39]Busch, *Karl Barth*, 81.

on the border, and on several occasions Barth himself took "home guard" watches in Safenwil proper.[40] In retrospect, however, the most jarring and impactful event for Barth was when ninety-three German intellectuals signed a public Manifesto in support of "the war policy of Kaiser Wilhelm II and Chancellor Bethmann-Hollweg" on October 4, 1914.[41] Barth was dismayed to find that his own teachers had signed the document, and it "shook to the very foundation an entire world of theological exegesis, ethics, dogmatics, and preaching, that until then I had held to be credible in principle."[42] In personal communication with Martin Rade, Barth makes clear that the primary affront was not only that his professors supported the war, but that they claimed God's support for war tactics as well. He rails to Rade that such theological justification for the war means that "Germans along with their big cannons may now feel mandated by God, as though in this moment they are permitted to shoot and burn with clear consciences. Not *that!* And you preach particularly this, a clear conscience now, now, where the bad conscience might be the only Christian possibility in the face of the worldly, sinful necessity that now exists."[43]

Barth's response to the war and to his teachers' failure to stand against it was to throw himself into a study of Paul's letter to the Romans. He writes what will ultimately be *The Epistle to the Romans*, the first edition of which was published just after the end of the war in December 1918.[44] In some ways, the whole of the book is one long explication of the above quote to Rade: namely, that in the face of sinful, worldly necessities, having a bad conscience might be the only faithful Christian possibility. Barth writes, "In Jesus, the communication of God begins with a rebuff, with the exposure of a vast chasm, with the clear revelation of a great stumbling block."[45] In the resurrection of Jesus, Barth says, God is speaking a strong "No" to the world, and it is only through receiving this No with its full force that humans might experience God's "Yes" within it.[46] What is God saying "No" to specifically? God says No to "everything that thwarts and damages the life that has been made by God."[47] One can hear Barth's critique of war, but one can also hear how Barth's critique is a sweeping condemnation of most of the powers and structures of this world that harm the creatures locked within them.

---

[40]Ibid., 81.
[41]Ibid.
[42]Tietz, *Karl Barth: A Life in Conflict*, 69.
[43]Ibid., 69.
[44]Johnson, *The Essential Karl Barth*, 4–5. While the first edition of *The Epistle to the Romans* was published in 1918, all citations in this text come from the highly redacted second edition, the sixth edition of which was eventually translated into English.
[45]Barth, *The Epistle to the Romans*, 98.
[46]Ibid., 38.
[47]Ibid., 43.

Those who are willing to receive Jesus Christ as God's No to the ways of the world, must learn to receive God's judgment and stand under it with "the courage of despair."[48] Barth explains, "In Christ, God offers Himself to be known as God beyond our trespass, beyond time and things and men; to be known as the Redeemer of the prisoners, and consequently, as the meaning of all that is ... He displays His mercy by inaugurating His KRISIS and bringing us under judgment."[49] Barth insists repeatedly that one cannot receive God's Yes unless one is willing to "affirm the No and be ready to accept the void and to move and tarry in negation."[50] Barth makes a distinction here between the judgment and wrath of God. God's judgment of the world as it stands is a good and important step to receiving God's kingdom, God's Yes, and God's alternative way of being in the world. The judgment of God only becomes the wrath of God when people are unwilling to accept God's protest and make it their own.

I hear Chaplain Love embedded in the crisis Barth describes. Her following of Christ into presence with incarcerated people has given her "the courage to stand and watch," but as she sees the stripping, handcuffing, and searching of human beings, she knows that God has said No to these tactics.[51] She wants to speak aloud God's No to "everything that thwarts and damages life," and yet she cannot figure out how to consistently speak God's No within the realities of prison life.[52] She consistently shows up and uses her physical presence to stand as a sign of God's judgment against strip search and cell search practices that dehumanize, but she acknowledges that the silence of that presence means there is a real possibility of misinterpretation. Her presence, at its best, communicates God's No to the prison's way of confining and controlling human persons, but it does not change the system. In following Christ, she is thrown into crisis.

Perhaps it seems that it should not be hard to speak God's No to prisons as one becomes an eyewitness to the abuses, both sanctioned and unsanctioned, that occur within them. But the chaplains in this study repeatedly and consistently named that it was difficult to discern how and when to address injustice in ways that might actually make a difference, did not undermine their ability to function well with other staff, did not create blowback on incarcerated people, and did not result in their termination. Father Michael told me a story that was characteristic of the frustrations that chaplains faced when attempting to report abuses internal to the prison system early in their careers.

---

[48]Ibid., 40.
[49]Ibid., 41.
[50]Ibid., 42.
[51]Ibid., 39.
[52]Ibid., 46.

Father Michael:

> I learned early on, I remember one time I witnessed—in the hole—real abuse going on. A prisoner, as I can remember, it was both physical and psychological abuse. It was just like, you know, people being beaten up, people being denied food, just being tormented. And I remember writing what I thought was a confidential memo to the superintendent, "I'm concerned that I saw this happen with this CO and this inmate."
>
> I get called to the investigator's office, and he said well ... let's see how he worded it ...
>
> "Well, we got a report that you said so and so is beating up inmates," and so basically the confidentiality wasn't respected. They just threw me under the bus, and of course the CO who I'd always gotten along with prior to that, after that it was, "Forget it!" He wouldn't speak to me, and it just put me in a really bad position.
>
> So I realized, there are times you really have to ... you're stuck in the system that's, that in many ways, can be demonic. So just learning how to be aware, and to help when I could, or find proxies who could report this and not have it come back to me. You learn the ways of getting the information out there, but I had to also realize I couldn't do that in my position. Because I either lose credit and credibility with the staff, which is terrible. Or worse is the inmates would see me as a rat. That would also be terrible. So it's really, it's kind of an everyday kind of a challenge that way, to kind of keep that balance. But I learned early on, not to trust the system. Because the system is not designed for fairness. It's not designed for correction or rehabilitation either.[53]

Father Michael goes on to tell stories about reporting prison abuses to outside organizations, advocates, and lawyers. He tells stories about talking directly to officers about their behavior, but he is clear that much of what he sees every day that he believes is wrong is simply how prisons operate. There is nothing to report.

Chaplain Tyrone, who began as a corrections officer and transitioned to chaplaincy, explains that part of why it often seems there is nothing to report and no one to report it to when it comes to the degradations of prison is that officer behavior is embedded in a wider American culture of "lock 'em up and throw away the key" that shapes the policies and practices of prison.[54] He explains that while a chaplain cannot change the wider culture

---

[53]Interview with the author on April 16, 2021.
[54]Interview with the author on March 15, 2021.

within their role, the chaplain can work with officers one-on-one to change individual attitudes and practices. He joins other chaplains in naming that one has to work to build trust with officers over time by staying late with them during prison crises, showing up during inclement weather, and helping with funerals for officers and their families. Only after earning trust, does one earn the right to speak into an officer's approach to their work in ways that might actually have an impact.

These changes in individual officers are important, but they ultimately do not make much of a dent in the wider culture of the institution. Chaplains responded to this "everyday kind of challenge" in a wide variety of ways. Some "stood their ground" and went head-to-head with CO's often. Some tried to "fly under the radar" at the institution and then report prison harms to outside organizations. Some worked hard to befriend officers and their chain of command in the hopes of either being able to impact individual officers or to have enough trust with their leadership to be able to report "real abuses" when they occurred. No one seemed to feel that they had landed on a "best practice" for addressing the harms they witnessed daily, and everyone affirmed that "the tension is always there."[55]

Barth calls this ability to see God's truth but not enact it "the impossible possibility" of Christian ministry, and he insists that there is no way to escape the bind. Because the way of God is so outside the structures of this world, enacting God's Yes is impossible, and yet, once one has experienced God's Yes, attempting to speak it and do it is the only possibility.[56] Barth writes, "If we do not ourselves hinder it, nothing can prevent our being translated into a most wholesome KRISIS by that which may be known of God. And indeed, we stand already in this KRISIS if we can but see clearly."[57]

As Barth looks around himself at an inescapable wartime reality, he is realistic that it cannot be changed, but he also refuses the inactivity of fatalism. He is realistic in saying that, if we are being honest, no one person can turn the world toward God's purposes, but neither can anyone escape the judgment of being unable to do so. He writes, "The world remains the world ... The whole burden of sin and the whole curse of death still press heavily upon us. We must be under no illusion: the reality of our present existence continues as it is!"[58] No one gets to opt out of living in a world turned against God's purposes; "everything human swims with the stream either with vehement protest or with easy accommodation, even when it appears to hover above it or to engage in conflict with it."[59] But Barth also avoids fatalism when he says that those who have eyes to see God's Yes

---

[55]Interview with the author on January 23, 2021.
[56]Barth, *The Epistle to the Romans*, 79.
[57]Ibid., 46.
[58]Ibid., 38.
[59]Ibid., 57.

and No in Jesus Christ are not permitted to simply throw their hands up in the face of this crisis. The only way to receive God's Yes and No while remaining embedded in a reality that stands against the ways of God is to stand under judgment oneself. "Every prison chaplain should have to think about the question of complicity," said Father Katy.[60] Or as Barth puts it, "We are enabled to take to ourselves the protest of creation against the world as it is, for we recognize that we stand under judgment, and we love the Judge."[61]

The Christian ability to protest the world as it is rests upon a willingness to stand under judgment oneself while loving the Judge and the judgments that are passed down. The acknowledgment of this tension does not resolve it. Rather, the chaplain is thrown into crisis by the knowledge of God on a daily basis. Barth addresses this directly when he travels on his seventy-fourth birthday in 1960 to speak to a conference of prison chaplains.[62] Barth explains that if the chaplain acts faithfully as a caregiver and advocate for incarcerated people, as called to by God, the chaplain will be thrown into a series of "mini-wars" with the authorities and staff at the institution.[63] These mini-wars are unavoidable. The only question is whether or not the chaplain will be "tired out" by them or continue to "fight from week to week, from year to year."[64]

One can acknowledge that a chaplain will never fully embody God's just judgments in prisons and still affirm the chaplain's ability to represent Christ within the prison. Barth explains that in the face of the Krisis created by Christ, Christians can continue to point to the one who creates the crisis. He writes:

> The activity of the community is related to the Gospel only in so far as it is no more than a crater formed by the explosion of a shell and seeks to be no more than a void in which the Gospel reveals itself. The people of Christ, his community, know that no sacred word or work or thing exists in its own right: they know only those words and works and things which by their negation are sign-posts to the Holy One.[65]

Prison chaplains practice the brave faithfulness of letting their inability to change the system point beyond themselves to a God who desires that change. Chaplains embody God's presence in prison, but they also receive

---

[60] Interview with the author on April 28, 2021.
[61] Barth, *The Epistle to the Romans*, 156.
[62] Karl Barth, *Barth in Conversation: Volume 1, 1959–1962*, ed. Eberhard Busch (Louisville: Westminster John Knox Press, 2017), 37–61.
[63] Ibid., 57.
[64] Ibid.
[65] Barth, *The Epistle to the Romans*, 36.

God's judgment on prison practices and on those who participate in them, including upon themselves. In his exploration of a chaplain's ministry of presence, Neil Holm uses the image of the chaplain as an icon to describe the "sacramental presence" that occurs in a ministry of presence.[66] Icons point beyond themselves to the Holy One they represent. Holm states honestly that chaplains are not perfect and cannot enact this representation perfectly, but he explains that even a "desecrated, damaged, or broken icon" can still point to the one it represents.[67]

I would go a step further to say that as a chaplain learns to stand under God's judgment for her failure to change the death-dealing structures in which she participates, the chaplain learns the art of receiving judgment for the sake of doing life-work. The chaplains in this study were resigned to their complicity in carceral systems, but they did not let that complicity stop their movement for life within the system. Instead, they became people who practiced daily discernment and weary bravery about when it was worth risking judgment—either God's or the prison system's—for the sake of embodying God in prison. Mini-wars, broken icons, standing under judgment, real presence … What does this actually look like in the daily work of chaplains? I turn now to a set of case studies about the ways in which chaplains are risking judgment by violating prison policy for the sake of ushering in the real presence of Christ.

Risking Judgment for the Real Presence of Christ

The chaplains in this study are clear that being a prison chaplain means following the policies and procedures of a prison. If one cannot follow policies with which one disagrees, one cannot be a prison chaplain. They also talk about how policy is often unclear. It must be interpreted, and one opportunity for chaplains to act toward life is to "stretch policy toward humanity and towards connection," even when the policy was not originally created toward those ends.[68] But all of the chaplains in this study also admitted that there are times when they move beyond stretching policy to breaking prison policy. All of the chaplains who were brave enough to name the specific ways in which they have violated policy also named that they knew they were risking their livelihoods, reputations, and even possible criminal charges in these violations. They stood ready to give an account of themselves to their superiors should they be questioned or even placed

---

[66]Neil Holm, "Practising the ministry of presence in chaplaincy," *Journal of Christian Education* 3 (2009): 34–5.
[67]Ibid., 34.
[68]Interview with the author on January 1, 2021.

under investigation. The most frequent reason that chaplains violated prison policy was to touch incarcerated people. The following excerpt is from an interview with Chap Lin.

Sarah Jobe:

> You mentioned dealing with the balance between the two sides of the job: the custody side and not losing the pastoral side of the job. How did you deal with that? How did you uphold policy? How would you advise younger chaplains about that balancing act within the job?

Chap Lin:

> You can't be scared of what people think of you. You've got to find your place because authenticity is the main thing. And prisoners will be looking to make sure that you seem to be fair or consistent or both.
>
> You know, I think for me, it's presence and spending time. I was so hard-nosed and so clear on policy when I was new. I was trying to do everything by the book. I was really clear that I had to read policy and know it, and I was so tough on that. I'm surprised that I didn't get shanked or something early on, but I think what saved me was the same guys that would be a little, you know, they would look at me askance, also saw me on the hospital floor as they were coming and going. And they'd see me with dying inmates. And I had no hesitation of holding their hand, even though you're told, "don't touch these guys, don't hold their hand." And I know that to be true. I know. But when somebody has gone from 200 pounds to 130, and they're chained to a bed … yeah, I mean, at some point, if they are in a three man hold or if they're, you know …
>
> You use it judiciously. I mean, there were times when they'd say, "I want to hold your hand," and I'd say, "You put your hand on that Bible, I'll put my hand on this Bible, and we'll be joined by that!"
>
> And there are times when you see somebody is clearly dying, and you have, you do not hesitate to hold their hand.
>
> And officers would criticize me for it. And I would just say, "You know what, if you were dying, I'd hold your hand, and this is what I'm going to do. This is a human being."[69]

---

[69] Interview with the author on January 6, 2021.

There are times when you see somebody is clearly dying, and you do not hesitate to hold their hand. Chap Lin is willing to violate prison policy and come under criticism by officers in order to hold the hand of the dying person before her. She knows that she is violating policy, and it is a policy that she believes is important and upholds at other times. Yet a basic ministry of presence brings her to prison deathbeds, and in those moments when she is being present with a human being who is passing from life to death she "does not hesitate" to extend her presence to physical touch. She told me the story with the sort of resigned bravery that characterizes people who have to make impossible choices every day. Chap Lin's sense that chaplains are "damned if I do, damned if I don't," did not lead her to opt for touch in every encounter. Rather, she enacted a rigorous, thoughtful, and world-weary wisdom about what would be best in each encounter, knowing that any choice she made could bring judgment.

Chaplain Noa, a woman who has worked for over forty years in women's prisons with all custody levels, expressed a similar set of concerns regarding touch. She explains her willingness to violate policy about physical touch during death notifications.

Chaplain Noa:

> Well of course I don't ever give them food unless I've gotten permission to do so. Not ever. When somebody says, "Chap, can I have?" I say, "You want me to keep my job? I love my job. I love coming here to see you. I want my job!" in a kind of funny way. So I don't ever violate things like, you know, bringing in food, unless I have permission to do so.
>
> But in terms of, for example, if somebody—you know we're taught in terms of professional boundaries and PREA—but what if I've just told somebody their mother has passed away?[70]
>
> And they, they just lose it, and just ... you know, they are devastated. Will I come over there and put my arm on their shoulder or even put my arm around them, you know, like this? Yes, I will.
>
> I don't advise my interns to do it, but I've been navigating this for 40 years or so.[71]

---

[70]The Prison Rape Elimination Act (PREA) prohibits sexual contact of any nature between a person in custody and a staff person or volunteer in a prison. Under PREA, there is no such thing as consensual sexual acts between an incarcerated person and a non-incarcerated person; all sexual acts are treated as nonconsensual and prosecuted as crimes. While this has cut down on prison rape, it has also further inhibited appropriate touch inside of prisons between staff and incarcerated people. Bureau of Justice Assistance. "Prison Rape Elimination Act (PREA)—An Overview." Accessed on January 27, 2023. https://bja.ojp.gov/program/prea/overview.
[71]Interview with the author on February 27, 2021.

Chaplain Noa makes clear that she understands the consequence of violating prison policy could be losing one's job. She does not violate policy lightly, and she does not violate food policies even though a few chaplains in this study mentioned their willingness to share food with incarcerated people even though it was against the rules. Even so, when she tells someone that their mother has died, Chaplain Noa will put her arm around the person as they cry. She does not advise her interns to follow her example, but she will touch an incarcerated person in the face of death. Her ministry of presence expands to incorporate physical touch.

When chaplains talk about touch as a site at which to occasionally violate prison policy, they talk about touch as a basic human need. They talk about the ways that prisons do not permit touch, even between incarcerated people. They talk about the way that sanctioned physical touch in prisons tends to be forceful if not violent—handcuffing, cavity searches, cell extractions—and they talk about the ways in which pastoral touch offers a counter-witness to the isolation of a touch-less life peppered with forceful or violent touch. While most chaplains spoke about violating policies on touch in the face of death or in the wake of death, Chaplain Moses describes purposefully violating his prison's no-contact rule every Sunday as men enter the Chapel for worship in his close-custody facility.

Chaplain Moses:

> Another really concrete example of this is that I became convinced that one of the most important things I did, maybe *the* most important thing I did, when I was doing worship every other week was that I would stand at the door of our Chapel, which was in the prison. You know in some places it's a separate building, but this is in the prison.
>
> As the men would come—not all of them, but especially as I became known more and built more relationships with people—they would come to the door, and I know you've seen this—the kind of prison greeting? You know, the handshake and then the kind of quick little, almost a chest bump, you know? Which by the book, I was not supposed to do, right?
>
> *(long pause)*
>
> It was ...
> just ...
> there was supposed to be zero contact.
>
> And I don't think I even knew that at the beginning, but I remember kind of being told at some point, "Hey, you shouldn't do that."

But I didn't stop, and it felt like one of those things like "undue familiarity" … I mean …

I, you know, the lack of positive contact …

The deprivation of positive contact …

most contact in prisons is intended to be at best controlling, at worst harmful.

And there's just something about that touch that seems so important to try to humanize each other.[72]

I became convinced that one of the most important things I did, maybe the most important thing I did, when I was doing worship every other week was that I would stand at the door of our Chapel and offer a handshake and a chest bump to each man who entered. Chaplain Moses understands this routine liturgical touch to be the most important thing he does. It is a clear violation of his prison's zero contact rule, and he does it week after week with each person who enters for worship. He is advised by staff not to do it. In our interview, he clearly felt put in a bind by the prison's no-touch policy, but he keeps choosing to violate policy in order to show with his body that men are welcome in the Chapel. *There's just something about that touch that seems so important to try to humanize each other.*

Chap Lin, Chaplain Noa, and Chaplain Moses are willing to risk standing under judgment in order to extend their ministry of presence to hold the hand of a dying person, to place an arm around a grieving person, or to shake hands with and bump chests with people coming to worship.[73] Their

---

[72] Interview with the author on April 23, 2021.

[73] In the year and a half between going on record for this study and reading a draft of this book, Chaplain Murray was placed under investigation and put on administrative leave for seven and a half months. She was given few details and not permitted to be at the prison, but she was ultimately made aware that her practice of hugging incarcerated people was among the charges against her. She was ultimately reinstated with no charges, but she was held under suspicion and kept from her ministry for months, at spiritual and psychological impact to both herself and the women incarcerated at her facility. Chaplain Murray shared with me about how she defended her practice of physical touch:

In my defense, I explained that I'm a Chaplain, not a Correctional Officer. My professional relationship with our residents is very different from the professional relationship of an Officer. I walk with these women through the lowest, darkest times in their lives—when their mother dies, when their kids go up for adoption, when their teenager commits suicide, when they are struggling with who they are and how they make sense of their life, when they are trying to find meaning and hope in a place of scarcity and hardship and pain. I am their Chaplain. And safe human touch is essential for a person's well-being. If they can't hug their Chaplain, who can they hug? Seriously—who can they hug? In the end, I was allowed to continue to hug 'in the

practice of the incarnation—an en-fleshed ministry of presence—stands in direct contradiction to prison policy. While they stand under God's judgment in upholding prison policy at most times, they also find moments in which a ministry of presence so forcibly and palpably calls for them to violate prison policy that they instead stand under the prison's judgment in order to offer some small counter witness to the way of God-with-us. Are these chaplains ushering in the real presence of Christ in these encounters? They do not say that explicitly. They say that they are insisting on the humanity of the person in front of them through their embodied presence. They are willing to risk themselves for the sake of that embodied presence. Which is to say, they are operating within the logic of the Eucharist.

It is worth noting that all of the above chaplains self-identified in their interviews as Baptists. When one of the Catholic chaplains in this study, Father Katy, shared about her chosen rule violation, I began to see how the real presence being offered by Baptist chaplains through physical touch might be commensurate to the real presence of Christ that Catholic and Episcopal chaplains understood themselves to be offering in the Eucharist.

Father Katy:

> I definitely broke some rules, as I feel like every good chaplain should. But I don't feel, I don't recall being put into any situation where the dilemma was to significance ... yeah ...

Sarah Jobe:

> What were the ones you felt you had to break?

Father Katy:

> Well, one I remember most vividly because I considered it the only miracle I've ever performed ... *(both laugh)*

> So that day they weren't allowing any wine in. So even if a priest came in to do mass, they wouldn't allow even one ounce, just for the priest to consume himself!

> And so at one of the masses, when I was having the Bishop come in and do baptisms and confirmations, I was, I was like, "This is ridiculous. It's stupid. Like one ounce of alcohol for religious purposes, can you please?"

---

context of pastoral care only,' as if pastoral care only happens in my office, not in the hallways or corridors or classrooms or living units. Nope, not there at all. (Correspondence with the author on March 7, 2023.)

And so I got a little bit and put it in my holy water bottle, and I went through the metal detector, and the guy's like, "Oh, is there some liquid in there?"

I was like, "Oh yeah, it's just, it's just some water."

So, Jesus turned water into wine; I turned wine into water! *(both laugh)*

And they let me through. It was great. So that was a small one.[74]

I will admit that when Father Katy first told me this story, I found it incomprehensible. She risked bringing in a contraband substance and lied directly to an officer just to have a Bishop consume wine in front of incarcerated people. As a Baptist, with a notably non-sacramental understanding of Communion, the risk-reward analysis of this rule violation may never make sense to me. When chaplains told me about touching incarcerated people around death or sharing food with incarcerated people, I could relate. The policy violations seemed appropriate. I could imagine doing them. I could not imagine risking my job for communion wine. But Father Katy was full of joy and conviction about her policy violation. She called it a miracle. She likened herself to Jesus, albeit with joking laughter, and I could not shake the memory of her telling this story.

Father Katy was willing to risk her job to bring into prison what she, as a Catholic, understands to be the real presence of Christ. For me, as a Protestant, because I cannot quite internalize the logic, it makes her rule violation somehow more profound, more excessive, and more explicitly about Christ's presence than the rule violations based around physical touch. Her story is also illustrative. It helps to make sense of what was happening in the other chaplains' policy violations. All of these policy violations are about the moments when a chaplain's ministry of presence tips visibly into ushering in the real presence of Christ. When the real presence of Christ is at stake or when making-real the presence of Christ is at stake, chaplains are willing to stand under judgment, saying No to prisons in order to say Yes to the person before them. In those moments, God's Yes and God's No in Jesus Christ are made flesh again as the body of the chaplain encounters the bodies of incarcerated people in death, in grief, in worship, and in Eucharist.

In this chapter I have sought to push the "ministry of presence" literature beyond easy affirmations that chaplains are Christ-like in their willingness to go and be with people where people are. While this may be true, a chaplain will, in this process, inevitably witness practices and structures that stand against the way of God, and the chaplain will have few ways to change those

---

[74] Interview with the author on April 28, 2021.

systemic patterns. I have joined Barth in his realism about this situation while resisting the fatalism of inaction, and I have suggested that Barth's idea that the chaplain stands under God's judgment gives a way forward in which chaplains can bravely risk rule-violation for the sake of real presence. I hope I have asked more questions than I have answered. The incarnation is only the beginning of Jesus' story, and if chaplains are inhabiting Christ in some real way in their work within prisons, they will be taking up his prophetic lifework of freeing, healing, comforting, and overturning unjust economies, as outlined in his inaugural sermon based on Isa. 61:1-3. Is prophetic lifework in prison an "impossible possibility"? Are chaplains participating in some mediation of the real presence of Christ behind bars? Are chaplains simply accommodating their theologies and ministerial practices to a system they cannot change, or are chaplains modeling a mode of resisting systemic, death-dealing powers one person at a time? These are the questions we will continue to push forward in the next chapter.

3

Risking Atonement:

Reconciling Race, Rank, and Religion

As a chaplain, I want to be in the middle, like Jesus on the cross in the middle.

—CHAPLAIN KING, INTERVIEW ON JANUARY 15, 2021

Karl Barth names the entirety of Volume IV of *Church Dogmatics* "The Doctrine of Reconciliation." In the standard English translation, G.W. Bromiley translates *Versöhnung* as both "reconciliation" and "atonement" depending on the context, but in Barth's original text, there was no distinction.[1] When Barth turns to the task of describing Christ's reconciling or atoning work, he asks three questions: How or in what way did God become human? Why did God become human? And what is the connection between how and why God became human and our current individual transgressions and systemic sins?[2] Barth answers the question of "how" God became human with a doctrine of the incarnation as described in the last chapter on a ministry of presence. The Christian God is a God who characteristically draws near to human beings, takes on flesh, and is "with

---

[1] Barth, *CD* IV/1, vii.
[2] Barth will primarily answer the first question, "*Quo iure Deus homo?*" in §59.1 "The Way of the Son of God into the Far Country" and the second question, "*Cur Deus homo?*" in §59.2 "The Judge Judged in our Place." He explains the logic of distinguishing between these questions—the person and work of Christ—in *CD* IV/1, 184. He then attempts to answer the third question, "How can that which has happened once, even if it did happen for us, be recognized to-day as having happened for us, seeing it did not happen to-day?" in §59.3 "The Verdict of the Father," *CD* IV/1, 284–7.

us." Prison chaplains inhabit the incarnation in their ministry of presence, but just as the work of Jesus is not accomplished in the simple fact of the incarnation, the work of prison chaplains is not accomplished by the simple fact of their presence in prison. What does Jesus do once incarnate? What is his work and ministry? *Why* has he become flesh? Similarly, what are chaplains doing when they choose to keep staying in prison even as it throws them into crisis? This chapter takes up the ways in which prison chaplains are inhabiting Christ's atoning work as they face wicked problems and reconcile divisions in both chapel programs and in their own bodies and identities.

When chaplains choose to stay inside prison systems that they cannot structurally change, they still believe that they can create pockets of life and moments of safety in an otherwise unsafe and death-dealing place. In addition to offering a "ministry of presence," they understand themselves to be doing that through faith-specific religious programming. They describe creating and sustaining chapel programs that are diverse, authentic, and free, and they claim that these programs offer a glimpse of the kingdom of God on earth. This chapter will describe those services, while naming how the systemic divisions of race, religion, and carceral status continually threaten to break into and overrun those life-spaces.[3] I will explore the way that chaplains are reconciling the "wicked problems" of racial, religious, and carceral divisions in both their professional tactics and their own bodies.[4] I will then explore how a chaplain's willingness to act with authority while risking themselves looks strikingly similar to how Karl Barth describes the work of Jesus Christ in his atoning work of becoming the Judge who is Judged in our place. We will explore how Jesus, Barth, and chaplains hold dueling identities within themselves: whatever reconciling work Jesus does for the cosmos, he does first by reconciling categories within his own body.

How are chaplains enacting Jesus' salvific work in their programs and in their persons as they confront wicked problems? How are chaplains winning and how are they losing against persistent social divisions? What difference

---

[3] As I describe the interfaith religious programs offered by prison chaplains, I am choosing to focus on the way that those programs take on wicked problems and enact God's reconciliation in incarcerated communities. This focus means that two important topics that emerged in the study with respect to religious programming will not be addressed in full. First, chaplains repeatedly named the difficulty of "balancing people and paper," i.e., managing the high amount of administrative work—documentation of services, memos for volunteers to enter prisons, volunteer training, response to resident's written requests—that often felt like it got in the way of, rather than facilitated, religious programs. Chaplains also shared a great deal of wisdom on both the tactics and theological framing for offering corporate observances in faith traditions that are not their own. These were both important aspects of the data collected in this study with respect to religious programming in prisons that fall outside the focus of this chapter.

[4] Horst W. Rittel and Melvin M. Webber, "Wicked problems," *Man-Made Futures* 26, no. 1 (1974): 272–80.

does it make in prisons today for Jesus, the just Judge, to have been judged in a Roman court? If the doctrine of atonement is being inhabited by chaplains in their creation of diverse, authentic, and free programming, what is the role of the chaplain versus the role of Jesus versus the role of incarcerated people in this drama of reconciliation? We turn now to those questions.

Diversity, Authenticity, Freedom: The Kingdom of God on Earth (One Program at a Time)

In his book *Down in the Chapel: Religious Life in an American Prison*, Joshua Dubler explains that the chapel in Graterford Prison hosts services and studies for thirteen different religious traditions each week.[5] The chaplains in this study ran weekly programming for as few as five religious traditions and as many as thirty.[6] A prison chapel, Dubler writes, is "arguably the most religiously eclectic sliver of real estate in the history of the world."[7] I went into this study speculating that Christian prison chaplains might understand their Christian commitments to be in tension with the interfaith and inter-denominational nature of prison chaplaincy, but I found instead that chaplains delighted in the diversity of their prison chapel communities and affirmed such diversity within their Christian theologies. Chaplain Moses said, "I tell the guys, this is a taste of the kingdom of God here on Earth, a representation of all God's people coming together and kind of putting down some of the differences. And some, some put down the differences better than others!"[8] Many chaplains named that getting to be a part of Christian worship between people of different ages, races, socio-economic backgrounds, denominations, and political commitments was one of the most nourishing aspects of the job and the thing that kept them coming back to work in the face of death and injustice.

Chaplain Maverick is an African American chaplain at a men's maximum custody prison. In telling me about his love for the diversity of the prison chapel community, Chap Mav explained that over his twenty years on the job, he came to "believe in the Christ beyond color."[9] While he begins by saying that the true Christ exists beyond any racialized depictions of him,

---

[5] Joshua Dubler and Vincent W. Lloyd, *Break Every Yoke: Religion, Justice, and the Abolition of Prisons* (Oxford: Oxford University Press, 2020).
[6] Each state prison system has different policies regarding what religious traditions the state recognizes for corporate worship in that state's prisons. This means that some states recognize fifteen religious traditions and other recognize more than fifty. Additionally, there are policies governing how many incarcerated people must be registered for a specific faith tradition for that religion to be granted a corporate worship time on the chapel's weekly calendar.
[7] Dubler, *Down in the Chapel*, 9.
[8] Interview with the author on January 23, 2021.
[9] Interview with the author on January 25, 2021.

Chap Mav goes on to name that the Christ beyond color also pushes him to acknowledge the dignity and worth of people of other religious traditions and their pathways to a Christ that exists beyond religious detail. He also names that this Christ exists beyond the divisions of "officer and inmate." Without detailing a specific doctrine of reconciliation, Chap Mav pointed to the idea that Christ stands beyond the social divisions of this world and that following Christ means somehow seeing beyond, reconciling, or existing in community amid those divisions.

Diversity in the chapel community was named as something that made Christian worship richer. Father Katy explained that the diversity of the community made it easier for her to empower residents in worship leadership, knowing that she was not equipped to lead in every tradition or in every language represented. When she describes her attempts at multi-lingual ministry to detainees in an Immigration and Customs Enforcement (ICE) ward of her prison, she shared that she would print out readings and prayers in Portuguese and Spanish for incarcerated people to read in the service. She depended on native speakers of those languages to reflect on the Word for their communities in ways that she could not. She says laughing, "I can still say the Our Father in Spanish decently, but I don't know, there was a little bit of a Pentecostal Holy Spirit thing going on, too!"[10] Diversity in language and citizenship status were not named as barriers to ministry but as opportunities for the Holy Spirit to work beyond the ability of any given participant.

Diversity was not the only characteristic of religious programming that made chaplains see these gatherings as a taste of the kingdom of God. Chaplains also named the authenticity and transparency of religion in prison as nourishing and even addictive. Many chaplains named that they had been "spoiled" by this authenticity and in some way found it difficult to engage in non-incarcerated religious communities in which such authenticity seemed less present.

Chaplain Moise explains:

> I think I've gotten completely spoiled by prison church, and I just don't even know if I'll ever be able to go to free church again because any time I tried to show up at free church—this sounds awful—but it just feels so fake. I just feel like everyone is faking it entirely. And I'm sitting around just like, "What?! We're just engaging in a charade!" We've come with this very manicured, put-together worship, and no one ever says anything about what's going on with themselves or their lives. And yeah, and everyone looks so good, just very put together.

---

[10]Interview with the author on April 28, 2021.

You know, and in prison, people roll out of bed. They're going to church with the same people they were just in the dorm with. Some women feel it is important to put on makeup to go to church. But there's only so much that you can do, right? You're going to be in your uniform, no matter what. So if you do your hair and makeup that's noticeable, but you are still in the same uniform as everybody else and there's just no pretending like you haven't hit rock bottom, right? You are in prison. You're being held against your will.

So there's no pretending. There's nothing at stake in acting like you have it all together. And so people are pretty honest about what's gone wrong, what's going wrong, what they need from the Lord, what they need from each other. And this kind of honesty, I just find it so refreshing and intoxicating, and frankly, I just feel like I'm pretty addicted to it now. I feel like I've learned to be a more honest woman as I watch incarcerated women be honest, sometimes because they have nothing left to lose.[11]

People are pretty honest about what's gone wrong, what's going wrong, what they need from the Lord, what they need from each other. Chaplain Moise calls this honesty in corporate religious practice refreshing, intoxicating, and addicting. Later in the interview she will call it nourishing. She will also name that she intentionally cultivates the chapel as a place of nonjudgment in which people are welcome to bring their broken, messy, and diverse selves knowing that the chapel is a safe space in which they will be accepted if they practice such vulnerability.

Finally, chaplains noted that these diverse, authentic religious communities had the power to transport both staff and residents out of the prison in some way for the duration of the service. Freedom and escape were frequently mentioned as one of the important benefits of participation in chapel programs. Chaplain Noa explained that she intentionally uses music as a device to transport participants away from the prison during programming. She says of music:

It's kept, it's kept, it's kept a lot at bay.
It's kept discouragement at bay …
for me and for them.
It keeps depression at bay.
It keeps enthusiasm.

And when you sing,
when you're really engaged in the arts,

---

[11] Interview with the author on January 1, 2021.

when you sing it does create endorphins in your brain and there is, there is a therapeutic value just in terms of making the sounds but …

When people sing, it just lifts them to another plane.

I just love the scene in a *Shawshank Redemption* where he locks himself in the warden's office—I've never done that, by the way—where he locked himself in the warden's office and plays this aria, you know. You remember that scene? And the men are on the yard just transfixed.

It just takes you to another plane,
another level,
and it makes people feel so human and so …
So …
Just so human, you know.
And like they, for a little while they can escape.
It's been a way of escape without going anywhere.[12]

It lifts them to another plane … for a little while they can escape. While Chaplain Noa was talking specifically about the use of music in Chapel programs, many chaplains expressed this idea that everything from educational classes to worship services to interfaith life enrichment programs had the power to transport people "out of prison" by offering a moment in which incarcerated people were treated as human beings. These moments were so counter to the usual experience of prison that it was possible, for an hour, to forget that one was incarcerated.[13] These moments did not change the wider, dehumanizing prison culture; they simply offered a brief antidote in which a person could experience themselves as a human being. Each of the chaplains who named the ability of programming to provide freedom was clear that this freedom was a time-limited experience, but they insisted that those moments were important to both staff and residents alike and served as a primary motivation for incarcerated people to attend religious services.

Chaplain Camillus explained this dynamic in detail and shared her own tactics for amplifying such freedom and escape:

Many people come into the services because they want to hear the Word. You know, they want to read the Gospel. They want to hear the Scripture. They want to hear the homily. They want to receive Communion. Definitely. But a lot of people walk into that room with none of those

---

[12]Interview with the author on February 27, 2021.
[13]For more on the creation of pockets of escape, both in prison programming and within an incarcerated person's inner life and mind, see Amelia C. Boomershire, *A Breath of Fresh Air: Biblical Storytelling with Prisoners* (Eugene: Cascade Books, 2017), 113–54; Sweeney, *Reading Is My Window*.

reasons. They're walking into that room to escape for an hour ... to be, to feel truly safe for an hour.

So I often started my services with a brief minute or two of meditation where I just ask people to close their eyes and imagine being in church ... to try to ignore the bars and the stark and the noise and the craziness ... You know the competing football games on the TVs (sometimes the guards decide to crank up to high volume during our service).

I say, "can you think of a time when you've been in a church or in a sacred place where there was safety and beauty?" And let's imagine, you know, create our own sort of bubble. Because I think to give people an hour of their day to just feel love and to feel valued ... that's probably the best that I can do.[14]

Chaplain Camillus encourages incarcerated people to use their imaginations to create a "bubble" in which they can experience the feelings of love, safety, and being valued for as much as an hour at a time. The use of imagination to escape prison life is a primary theme in Meghan Sweeney's *Reading Is My Window: Books and the Art of Reading in Women's Prisons.*[15] Sweeney documents how incarcerated women use reading as a vehicle to cultivate a robust imagination that allows them a brief "window" out of prison life. Similarly, Kevin Quashie describes the ways in which an active and detailed inner life can serve as a bulwark against the impacts of anti-Black racism and systemic oppression in *The Sovereignty of Quiet: Beyond Resistance in Black Culture.*[16] The neuroscience of meditation suggests that these moments of escape are not simply a coping mechanism but can rewire neural pathways impacted by traumatic experience. Rick Hanson explains that intentionally cultivating positive, safe, and affirming mental experiences and savoring them for a few minutes at a time—similar to the meditation described above by Chaplain Camillus—can create a stronger immune system, lower the cardio impacts of stress, increase optimism and resilience, and "help counteract the effects of painful experiences, including trauma."[17] Though not bodily freedom from prison, the freedom experienced in worship does have a reality of its own. It can have healing and freeing impacts on the bodies and minds of both staff and residents in prisons.

---

[14]Interview with the author on September 22, 2021.
[15]Sweeney, *Reading Is My Window*, 129–39.
[16]Kevin Quashie, *The Sovereignty of Quiet: Beyond Resistance in Black Culture* (Piscataway: Rutgers University Press, 2012).
[17]Rick Hanson with Richard Mendius, *Buddha's Brain: The Practical Neuroscience of Happiness, Love, and Wisdom* (Oakland: New Harbinger Publications, 2009), 75.

Threats to a Reconciled Community: Wicked Problems in the Prison Chapel

The kingdom of God on earth. The Christ beyond color. Sacred places of safety and beauty. Freedom and escape. These descriptions can start to sound Pollyannish, but prison chaplains are not given to rose-tinted glasses. Even as the chaplains in this study described the possibilities of religious programs to provide diverse, authentic, and liberating experiences—glimpses of a reconciled kingdom of God—they also named a host of internal and external factors that threatened the realization of those ideals in religious services. Chaplains described how residents often came to religious services not for religion but to see friends who lived in other, inaccessible parts of the prison complex. They would come for food that was being offered after a service. Some incarcerated people register to be Jewish to get transferred to a prison across the state that happens to have a Kosher Kitchen, to be Muslim to get to wear a hair wrap in the dayroom, or to be Native American Traditionalist to use tobacco on otherwise tobacco-free campuses.[18] These "uses" of religion thwart the authenticity of experience that most chaplains are trying to cultivate, but most chaplains in this study acknowledged that resources and agency are scarce in prison. There are few ways to choose one's own diet or clothing, and using religion toward the end of personal choice was largely deemed acceptable and understandable.

The real threats to religious programming as a space of life, health, and freedom were the systemic social divisions of racism, religious extremism, and carceral status. These divisions threatened the reconciling work of the chaplain in at least four characteristic ways: (1) in explicitly race-based arguments among Christians; (2) in gang activity during religious programming; (3) in tensions between officers and incarcerated people in the chapel; and (4) in racial extremism bound up with specific religious groups like Odinism, Asatru, Rastafarianism, Moorish Science Temple of America (MSTA), and Nation of Gods and Earths (Five Percenters). Throughout this chapter, I will refer to racism, religious extremism, gang activity, and general us-versus-them mentalities as "wicked problems." I am using this term in its technical sense as developed by Horst Rittel and Melvin Webber.[19] Wicked problems are problems that resist solution because they are socially complex, systemic in nature, and have no clear beginning or end. Because wicked problems like climate change, homelessness, or drug trafficking seem too big and unwieldy for any given person to address, wicked problems

---

[18] Arguably, friendship, food, and the benefits of material practices are part of what create "religious experience," writ broadly, and are thus properly religious; but the chaplains in this study named these as "uses" of religion rather than part of religious experience itself.
[19] Horst W.J. Rittel and Melvin M. Webber, "Dilemmas in a general theory of planning," *Policy Sciences* 4, no. 2 (1973): 155–69.

are often met with a certain fatalism or "organized irresponsibility."[20] What I find interesting about prison chaplains is that they are facing these wicked problems head-on whenever those systemic problems threaten the integrity, authenticity, diversity, and safety of chapel programming. Far from embracing fatalism, chaplains are addressing these wicked problems directly with both practical tactics that rely on their own authority as prison staff people and solutions in which they risk their own bodies and identities. After I describe some of the characteristic ways in which wicked problems threaten chapel life and the tactics that chaplains use to counteract that, we will turn to the ways in which chaplains seem to be enacting the tactics and identity of Jesus in their approaches.

Singing (and Fighting) across Racial Difference

Many chaplains named the prison choir as a particularly combustible site of racial difference. As described above by Chaplain Noa, music has the ability to transport people, yet most Christians are accustomed to the "transporting" nature of worship music coming to them in a racial and cultural specificity that matches their own identity. As Martin Luther King, Jr. famously noted in 1963, "the most segregated hour of Christian America is 11 o'clock on Sunday morning."[21] The majority of Christians are used to singing in racially homogeneous groups. Prison chapels, unlike churches, are legally prohibited from segregating in this way. Christian worship in prison is racially and denominationally diverse by law and by necessity. Because of this, chaplains encourage their prison choirs to select a wide array of worship music from a variety of denominational contexts. Chaplain Noa explains, "It's really challenging, because if you present too much of either the traditional white Southern church music or the traditional Southern African American church music, you're going to lose somebody. At some point in time each of these different groups have to feel some kind of home-ness in the worship service, or they're just not going to come."[22] Chaplain Noa is explaining how diversity in worship music makes a space for each person to feel "home-ness" at some point, but she is also naming that one person's "home" music will feel alienating and strange to others at the same time.

Chaplain Levine explained how the navigation between one person's "home-ness" and another person's alienation built so much tension on his choir that it could lead to physical altercations.

---

[20]Dean Curran, "The organized irresponsibility principle and risk arbitrage," *Critical Criminology* 26 (2018): 595–610.
[21]Gerald W.C. Driskill, Alexandra Arjannikova, and John Meyer, "A dialectic analysis of a community forum on faith: The 'most segregated' or separated hour?" *Journal of Applied Communication Research* 42, no. 4 (2014): 477–96.
[22]Interview with the author on February 27, 2021.

Chaplain Levine:

So I was in charge of the choir. Okay, I wasn't in charge of the choir, but I was there to provide structure. As you probably know, just incredible talent, oh my gosh, just some amazing musicians. But man, herding those cats, it was one of the hardest parts of the whole job! I mean that's where I had, I had to literally break up fights, you know. That's where the rubber hit the road! And I did a lot of that, and often that was on racial lines. It was racial/cultural. You know, style of music, but all that stuff has racial components to it.

And that's probably where the real sort of rubber-meets-the-road-racial stuff happened ... and just trying to, trying to promote a different understanding, and also just the tools of conflict transformation.

Sarah:

So, how did you navigate it?

Chaplain Levine:

By the seat of my pants most of the time! *(both laugh)*[23]

Despite the joke, Chaplain Levine goes on to describe using his authority to draw a hard line in which men would be dismissed from the choir or put on a temporary suspension if they could not work together across lines of racial and cultural difference. He also acknowledges that asking men to work across lines of racial difference to create worship music for a diverse-by-force congregation is difficult work. He explains:

These men are coming from different backgrounds, different races,
to come together,
and work together,
and create something together.
That's hard for anybody.
And I would talk about it that way.
I would say,
"This is not about whether you have an identifiably good voice.
I don't really care, you know?
Does music stir your heart?
and are you interested in learning from this group of people and growing and expanding your capacity for love and collaboration?

---

[23]Interview with the author on April 23, 2021.

If you're interested in those two things, come."

Finally, he takes some of the responsibility for defusing the tensions of cross-racial collaboration on himself by being especially "vigilant" during choir practices. He explains, "I was always at the practices, and I had to be really proactive when things started going south, kind of intervening, because it could get explosive fast." Hyper-vigilance and the physical presence of a chaplain willing to intervene help to create the conditions for the possibility that a racially diverse group of incarcerated men might overcome the tensions of cross-racial collaboration to create the diverse, authentic, and freeing worship spaces described in the first part of this chapter.

Kicking the Money-Changers out of the Temple: Gang Presence in Christian Worship

After forty years of prison chaplaincy, Chaplain Noa noticed a rise of gang activity in her women's prison around 2018. Many chaplains name the ways in which religious life—specifically the opportunity to gather in a congregate setting across dorms—can be used to carry out gang activity through communication, handing off contraband materials, and even drug trafficking.[24] Chaplain Noa noticed that as competing gangs came to have a visible presence sitting together in Christian worship, incarcerated women who were not affiliated with gangs began to drop off in their worship attendance. When those groups began to disrupt worship services by talking over the worship leaders and religious volunteers, Chaplain Noa took a proactive role in what she called "kicking the money changers out of the temple."[25]

Chaplain Noa's approach to driving gangs out of the worship space was a multi-pronged attack that used everything from corrections officers to a worship theme to her own body. While she was not required to be present every Sunday, she committed to coming in every weekend to oversee this process. She worked with incarcerated women to decide on a worship theme of "shifting the atmosphere," and on the first day of her anti-gang campaign, she displayed a banner painted by incarcerated women over the altar saying just that. She addressed the issue directly from the pulpit saying, "Good morning to all! Our theme this year is going to be shifting the atmosphere, and we're taking this church back and making it a very holy place." She went

---

[24]Jim Thomas and Barbara H. Zaitzow, "Conning or conversion? The role of religion in prison coping," *The Prison Journal* 86, no. 2 (2006): 242–59; Stefano Bloch and Enrique Alan Olivares-Pelayo, "Carceral geographies from inside prison gates: The micro-politics of everyday racialization," *Antipode* 53, no. 5 (2021): 1319–38; Taylor G. Stout, "The costs of religious accommodation in prisons," *Virginia Law Review* 96, no. 5 (2010): 1201–39.
[25]Interview with the author on February 27, 2021.

on to say that this holiness would be achieved by people no longer being able to sit where they wanted. Women would instead have to sit according to their assigned dorms, a seating arrangement that would be enforced by corrections staff. If a group of people still displayed disruptive behavior, Chaplain Noa would sit down in the middle of them. Her physical presence was normally enough to calm disruption, but at one point a woman spoke back saying, "I don't see why we have to come over here and be harassed." Chaplain Noa responded, "You are free to leave. You do not have to sit here. If you feel like you're being harassed, you do not have to sit here." The women got up and left.

At first these tactics produced a sharp drop in attendance. One can understand why. The freedom that seems so important and prized in prison worship was replaced with intensive behavioral policing. "But then what happened," Chaplain Noa explained, "is the people who had been scared to come to church and who had been hesitant to come to church because of all the frou frou, started coming back to church and said, 'Thank you, Chaplain Noa, for straightening this out. We just didn't want to come to church because we just, we were scared.'" Through worship practices, seating arrangements, use of correction officer presence, and the placement of her own body in the middle of sites of conflict, Chaplain Noa interrupted the gang activity in Christian worship in her prison. But Chaplain Noa is clear that she paid a price for the restoration of peace and safety in the Chapel. She explained:

> I felt like Jesus and the money changers,
> but we got it straightened out.
> But I admit,
> I had to get up at five o'clock in the morning,
> and be there every Sunday morning
> (as opposed to letting volunteers just come in and conduct the services.)
> So yeah…
> so yeah it did impact.
> It did impact.
> And I had to kind of step in and do a lot more
> to kind of straighten it back out
> and get it back into a worshipful attitude.

Chaplain Noa is willing to both stand in her authority as a prison staff person and sacrifice her own weekends to protect the safety and freedom of incarcerated people coming to Christian worship.

"Cop or Convict?": Navigating Carceral Status in Prison Worship

While all chaplains in this study talked about the tensions between staff and residents and their attempts to stand in the middle of those groups, a few chaplains explicitly talked about the ways in which those tensions sometimes erupted during chapel programming. Chap Mav, introduced above, told me a story about a white officer who had been assigned to supervise a Christian worship service. The officer made a racist comment toward an incarcerated person in a way that disrupted the service. When I asked how he handled the situation, Chap Mav responded succinctly, "With reason and administrative protocols."[26] He did not address the situation when it occurred, and he did not speak to the officer directly about the incident. Rather, he went to the officer's supervisor—not with a charge of racism—but simply saying that the officer was not a good fit for supervising religious services.

Chap Mav:

> I was able to go talk to his supervisor and say, "This person disrupted a service. I don't think they're understanding enough of the service or being respectful enough of the service to be assigned that post." And they just replaced him. But I didn't even touch on race, per se, but my goal was met. My goal was to get him out of there. Instead of saying, "He's a racist. I don't want him in there." I said, "He's disturbing the service. He doesn't respect the service. Can we get someone else?"[27]

Chap Lin, an Asian American woman serving in a men's maximum custody prison, took a different approach to navigating tensions between an officer and the incarcerated people who felt belittled in worship by that officer. She had been telling me about how tensions between officers and residents arise each shift, and all the ways that she tries to walk the line between officers and incarcerated people while remaining accessible for all.

Chap Lin:

> I think everybody has to carve out a space and realize you're going to make mistakes. But if you value people and both sides …
>
> I remember inmates complaining to me early on because this tough, mean, correctional officer was coming to chapel and just listening to our sermon, you know. And they're saying, "How can you let him in? He won't even shake hands."
>
> Well, I knew this guy, and I had spoken with him. He didn't shake hands because he said that was the way he could keep … if he shook hands that was reserved only for friendship, and he thought his

---

[26]Interview with the author on January 25, 2021.
[27]Ibid.

boundaries would get all messed up if he shook the hands of a prisoner. And he was known to be tough and rough.

And I said, "You know what, this is a sanctuary. And Jesus healed the centurion's slave just like he did Jairus' daughter, so you know what? You're going to have to deal with it because this is a chapel, a sanctuary for all people."

And that, I think that that helped them.[28]

Jesus healed the centurion's slave just like he did Jairus' daughter. Chap Lin goes to Scripture, and particularly to the witness of Jesus as he offers healing to people of differing ethnicities and social positions. The centurion is part of the Roman military that is serving as an occupying force in Judea, much like the role of a corrections officer inside of a prison, and Jesus extends welcome and healing to his household anyway. Jesus even holds the centurion up as an exceptional example of faith to the very people that the centurion is oppressing (Lk. 7:9-10). Chap Lin's story does not resolve the tension, but she offers the witness of Jesus as justification for keeping the chapel open to all, even in the face of the way that differences in carceral status were disrupting peace.

None of the chaplains in this study seem to think that they are resolving or winning against the wicked problem of mass incarceration and the way that it divides people according to carceral status: prisoner and free, staff and inmate, officer and offender. But most of the chaplains in the study encouraged some sort of "middle way"—some sort of resistance to the common idea that the chaplain must choose sides between officers and incarcerated people. Father Michael put it starkly when he said, "Somebody told me early on that if you're in this line of work, you either become a cop or a convict. And so I always wanted to err on the side of identifying with the convicts, but not overly identifying, and not necessarily to see myself as against the cops either. But I found that the tension between custody and pastoral care is real."[29] Later in our conversation, I would ask Father Michael how he navigates these tensions and how he is able to stay present and sane in the middle of such tension. He told me about praying prayers of protection over himself and the prison before going through the gate, a practice that he takes so seriously that he prays again after his lunch break before re-entering. He told me he prays to two saints: Saint Dismus, "the good thief" and the patron saint of condemned people, and Saint Michael the Archangel, the patron saint of cops and firefighters.

---

[28] Interview with the author on January 6, 2021.
[29] Interview with the author on April 16, 2021.

Father Michael:

> The power is not so much in the prayer itself, but in the awareness that we're up against stuff that is much bigger than we are—systems and the demonic. The demonic stuff is not like individual evil or devils. It's systemic evil which goes back to racism and other stuff. It's a system, and we're in the system. And we can't, we're not bigger than it. And I think it's the same way with, you know, whatever the evil is in the world. It's not that the evil's in charge of the world, but it's systematized, and it's big, and it's bigger than we are. And I mean the good news is that God is bigger than that. You know, and God has already triumphed over it. But, but we haven't, you know, in our own individual lives. So I think it's just to be aware of that—there's something bigger out there than we are, and we don't have all the answers. That's important.[30]

"It's a Front": Racial Extremism in Religious Practice

While the above examples from Christian worship show the way that chapel life insists on the navigation of racial and carceral difference in diverse groups, the accommodation of certain faith traditions—like Odinism, Asatru, Rastafarianism, Moorish Science Temple of America, and Nation of Gods and Earths—creates pockets for racial homogeneity and solidarity within the overall diversity of prison life. While much has been written on the role of race-based gangs in the governing of prison life, much less has been written about the way in which particular religious groups are essentially used as fronts for racial extremism in prison.[31] Chaplains acknowledge these race-based religious groups as both a good and as a potential seed-bed for race-based religious extremism, and they use a wide variety of tactics to amplify the good while keeping overt racism or race-based violence out of prison chapels.

The 1990s saw a rise of white nationalism and neo-Nazi organizations, and one manifestation was the rise of Norse or pagan religious practices.[32] In the resurgence, ancient European, earth-based traditions like Odinism and Asatru are merged with white-supremacist ideologies. While it is illegal in most prison systems to participate in a white supremacist gang, it is a protected right to practice Odinism or Asatru. Chaplain Tyrone is a Black

---

[30]Ibid.
[31]David Skarbek, *The Social Order of the Underworld: How Prison Gangs Govern the American Penal System* (Oxford: Oxford University Press, 2014).
[32]Mattias Gardell, "White Racist Religions in the United States: From Christian identity to Wolf Age Pagans," *Controversial New Religions* (2005): 387–422; John Pollard, "Skinhead culture: The ideologies, mythologies, religions and conspiracy theories of racist skinheads," *Patterns of Prejudice* 50, no. 4–5 (2016): 398–419.

chaplain who oversees the Odinist worship in his maximum-security prison. He had been politely and professionally explaining to me how he ensures that Odinists have space and materials to practice when I asked him if he ever had to navigate white supremacist behavior directed against him in providing services to the group. He smiled sheepishly.

Chaplain Tyrone:

Well ... let me see ...

oh ... how to describe it ...

yeah ... basically ...

it is pretty much like a front. *(laughs and shakes his head)*

I mean that's, that's the, that's the God's honest truth. I have yet to come across an Odinist or Asatru follower or even a person of any pagan religion, that are accepting of having a black chaplain sit in on their services. They're not. It's a front.[33]

Chaplain Tyrone goes on to explain that he navigates the racial tension between a white religious group and himself as the black chaplain overseeing that group through direct conversation with them, fair provision of their space and materials, and a clear policy that if white supremacy is mentioned outright an officer will be called and the service disbanded. But he also acknowledges that his prison is predominantly Black and that the Odinists are mostly trying to "stay to themselves." As Father Michael put it, "They (Odinists) are really looking for safety and community."[34] Because Chaplain Tyrone can see the need of white men for safety and community in a primarily Black prison, he is willing to overlook undercurrents of racial extremism if they are not made explicit. "We have an understanding," he explains, "I won't tolerate any of their white supremacy discussions, and they won't try to incite any type of ruckus, you know, while they're there. It's an even trade: I respect you, you respect me."

Chap Mav, introduced above, took a different approach to white religious groups that seemed to him to be overtly racist.

Chap Mav:

There was a church called the Church of the Creator, which is a racist church that was organized in America, and there were some people who

---

[33]Interview with the author on March 15, 2021.
[34]Interview with the author on April 16, 2021.

tried to become adherents of that in the prison, white men. And, you know, you can't deny people their religious affiliation. But if a certain religion ... well there were two religions ... all right, so one is called Odinism and then Church of the Creator. So it turns out the Church of the Creator really did say some racist stuff in their rhetoric, and so I was able to get them classified as a gang, and then they couldn't practice.

The Odinists successfully litigated in other facilities and therefore needed to be respected, but I was able to put a requirement of there being a volunteer.

Sarah:

For them to meet for corporate worship?

Chap Mav:

Right. And they couldn't find a volunteer because they're not that organized on the street.[35]

Using prison policy, Chap Mav legislates white supremacist religious groups out of operation. One is classified as a gang and thus prohibited. The other, while still technically permitted, is not allowed to meet unless they have an outside volunteer to supervise them, a bar that Chap Mav knows the group will not be able to meet. This is similar to how Chap Mav handled racism when he encountered it in corrections officers. Rather than naming what he saw in the officer's behavior as racism, he uses the policies of the prison to simply legislate the overt racism out of the spaces and programming that he oversees.

White supremacists are not the only racially extreme group using religious identity as a means to organize in prison. Father Michael is a white Catholic priest in a men's maximum custody prison, and he shared about similar trials with the Nation of Gods and Earths or "Five Percenters," a Black radical movement.[36] In some prison systems, this group is characterized as a "security threat group" or gang and is not permitted to meet. In Father

---

[35]Interview with the author on January 25, 2021.
[36]Khatija Bibi Khan, "Erykah Badu and the teachings of the Nation of Gods and Earths," *Muziki* 9, no. 2 (2012): 80–9; Yusuf Nuruddin, "The Five Percenters: A Teenage Nation of Gods and Earths," in *Muslim Communities in North America*, ed. Yvonne Yazbeck Haddad, and Jane Idleman Smith (State University of New York Press, 1994), 109–132; Göran Larsson, "The Five Percenters: Islam, Hip Hop and the Gods of New York by Michael Muhammad Knight," *Alternative Spirituality and Religion Review* 1, no. 1 (2010): 91–3.

Michael's system, Nation of Gods and Earths was a recognized religious tradition. He had just finished explaining his approach to the racial extremism of Odinism: he makes sure they get the space and items that they are guaranteed and upholds a commitment to "meeting people where they are." He then turned from his experience with white religious extremism to Black religious extremism.

Father Michael:

> Yeah I mean, I had the same problem with the Nation of Gods and Earths, the Five Percenters.
>
> I actually got along well with them in my first prison, but I ran into trouble on Death Row with a couple of them because I wanted, I tried to help them, but they are so impossible to work with these guys. No matter what I did it wasn't enough, and eventually one of them ended up suing me and the Department because we're racist. I thought, "I should have just done what the other chaplains did and took one look at the guy and ran the other way and just never encounter them!" But I thought naively that, well you know, I work with the Odinists, I can help these guys too, but ... it proved to be really difficult. But it might have been more him than the Nation of Gods and Earths in general. Because I mean, I kind of understand where they're coming from. And obviously I don't believe what they believe, but I can, I can sympathize or empathize to some degree with what a guy growing up in a ghetto would think ... at least from what they've told me.[37]

Father Michael, a white man, faces a lawsuit in his attempts to resource a religious group known for anti-white extremism. There is a very real dialectic here between power and risk. The chaplains described above use their power and authority to keep wicked problems from overtaking the chapel: kicking people out of choir, having religious groups labeled as gangs, closing services, partnering with corrections officers to arrange seating in worship, and getting disruptive officers reassigned. They are standing in their full authority as staff people with power that can be used over and against other people, and they are leveraging that power against social divisions as they manifest in the prison chapel. At the same time, they are risking themselves: breaking up fights, sitting in the middle of a gang, overseeing extremist groups that hate their race, and being sued. When chaplains confront wicked problems, they simultaneously leverage their own power and risk their own lives and livelihoods in real ways. They judge and are judged. They risk and

---

[37]Interview with the author on April 16, 2021.

are risked. Chaplain King was explicit that when chaplains are inhabiting these various dialectics—between power and weakness, staff and resident, black and white—they are following the "middle way" of Jesus.

Chaplain King is a Black chaplain who has served at a men's mixed custody facility for ten years. He can remember white men leaving Christian worship when he came, and he can remember Black men leaving when he welcomed Hispanic men overtly into worship. He told me about leading a service after the shooting of Trayvon Martin and beginning with the words, "Some of you say I'm too black. Some of you say I'm not black enough. And some of you, I just can't please at all."[38] He names that "the faith groups like the Nation and Rastas and Moors (MSTA), they would want me to be a black radical man, you know, and I did wear my dashiki on occasion," but those groups grew frustrated with him when he sought unity between races and religions on the prison compound. His "middle way" was not limited to racial and religious difference. Chaplain King extended this logic to the carceral divisions that characterize prisons. He told me the story of trying to explain this "middle way" to his wardens.

Chaplain King:

> I've come to the point where I'm bold enough to say, and I've said this to all of my wardens, and I've had about seven wardens in the last ten years: "Hey warden, I'm here to work with you and serve, but I want you to know whose side I'm on. And I'm not on the inmate side. I'm not on the staff side. I'm on God's side." And so as a chaplain, I want to be in the middle, like Jesus on the cross in the middle, you know. I think that's a good place to be as a chaplain.[39]

I want to be like Jesus, on the cross, in the middle. Chaplain King makes explicit that this balance of authority and risk, the willingness to stand between competing categories and repeatedly try to draw them together, was a way to be like Jesus. He is clear that such a middle way will both make everyone mad and preserve the ability for anyone to come to the chaplain when they need him. He claims that this middle way is being like Jesus, and I think Karl Barth agrees. Barth calls this "middle way" the Doctrine of Reconciliation, and he uses that doctrine to describe both the person and work of Christ and the ways in which Christians can participate in what Jesus has already accomplished.

---

[38] Interview with the author on January 15, 2021.
[39] Ibid.

The Judged Judge: Reconciled Divisions in the Body of Christ

As noted previously, Karl Barth names the entirety of Volume IV of *Church Dogmatics* "The Doctrine of Reconciliation" which can also be translated "The Doctrine of Atonement."[40] So what does Barth mean when he refers to a doctrine of reconciliation or atonement? Barth begins section §59 "Jesus Christ, The Lord as Servant," saying,

> The atonement is history ... the very special history of God with man, the very special history of man with God ... What takes place in this history—the accusation and conviction of man as a lost sinner, his restoration, the founding and maintaining and sending of the community of God in the world, the new obedience of man—is all decided and ordained by Him as the One who primarily acts and speaks it.[41]

Atonement, or reconciliation, is how God enacts God's judgment against human beings while bringing human beings into right relationship with God. Paul Fiddes brings the senses of the English terms "atonement" and "reconciliation" together when he notes that the etymology of the word "at-one-ment" suggests the idea of "making one" out of those that were previously divided.[42] In less theological terms, *The Oxford Languages Dictionary* defines "atonement" as "reparation for a wrong or injury." In short, a doctrine of atonement asks, "How does God repair the wrongs that we have done and are doing?" Or put more systemically and less in the register of individual action, "How does God annul, repeal, or abolish the sin of the world?"[43]

When Barth turns to answer this question, he joins a long-standing Christian theological tradition of using a juridical framework, i.e. the language of a court system. In part, he uses court language to describe the person and work of Christ because that is what he sees the Gospels

---

[40]Barth, *CD* IV/1, vii.
[41]Barth, *CD* IV/1, 157–8.
[42]Paul S. Fiddes, "Salvation," in *Oxford Handbook of Systematic Theology*, ed. John B. Webster, Kathryn Tanner, and Iain Torrance (Oxford: Oxford University Press, 2007), 178.
[43]See Barth, *CD* IV/1, 247–53 or Barth, *KD* IV/1, 272–9. With respect to sin, Bromiley translates *aufheben* as "overcome." In *Obedience from First to Last: The Obedience of Jesus Christ in Karl Barth's Doctrine of Reconciliation*, Edmund Fong reclaims some of the juridical sense of the term by translating it as "abolish." *Aufheben* could be translated as abolish, annul, repeal, revoke, or reverse—all terms that stay within the wider register of the juridical in which Barth places his doctrine of atonement. Edmund Fong, *Obedience from First to Last: The Obedience of Jesus Christ in Karl Barth's Doctrine of Reconciliation* (Eugene: Pickwick Publications, 2020), 198–203.

doing.⁴⁴ Writing about the Passion Narratives in the final chapters of each Gospel, Barth names that, "what these chapters bring before us is an arrest, a hearing and prosecution in various courts, a torturing, and then an execution and burial."⁴⁵ Barth notes that the Gospels do not describe the theological significance of this arrest, sentencing, execution, and release, they simply present them as fact, as something of a court transcript of the accused Jesus Christ.⁴⁶ Barth looks at this court transcript and says that in order to understand how this court scene relates to the salvation of the cosmos or the annulment of sin, three questions must be addressed: How or in what way did God become human? Why did God become human? And what is the connection between how and why God became human and our current individual transgressions and systemic sins?⁴⁷

Barth answers the question of "how" God became human with a doctrine of the incarnation as described in the last chapter on a ministry of presence. The Christian God is a God who characteristically draws near to human beings, takes on flesh, and is "with us." The simple taking on of flesh already begins some of the work of reconciliation insofar as human and divine are brought together in one body in Jesus Christ and God's Yes and God's No to the human condition are also united in Christ. But just as the work of the chaplain is not completed by their simple presence in prison, the work of Jesus is not accomplished in the simple fact of the incarnation. What does Jesus do once incarnate? What is his work and ministry? *Why* has he become flesh? Barth's answer, in brief, is this:

> Why did the son of God become man, one of us, our brother, our fellow in the human situation? The answer is: In order to judge the world ... What took place is that the Son of God fulfilled the righteous judgment on us men by Himself taking our place as man and in our place undergoing the judgment under which we had passed ... He judged, and it was the Judge who was judged.⁴⁸

---

⁴⁴Barth, *CD* IV/1, 273–83.
⁴⁵Ibid., 226.
⁴⁶Ibid., 224.
⁴⁷Barth will primarily answer the first question, "*Quo iure Deus homo?*" in §59.1 "The Way of the Son of God into the Far Country" and the second question, "*Cur Deus homo?*" in §59.2 "The Judge Judged in our Place." He explains the logic of distinguishing between these questions—the person and work of Christ—in *CD* IV/1, 184. He then answers the third question, "How can that which has happened once, even if it did happen for us, be recognized to-day as having happened for us, seeing it did not happen to-day?" in §59.3 "The Verdict of the Father," *CD* IV/1, 284–7.
⁴⁸Barth, *CD* IV/1, 222.

Jesus became flesh to render a just judgment on the conditions of the world through his words and actions, but he then does the unthinkable and steps down from his place at the bench in order to take the guilty verdict and sentence himself. Barth presents his theology of Jesus the Judged Judge as an exegesis of the synoptic Gospels.[49] As we have seen before, Barth understands the Gospels to operate in halves: the first half establishes Jesus' authority as a righteous judge and shows the content of Jesus' judgment through Jesus' words and actions. The second half, the Passion narratives, flips the script as Jesus becomes silent, acted upon, and literally judged in court scenes. Commenting on the earthquake that happens at Jesus' execution in Mt. 27:51, Barth writes, "The cosmos had to register the strangeness of this event: the transformation of the accuser into the accused, and the judge into the judged, the naming and handling of the Holy God as one who is godless."[50]

I agree with Barth's assessment that the Gospels present Jesus as both a judge and as one who is judged. I also agree that at one level it is a "strange and scandalous reversal" for the God of heaven and earth to be put on trial in a Roman court.[51] But I want to notice, more than Barth does, that the first half of the story *leads* to the second. The specific ways that Jesus confronts the powers of this world—i.e., executes God's judgment—are what build the tensions between him and authorities that ultimately lead to his arrest, trial, and conviction. The judgment that Jesus renders leads to him being judged. In other words, it is because Jesus sets out to bring good news to poor people, release to prisoners, recovery of sight to the blind, and release to the oppressed (Lk. 4:18, Isa. 61:1), and because he offers those things in ways that press beyond ethnic, religious, and carceral divisions, that he is targeted as a disruption to the status quo of economic, carceral, and ethnic disparities. Jesus confronts wicked problems and divisive binaries in such a way that he falls victim to them—the judge gets brought up on charges by the system he came to judge.

As with prison chaplains today, Jesus confronts ethnic and religious divisions by refusing to give preference to his own categories. When he announces his Isaiah 61 mission to prisoners, the poor, the blind, and the oppressed in Luke 4, his hometown people in Nazareth initially "marveled, wondered, or were amazed" (θαυμάζω) by his teaching (4:22). It is only when Jesus specifies that he is not coming to offer these freeing, healing, economy-shifting powers only to Israel that the crowd ἐπλήσθησαν πάντες θυμοῦ, were all filled with "anger, hot anger, or rage" (4:28). Like Chap Lin, Jesus cites the Scriptures as creating precedent for his behavior. Jesus tells his hometown that in Elijah's day there were widows in Israel, but Elijah goes

---

[49]Ibid., 224–8.
[50]Ibid., 239.
[51]Ibid.

to the widow in Zarephath; in Elisha's day there were Israelites with leprosy, but Elisha heals Naaman the Syrian (4:25-27). Jesus situates himself inside of a prophetic line of healing and feeding that crosses ethnic and religious lines and refuses priority to one's home people. In response, his home people try to push him off a cliff, and for the duration of Luke's Gospel, Jesus is homeless. He wanders from place to place depending on the hospitality of others for his basic needs.

Similar pressure begins to build early in John's Gospel when Jesus is willing to talk and share a drink with a Samaritan woman in Jn 4:1-42. Jesus and the woman discuss the differences between Samaritan and Jewish religious practices bound up with regional identity, and the woman is moved by the conversation to share with her people that Jesus might be the Messiah. When Samaritans follow her back to hear Jesus speak, these Samaritans proclaim that Jesus is the "Savior of the world" (4:42). This is the first act of proselytizing and mass conversion in John's Gospel, and the success in drawing followers to Jesus is attributed to a Samaritan woman, even as the story is threaded through with surprise that Jesus is willing to sit and talk with her across ethnic, religious, and gender difference (4:9, 27). The Synoptic Gospels do not contain this story, but Luke's Gospel contains the story of the Good Samaritan in which Jesus again upholds the compassionate witness of someone ethnically and religiously different from himself and his listeners (10:25-37). Jesus says that while a Jewish priest and then a Levite showed no compassion to one of their own who had been beaten and robbed, a Samaritan reaches across social divisions to bind the person's wounds, to deliver them to an inn, and to pay for their continued care. Jesus looks out at his Jewish listeners and tells them to follow the example of the Samaritan: "go and do likewise" (10:37).

In addition to reaching across ethnic and religious difference, Jesus reaches across carceral divisions. Here I use the term "carceral" broadly to indicate people who are confined, controlled, and policed in distinction to people who either are free from this or are doing the policing and confining. Luke's Gospel tells two stories in Luke 7 and 8 showing that Jesus' healing and freeing ministry will be offered both to soldiers serving as an occupying police force and to people held by officers with physical restraints. Chap Lin introduced us to the story of Jesus healing the centurion's slave as an example of Jesus accepting "officers" (Lk. 7:1-10). A centurion (ἑκατοντάρχης) is simply a non-commissioned officer (NCO) in the Roman army, and this centurion has been assigned to Judea, an occupied territory of the Roman Empire. It is worth noting that when the centurion sends Jesus a request for healing, he sends it through the "elders of the Jews" rather than coming himself. These leaders explicitly tell Jesus that this particular centurion "loves our nation" and helped "to build our synagogue" (7:5). They feel the need to make an argument excusing or explaining the centurion's ethnic, religious, and carceral status to justify why he might "deserve" this healing in spite of social divisions (7:4-5). When the centurion hears that his request will be honored, he uses an analogy from his own military background to send a new message that Jesus need not make the trip but simply speak the word and his slave will be healed. As an officer, he understands the power of a person in authority to simply command others and be obeyed, and he asserts that Jesus has this sort of authority to command healing. Jesus does as suggested and says to the Israelites around him, "I have not found faith like this in Israel" (4:9-10). Jesus not only heals a Roman centurion's slave, but he receives a comparison of himself and the NCO and holds the officer up as an example of faithful behavior to the very people the centurion is policing.

In the very next chapter of Luke, Jesus enacts a healing on the other side of Father Michael's cop/convict binary. Jesus encounters a man who had been "chained hand and foot and kept under guard (8:29)." The man has escaped his imprisonment and is living in a graveyard.[52] The lingering impacts of his incarceration are evident: when the man sees Jesus, he begs him not to torture him. Jesus sends the demons within the man into a herd of pigs and heals his mind (8:28-33). The keepers of the pigs report what has happened. When a crowd finds the formerly incarcerated man "dressed and in his right mind," they do not react with joy at this restoration. Jesus has overturned carceral divisions and assumptions, restoring sanity and dignity to someone who had been locked up, and the crowd "is afraid" and "asks or begs" (ἐρωτάω) Jesus to leave town (8:34-37). The formerly incarcerated man "begs" to go with Jesus, perhaps from gratitude or perhaps knowing that he would not be received in his restored state. Jesus commissions the man to become an apostle and tell others, "what God has done for you" (8:38-39). Paired with the chapter before it, the reader is given an image of a Jesus who offers healing to both officers and incarcerated people alike and then enrolls both groups in the ongoing work of God's kingdom.

Like chaplains, Jesus crosses ethnic, religious, and carceral divisions to offer healing, conversation, and restoration. Like chaplains, Jesus is willing to bend and break rules to do so (Mk 3:1-6, Mt. 12:10, Jn 5:1-18, etc.). And like chaplains, these actions build tension around the body of Jesus with both the crowds who witness these acts and the authorities responsible for policing and maintaining both the official rules and the social divisions. The series in John in which Jesus talks to the Samaritan woman (John 4), heals a lame man on the Sabbath (John 5), and feeds 5,000 people (John 6) culminates with the authorities sending guards to attempt to arrest Jesus (7:32). The Synoptic Gospels narrate Jesus kicking the money changers out of the temple as the last straw that moves authorities from simply trying

---

[52]For a treatment of this story as a carceral text, see Soering, *The Convict Christ*, 17–23.

to arrest him to planning to kill him (Lk. 19:45-48, 20:19). Like Chaplain Noa and her own attempts to "cleanse the temple" of gang activity, Jesus is using his authority to challenge wicked problems in a way that puts himself at risk of arrest and death. Even as tension builds, he continues with this mission until he is ultimately arrested, and the Gospels transition to the passion narratives in which the Judge becomes judged. The kind of judgment Jesus could rightfully give, he receives first in his own body as an arrested person placed on trial. He stands between judged ones and their accusers, Samaritans and Jews, a Roman Centurion and occupied Judeans, but he does not simply stand between them. The type of reconciling work he wants to do between these social divisions, he does by taking them into his own body as the Judge who becomes a Judged one. Jesus incarnates human and divine, God's Yes and God's No, and now also the identities of Judge and Judged—or perhaps Father Michael's Cop and Convict—within himself. Jesus is "with us" and "for us" *all*, without distinction, across every persistent and pernicious social divide.

I want to pause here to note two significant ways in which Barth is modifying penal substitutionary atonement.[53] These will be taken up more explicitly in the Postlude, but for now it is worth noting that the judgment to which Jesus submits is human rather than divine and that the first person of the Trinity drops out of the economy of judgment in Barth's doctrine of the atonement. While Jesus being judged has cosmic significance, it is not cosmic or divine judgment that is meted out upon him. Jesus simply undergoes an arrest, hearing, and sentencing process that any other person disrupting the peace would undergo. There is divine abandonment (Barth notes this in Jesus' cry, "My God, why have you forsaken me?"), but there is no judgment by the First Person of the Trinity against Jesus.[54] In Barth's economy of atonement, the Father is not the Judge. Jesus is the Judge *and* the Judged, and he is judged not by his Father but by religious leaders Annas and Caiaphas and the governor Pilate. As the First Person recedes in Barth's telling of the story, there is no indication that the Second Person of the Trinity is somehow satisfying the wrath of the First Person, being sent to his death by the First Person, or being punished by the First Person. Rather, the Second Person Jesus has simply drawn so fully into the affairs of human beings in taking on flesh to judge and disrupt sinful systems that he becomes implicated in the full impacts of those systems. Somehow, the salvation of the cosmos happens in a mundane Roman trial and sentencing process. Atonement in this telling is more about drawing near and becoming

---

[53] Neither of my specific points is noted in the following, but for a longer treatment of whether Barth's doctrine of atonement as expressed in CD IV/1 falls properly within the category of penal substitutionary atonement, see Fong, *Obedience from First to Last*, 200–7.

[54] Barth, CD IV/1, 215. See also Barth, CD IV/3.2, 637.

implicated than about cosmic exchange or satisfying a divinely ordained punishment.

Blurring the Binaries: Barth, Jesus, and Chaplains Have Criminal Records

While at one level, the above is a straightforward re-telling of the Gospel accounts, Christians do not usually call Jesus a justice-involved person, i.e., a person with a criminal record.[55] Though many churches enact his court drama annually during Holy Week, Christians do not always take the next step with Barth to notice that Jesus, "is not dying a hero's death, but the death of a criminal,"[56] or that Jesus "was sought out and arrested as a malefactor ... accused as a blasphemer ... and agitator."[57] Christians do not often say that salvation history is carceral history or that the only incarnate God is an incarcerated one. The truth that Jesus was classified as a criminal is often hidden in plain sight. But Barth sees Jesus' justice-involvement, amplifies it, and centers his doctrine of reconciliation on it.

I think that at least one reason Barth can see Jesus as a judged person is because Barth is one himself. In April 1934, Barth was detained by the Nazi government and put through a three-hour interrogation by the Gestapo concerning his resistance against the Nazi regime and his refusal the month before to open his classes with a Nazi salute.[58] At that time, Barth was released from custody without formal charges.[59] One month later, in May 1934, Barth participated in writing the Barmen Declaration, a document that was meant to strengthen and unify the Confessing Church in its stance against the German Christians.[60] In October of 1934, Barth participated in a gathering of the Confessing Church that was disbanded by the police.[61] Immediately after, in November of 1934, Barth refused to give an unqualified oath of loyalty to the Führer. He was suspended from his teaching post by the end of the month, and by the next month, December 1934, he was put on trial in Cologne.[62] In 1963, almost thirty years after

---

[55]For a substantial treatment of taking Christ's involvement in the criminal legal system seriously, see Mark Lewis Taylor, *The Executed God: The Way of the Cross in Lockdown America*, Second Edition (Minneapolis: Fortress Press, 2015).
[56]Barth, *CD* IV/1, 226–7.
[57]Ibid., 239.
[58]Johnson, *The Essential Karl Barth*, 9.
[59]Busch, *Karl Barth*, 242–5.
[60]Ibid., 245–8.
[61]Ibid., 252.
[62]Ibid., 255–8.

that court experience, Barth stands before an incarcerated congregation in Basel prison to preach a sermon about Jesus as the Judged Judge. He starts his sermon about Jesus' court experience with a testimony about his own arrest, trial, conviction, and punishment. Barth says:

> My dear friends, we all know what it means to appear *in court*. I can quite easily include myself too as I say this, for nearly thirty years ago now, in the days of Hitler, in Cologne on the Rhine, I too once appeared in court. I was accused and charged there by a wicked lawyer who said that I had done what was not allowed in the Germany of the day and had not done what ought to be done in the Germany of the day. Three judges sat opposite me and looked at me with serious, suspicious faces. And an able young lawyer sat next to me and took great pains to prove that everything was not as bad as all that. Everything took its inevitable course. I was found guilty and sentenced to be dismissed as an unreliable state official and as a bad teacher of German youth. Now that is a long time ago and as you see I have survived it pretty well up to now.
>
> I am telling you this simply to remind you about something you know more about that I do: what it is like to come up before a *human* court.[63]

Karl Barth knows what it is like to stand before a judge and be declared guilty. This is the most detailed first-person account in the historical record of Barth's justice-involvement. That he only shares it in such detail to other men with records some twenty-nine years after his conviction is notable.[64] Arguably even more notable is the fact that, in this sermon, Barth links his personal experience of being in court to his understanding that Jesus being judged in a court is the foundation of reconciliation or atonement, i.e., the repairing of wicked problems today.

When Barth is classified as a criminal, even though he breaks the law for admirable reasons, neither the church government in Berlin nor the Confessing Church supports his appeal. Eberhard Busch records Barth saying, "When I approached the Provisional Church Government and the Council of Brethren of the time, who had brought this trial upon me, and asked for their formal support, I was left in the lurch by both these bodies and had to fight the whole battle by myself."[65] It is important to keep in mind that Barth was not widely lauded or supported by his professional or ecclesial peers at the time of his court-involvement. This is important because history has, in many ways, de-criminalized people who stood against the Nazi regime. These criminal charges are now understood to

---

[63]Barth, *Call for God*, 88. Italics in the original.
[64]Ute Frevert, *The Politics of Humiliation: A Modern History* (Oxford: Oxford University Press, 2020), 1–75, 121–5.
[65]Busch, *Karl Barth*, 258.

have been "the right thing to do." We imagine that even if people broke the law in Germany attempting to stand against the Nazi regime, they broke the law justly. This narrative is a way of distinguishing between "real criminals" and justice-involved people who might disrupt common assumptions about criminality.

There are many problems with glossing some justice-involved people as "real criminals" and others as not.[66] For our purposes here, I will simply note that this retrospective narrative erases the little data we have about the way that Barth's arrest, trial, and conviction marked him as a "criminal" and the impact that might have had on him. In the sermon in which Barth names his own justice-involvement, he also indicates that he experienced the dynamics of shame, suspicion, and fear that the drama of the courtroom generates for those put on trial.[67] Barth was not shielded from those dynamics simply because he believed in the ways he had broken the law. Barth describes the faces of the judges who looked at him as "suspicious." He says that to be accused means to be "in the middle of a lot of people—and with everybody's eyes on him."[68] He acknowledges that once one is found guilty of a crime, "We don't even see ourselves as we really are. And others do not see properly either."[69] He describes appearing before a judge as a *krisis* and names fear as the primary emotion multiple times.[70]

The drama of arrest, trial, and conviction is aimed at criminalizing the accused. It is not enough to render a verdict. The process must convince all participants and the general public that the person found guilty can legitimately be stripped of their rights, freedoms, and privileges. Barth experiences this. As is common with criminal charges, Barth loses his job and becomes targeted for future actions against him by the state. Just two months after his conviction in March 1935, Barth is given verbal notice by the Gestapo that he may no longer speak in public in Germany at all.[71] In June 1935, Barth formally won his appeal. The Cologne verdict is dismissed, but Barth is simultaneously found guilty of other charges, fined a fifth of his annual salary, and dismissed from his teaching post a week later by the Minister of Cultural Affairs.[72] Barth leaves Germany within the month and seeks refuge in Basel, Switzerland.

---

[66] There is a long-standing tradition of glossing class and racial differences among justice-involved people by designating some people as "real criminals" who conform to social (race and class) stereotypes for who should be incarcerated as "real criminals." For a systemic treatment of the impacts of this dynamic in shifts in American carceral trends in the 1990s through early 2000s, see Jill McCorkel, *Breaking Women: Gender, Race, and the New Politics of Imprisonment* (New York: New York University Press, 2013).
[67] Ashby Jones, "The 'Perp Walk' Debate: Prejudicial or Legit?" *The Wall Street Journal*, June 19, 2008.
[68] Barth, *Call for God*, 88.
[69] Ibid., 89.
[70] Ibid., 90, 91, 93.
[71] Busch, *Karl Barth*, 259.
[72] Ibid., 261-2.

Perhaps it is then not too much to suggest that Barth can grasp the truth of Jesus as a judged and criminalized person because he was among those who have been forced to know in their own bodies that those classifications are false binaries. Judge/judged, cop/convict, felon/free are social divisions aimed not at truth but at social control. Jesus is transformed from, "the accuser into the accused, and the judge into the judged, the Holy God as one who is godless"[73] in a similar way to the manner in which Barth was classified as a good teacher and a bad one, as a reliable state official and an unreliable one, as one with authority and one stripped of it, as one recruited to teach in Germany and one exiled back to Switzerland. Barth holds in his own body and history the same types of divisions and binaries that Jesus does. One of the surprises of this study was that prison chaplains do too.

I did not ask chaplains about their own criminal records, but three of twenty chaplains self-disclosed that they had criminal records themselves. Perhaps more have records and did not feel safe to disclose it. I, for instance, have a criminal record, but I did not mention it on record in my interview for this study. Two additional chaplains self-disclosed that they had been institutionalized in psychiatric facilities prior to their service as chaplains. Three more indicated that they had immediate family members who had been incarcerated. Nine of the chaplains in this study named that they came into prison chaplaincy out of crisis conditions: job loss, sexual harassment in a prior position, and inability to find jobs as clergy in their denominations because of their gender, sexual orientation, or divorced status. Six chaplains named that they were survivors of rape, sexual assault, or childhood abuse. Almost all of the above social histories were shared with me when I asked what formal or informal training, education, or experiences had prepared them for the job. These criminal histories and traumas are identities and experiences that chaplains believe make them better chaplains.

Like Barth and like Jesus, these chaplains already hold within themselves some of the dueling identities that prisons (and wicked problems writ broadly) insist are distinct. They are healers who have been victims of assault. They are prison staff who have been arrested and detained themselves. They uphold policies that separate incarcerated people from their families, and they are the family members of incarcerated people. They are Pakistani, Innuit, Asian American, and Native American who are treated (often) as if they are white. They are Black men called too white, and white men called black for intentionally welcoming everyone into the chapel.[74] They are ordained Christian clergy intentionally offering interfaith services who are accused of being "not Christian enough" by conservative religious volunteers while simultaneously being sued by incarcerated people who accuse them of showing Christian favoritism.

---

[73]Barth, CD IV/1, 239.

[74]This last point is phrasing things politely. The two white men who expressed this indicated that they had been called derogatory racial slurs by white officers for their welcome of Black incarcerated men into their offices and the chapel.

They are not choosing to inhabit the "middle way" of Jesus out of some sense of martyrdom or duty; they simply do hold social divisions within themselves. Like Jesus, they risk and are risked. They judge and are judged. They have authority, and they are under it. They know and inhabit their own racial and religious identities, but they refuse to give priority to their homepeople. The reconciliation that they try to build in their prison chapels, they are doing first in their own bodies, minds, and social histories. They are inhabiting Chap Mav's "Christ beyond color." They are, as Chaplain King said, "like Jesus on the cross in the middle." They are a living witness of Christ's work of atonement or reconciliation, but they are not accomplishing it. The distinction is important.

Barth is clear that while Jesus gives us an example to follow in his reconciling work as a Judged Judge, Jesus also accomplishes a cosmic repair that does not need our successful inhabitation of the pattern to be real, complete, or effective. Barth writes:

> Jesus Christ is the fellow-man who goes before us as an example and shows us the way. It is true that there is a discipleship, a fellowship with Him ... but Jesus represents us without any co-operation on our part. In the event of His, the Gospel history, there took place that which permits and commands us to understand our history as a history of redemption and not perdition. It has happened fully and exclusively in Him, excluding any need for completion.[75]

Both sides are important: Jesus has accomplished a reconciliation of divisions that humans cannot accomplish on their own, and humans are invited to participate in the pattern of reconciliation by becoming a sign to how housing all of these divisions within oneself can be experienced as "redemption" rather than "perdition." In addressing what Jesus has done for humans, Barth says that Jesus has crowded humans out of both their false role as judge *and* crowded them out of the judgment they would rightly receive for their actions. Being both barred from the impulse to judge others and having our own sentences vacated means that there is a freedom to move against wicked problems. Humans are freed from one of the basic lies of wicked problems: namely, that social categories create clear divisions among people across which we are invited to judge one another. Humans are also freed from an immobilizing fear of being judged when one inevitably fails against the impossible possibility of standing up against systemic evil. One can step with confidence into a site of social division—the middle way of chaplains—because Jesus is already there, refusing the binaries by taking them into himself. We can "be with" Jesus in the middle, but Jesus is "for us" in a way that our obedience or disobedience, failure or success, never

---

[75]Barth, *CD* IV/1, 229–30.

touches.[76] His act of reconciliation will always stand for all whether we step into the pattern, successfully enact it, or simply point to the need for it with our failure.

There are comfort and power in knowing that God can hold the divisions of the cosmos within Godself in a way that any given individual cannot. When facing wicked problems inside of prison, enacting any sort of diverse, authentic, and liberating community legitimately seems like an "impossible possibility" most days. As Chaplain Levine says, "every day you are wading into personal trauma, but also the racial and historical trauma, generational trauma."[77] Chaplain Love said:

> I'd say most of the chaplains I met were doing the best they could under impossible circumstances...
> and doing really beautiful work.
> but there were some days that I thought,
> "Oh my goodness. This is tough."
> You know the institution itself thinks in either/or terms.
> It thinks ...
> it doesn't think in complexity.
> But I think chaplains,
> by the very nature of who we are in that institution,
> we have to do complex thinking.
> We have to look at many sides,
> not just either/or ...
> *(long pause)*
> It makes it exhausting.[78]

The work of standing in the middle is draining, lonely, and never complete. The stories of success are the same stories as the stories of facing and failing to eradicate pernicious social divisions. The stories of winning against wicked problems—freedom in worship, people singing together, a glimpse of the kingdom of God on earth, chaplains protecting the chapel from violence and extremism—are the same stories that show the persistent power of wicked problems—chaplains being sued, fights breaking out in choir, gangs derailing worship, racial extremist groups finding ways to meet in the chapel. What has actually been accomplished by Jesus in the ministry of reconciliation if these social divisions persist even as chaplains are brave to stand like Jesus and draw groups together using their own bodies? Barth says that the most important and ineradicable change accomplished by

---

[76] Ibid., 230–1.
[77] Interview with the author on April 23, 2021.
[78] Interview with the author on March 12, 2021.

Jesus' ministry of reconciliation is that now that Jesus has come to stand in places of God-forsakeness where wicked problems rule, there is no God-forsaken place. Social divisions, wicked problems, either/or thinking, racism, and religious extremism can persist, but when they do, they do not get to create conditions of God-forsakeness. Those social evils have been enveloped into the body of God as Jesus—human and divine, Yes and No, Judge and judged—comes to stand right in the middle of them and to take on their full implications. Barth writes:

> Jesus did become—and this is the presupposition of all that follows—the brother of man, threatened with man, harassed and assaulted with him, with him in the stream which hurries downwards to the abyss, hastening with him to death, to the cessation of begin and nothingness. With him He cries—knowing far better than any other how much reason there is to cry: "My God, my God, why hast thou forsaken me?" (Mk 15:34). *Deus pro nobis* (God for us) means simply that God has not abandoned the world and man in the unlimited need of his situation, but that He willed to bear this need as His own, that He took it upon Himself, and that He cries with man in this need.[79]

I think Barth is pointing to the same truth that Chap Lin articulated in the last chapter: that the chaplain shows by their presence that "there is no godforsaken place. There is always a representative of the Holy, even in the midst of unholy things."[80] A ministry of presence inhabits the logic of the incarnation, but a chaplain's creation of diverse, authentic, and free programming and her willingness to face wicked problems with authority while risking herself in the process, is an enactment of the doctrine of reconciliation.

Standing in the middle and drawing groups into reconciliation with your own body is draining and lonely, but because Jesus has already done it, the chaplain is not alone and has a limitless source of power. When one steps into the pattern of reconciliation, "acting as a faint but not obscure reflection,"[81] one is always stepping into a place where Jesus already is. Now, when anyone steps into places that seem God-forsaken like holding cells, court rooms, prisons, or even death—as we will get to in a few chapters—Jesus as God is already there, both experiencing God-forsakenness and eradicating our experience of God-forsakeness by His willingness to be present in such places, fully exposed alongside us to the conditions created by wicked problems. The chaplain can show by the presence of her own body in those same spaces that there is no God-forsaken place, no God-

---

[79]Barth, *CD* IV/1, 215. See also 185, 239, 306. Parenthetical translation mine.
[80]Interview with the author on January 6, 2021.
[81]Barth, *CD* IV/1, 244.

forsaken person, but the chaplain can do that draining, lonely, impossible, and soul-fracturing work because of the bedrock truth that God has already chosen to be with her, in her, before her, and around her in precisely those draining, lonely, impossible, and fracturing conditions.

A Closing Image: Standing between Divided Sacrifices

In trying to name what chaplains are doing in this work of reconciliation and atonement in prisons, Chap Lin shared an image that has stuck with me.

Chap Lin:

> You see the divisiveness,
> and I would say that the role of a chaplain is, is,
> is to try to,
> what is that Bible verse?
> Where you walk in between the divided animals and the sacrifices
> and just, you just,
> try to contribute to wholeness,
> and to realize
> when Jesus says, "Be ye therefore perfect as your Father is perfect,"
> that really means
> complete or wholeness.
> And so our job as chaplains is not to be flawless,
> but to support the wholeness.[82]

Chap Lin is referencing the story in Genesis 15 in which God makes a covenant with Abram. In the story, God tells Abram to look up at the stars and promises that Abram's descendants will be as numerous as those stars (15:4-6). God then promises that God will give the land on which they are standing to Abram (15:7). When Abram asks how he can know that the Lord will do this, God enacts the ritual associated with a Hittite suzerainty treaty.[83] A suzerainty treaty is made between a powerful entity (the suzerain) and a less powerful entity (the vassal). The vassal would make promises to the suzerain, and the suzerain would protect the vassal while those promises were fulfilled. One animal would be split in half for each promise made, and the divided animals would be laid out for the vassal to walk through. Threat

---

[82]Interview with the author on January 6, 2021.
[83]David Noel Freedman, "Divine commitment and human obligation: The covenant theme," *Interpretation* 18, no. 4 (1964): 419–31.

is implicit in the ritual: if the vassal is not faithful to the suzerain, they will be cut down like the divided animals through which they walk.

David Freeman notes two uncharacteristic and role-reversing facts about the suzerainty ritual in Genesis 15.[84] First, only God the suzerain takes on any promises. The vassal Abram is not required to promise anything in return. Second, God in the form of a flame is the one to walk through the divided animals, taking the place reserved for the weaker party in the ritual.[85] Like Barth's Judged Judge, the suzerain takes the place of the vassal, the divine steps into the place of the human, the powerful one steps into the place of threat and risk. And now, Chap Lin imagines herself walking between the divided pieces of a prison like God did. She is not taking God's place. She is not superseding the story. Her life and witness point back to the story, and as she draws closer and closer to God, she comes to look more and more like the God she serves. She stands in the place of risk where God stood, flipping social identities and surrounded by divisions, but there is no longer any way for her or any other person to stand in places of risk and division alone. The flame of God is already between the sacrifices. Jesus has already gotten off the bench and stood at the bar to take the sentence.

While never alone, there is a high cost to standing with God in a sacrificial fire or to standing with Jesus in a place that got him killed. How does it impact a person to enact a ministry of reconciliation when reconciliation means taking social divisions into oneself in acts of both authority and risk? What are the mental, physical, and spiritual impacts of journeying daily into places where it seems like wicked problems are winning? We turn now to the impacts of risking death for lifework.

---

[84]Ibid., 425.
[85]For a full treatment of fire, flame, and *kavod* (glory) as the "body" or physical presence of God in the Hebrew Bible, see Benjamin D. Sommer, *The Bodies of God and the World of Ancient Israel* (Cambridge: Cambridge University Press, 2009), 58–79.

4

Counting the Cost:

Being Made Sin for the Sake of Salvation

Am I going off the deep end?
—CHAPLAIN MOSES, INTERVIEW ON JANUARY 23, 2021

What would be the value to us of His way into the far country if, in the course of it, He lost Himself?
—KARL BARTH, *CHURCH DOGMATICS IV.1*, 185

Chaplain Harald told me the following story on May 6, 2021:

> It was a bad situation. These two guys had gotten a hold of hard pens.
>
> And when it came time to move them and open the door to their cell, they jumped the officer, and stabbed him in the back, and made a run for it.
>
> Now in the wings at the prison, not only are you locked in your cell, you're locked in the wing. And it's locked with different keys from the inside than from the outside, and the officers don't have both keys.
>
> So they stabbed this poor officer and couldn't get past the door!
>
> I was on the next level in that wing.
>
> I heard the alarm.
>
> I heard security screaming.

And I wasn't sure in this situation, because I didn't know what was going on, what am I supposed to do?

I stayed right where I was with my back against the solid wall, not against the door, not against the opening in the door, the solid wall. I set my stuff on the floor and stood still. I didn't know what the right thing to do was, but I knew better than to try and do something without knowing the situation or what was going on.

But the officers forgot that I was there!

(long pause)

I found myself starting to have trouble breathing.

They had cleared the officers out of that area around the guard station and got them all behind the glass and had released the gas to bring these guys under control.

Well, I'm all the way down at the end, and all that gas is rafting in my direction. And all of a sudden, I'm starting to be dizzy, and I couldn't breathe.

I dropped to the floor because I knew that's where my best chance for air was. I crawled out on my hands and knees because I didn't want to put my head too high because then I'd be getting too much gas. With my face against the floor, I crawled as best I could, pushing myself with my legs to the center area where the gas was coming from.

They didn't realize I was there. They forgot I was there.

Well, next thing you know, I've got the warden and both assistant wardens, the director of nursing on the outside door. And they've got the masks on, and they're trying to get to me, to get me out of there.

When I finally got outside the building, the lead chaplain said, "Well, all things considered, we're going to give you the rest of the day off with pay. But you better be back here tomorrow." *(laughs)*

You never know …

never know what to expect.

So we have to be ready.[1]

---

[1] Interview with the author on May 6, 2021.

You never know what to expect ... so we have to be ready. The confinement of human persons relies on use of force. Prisons are, therefore, places blanketed in state-sponsored, legal use of force in which illegal use of force is simmering right below the surface, occasionally erupting into episodes like the one described above. Chaplain Harald tells a story in which his coworker was stabbed in the back with a pen. Chaplain Harald is not stabbed, but the fact that he knows someone who has been stabbed on the job creates a sense of threat. He goes to work knowing that an assault on his person is a real possibility because it has happened to his coworker.

In this story, an attack against another staff person is not Chaplain Harald's only exposure to violence. Chaplain Harald is gassed. He is not attacked by an incarcerated person. Rather, the institution itself, its policies for resolving threat, and the officers who forgot about his presence in the midst of crisis release poisonous gas against him and the incarcerated men confined with him. Chaplain Harald works in a place in which he has been physically harmed not just *on* the job but *by* his employer. Finally, Chaplain Harald names the hyper-vigilance that comes from working in an environment in which there are both real possibility of being attacked and a personal history of having been harmed by the institution. Hypervigilance, the elevated sensory state of constantly assessing threats, can be a result of experiencing trauma, but as Chaplain Harald names, prison staff are trained in hypervigilance as a precautionary measure.[2] Chaplains "have to be ready" in the hopes of noticing the early warning signs of violence in order to de-escalate episodes and to reduce harm whenever possible. This sort of exposure to violence at the three levels of eye-witness, first-person experience, and bodily habituations of hyper-arousal has a direct impact on how chaplains navigate their own behavior toward other staff and incarcerated people and how chaplains experience their own minds, bodies, and spirits on and off shift. There is a cost to prison chaplaincy that is paid in the mind, body, and spirit of the chaplain.

Even chaplains who never experience an episode like what Chaplain Harald describes are impacted by these dynamics. Chaplain Harald works at a men's maximum custody prison. Chaplain Armstrong works at a women's minimum custody prison, and she explained to me the ways that episodes in one prison impact prison policy statewide. She explained how officers in her facility were being made to wear stab-proof vests at all times on every shift because of a stabbing that happened across the state at a men's maximum custody prison. Officers were hot and uncomfortable. The vests communicated in a palpable way that each officer was at risk, even though

---

[2]Matthew Kimble, Mariam Boxwala, Whitney Bean, Kristin Maletsky, Jessica Halper, Kaleigh Spollen, and Kevin Fleming, "The impact of hypervigilance: Evidence for a forward feedback loop," *Journal of Anxiety Disorders* 28, no. 2 (2014): 241–5; Charlotte Fritz, Leslie B. Hammer, Frankie Guros, Brittnie R. Shepherd, and David Meier, "On guard: The costs of work-related hypervigilance in the correctional setting," *Occupational Health Science* 2, no. 1 (2018): 67–82.

staff assaults were exceptionally rare at her facility. The vests communicated to incarcerated women that they were perceived as a threat, even though they rarely engaged in physical violence. All of this served to elevate tension in the prison rather than de-escalating it.

Chaplain Armstrong:

> I think the main thing that affects me personally in our prison as far as riots and safety and security issues and all those things, is that it's a shame that whenever something bad happens somewhere else, it affects minimum-security women's prisons. We end up with the same policy as a maximum-security men's prison where, you know, five people just got killed.
>
> Our staff—and not just the staff, the women—the policies don't make sense to us. To have the extreme measures ... and the vest is just an example of that. You know those came out after deadly assaults on officers at another prison.
>
> That same year there was the young sergeant, the female sergeant who was killed with the fire extinguisher.
>
> You know ... the stabbings happened with scissors.
>
> I have three pairs of scissors.
>
> And now they're in a locked box up on the wall, and you know, I'm supposed to check it every day and say, "Yes, I have all my scissors." And that all came as a result of those stabbings because that's how they killed those people, with, with scissors. And so I get it. I understand that they have to cover themselves, and there were lawsuits and all of that. I get it, in my brain, but ...
>
> I'll do anything to keep from using a pair of scissors! *(laughs)* Because I have to unlock it and take them out and sign them out and use the scissors and then put them back in there and sign them back in and lock the box up! And so we don't sit around and cut out flowers and whatever anymore, because it's just a pain.
>
> And recently when the officer came in to pick up my little sign-out sheet where I'm supposed to check every day that I have all my scissors, I said, "You do know that if somebody was going to kill me, they are not going to do it with the scissors. They're going to do it with this—this ID that I have hung around my neck here. They're going to slit my throat with it because they sure use it to open boxes every day because we

don't check the scissors out to open the boxes, that's for sure. We use our ID's for that!"

And I said, "Furthermore, you see that fire extinguisher right there beside the office door? I'm glad to have a fire extinguisher in case we have a fire, but if somebody wants to kill me, they're going to use the fire extinguisher!" And that has happened, but nobody took our fire extinguishers.

There's just this ... the disconnect is hard to understand.

So we don't have the assaults, but we have the effects of the assaults as far as policy goes.[3]

We don't have the assaults, but we have the effects of the assaults. Chaplain Armstrong works in a system where a handful of staff were stabbed to death with scissors at one prison and at a different prison an officer was killed with a fire extinguisher. One of those episodes resulted in statewide use of stab-proof vests and cumbersome policy around the use of scissors. These policies mean that staff deaths are at the forefront of every staff person's mind on each shift. And yet even as Chaplain Armstrong locks and unlocks her scissors, counts them, or avoids using them, she looks at a fire extinguisher hanging on the wall that she knows was also used to kill a staff person that same year. The prison's attempt to mitigate threat makes her job harder, but neither her safety nor her sense of safety is increased. Rather, what increases is her bodily habituation into the practice of threat assessment, her conscious awareness of the possibility of death on the job, and her frustration in performing basic daily tasks. These all elevate the stress-level of working in prison, a cost that is born in the body of every person who lives and works there.

In Lk. 14:25-33, Jesus acknowledges that there is a real risk of death in Christian discipleship. He explains that following him involves breaking rules for the purpose of healing (14:1-6), overturning social hierarchies that place some people above others (14:7-11), and creating a feast in which people are invited to eat together across divisions of wealth, health, and ability (14:12-24). These tasks are strikingly like the work described in chapters two and three, in which chaplains enact healing ministries of presence and create worshipping communities that are diverse, authentic, and free. As we saw in previous chapters, chaplains are risking rule violations, lawsuits, and their own physical safety to follow Jesus in this work. After describing the work of the kingdom of God in Luke 14, Jesus is honest that such work

---

[3]Interview with the author on July 9, 2021.

will create divisions in families and risk the execution of the one doing the kingdom work. Jesus then tells his listeners to "count the cost" before embarking on the work. This chapter is an attempt to "count the cost" of inhabiting salvation.

How are prison chaplains impacted by risking death for lifework? I begin by discussing the ways that prison chaplains change their professional identities in response to repeated exposure to threat and harm. Do chaplains try to change the system when they experience its violence? Do they seek safety in forming bonds with other staff people, with incarcerated people, with neither group, or with both groups? Do they use strategies of avoidance, keeping away from areas or people in the prison that are understood to be particularly risky? Rather than categorizing some chaplains as "social justice chaplains," others as "pro-prison chaplains," and still others as "state-employees riding a desk," my research showed that chaplains alternate between advocacy, institutional alliances, and avoidance strategies when trying to navigate the daily threats of prison.

Jesus similarly navigates bodily threat to be with human beings and to reconcile divisions. As Barth tries to describe the cost of Jesus not just taking on flesh but drawing into the worst of the human condition, he says that Jesus becomes the Prodigal Son.[4] Barth acknowledges that Jesus as Prodigal Son is God drawing into solidarity with humans to the point of becoming unrecognizable.[5] Horror and holiness come to inhabit one body. Barth says that this is what it means to be "made sin" for the purpose of reconciliation.[6] How are chaplains being "made sin" as Jesus is "made sin" when he exposes himself to the full weight of systemic violence?

Finally, what are the impacts, not just on a person's identity and role, but on a person's mind, body, and spirit from repeatedly experiencing violence and threat in the pursuit of God's healing and reconciling ministry? What does it look like, not simply to sin or be made sin, but to be made sin-sick by exposure to systems of confinement and control? Is that sin-sickness a necessary byproduct of salvific work? Can it be mitigated or reversed by self-care practices, or is sin-sickness simply the cost of engaging salvation? Is the cost of salvation limited to Jesus, or can one see the same costs being born by all those who follow him into the work of reconciliation? And finally, what does it mean for those who inhabit salvation that when Jesus is made sin, he is rendered an incarcerated person, not a chaplain? These are the questions to which we now turn.

---

[4]Barth, *CD* IV/1, 157–210.
[5]Barth, *CD* IV/3.1, 394–406.
[6]Barth cites 2 Cor. 5:21 to discuss the concept of Jesus "being made sin" 15 times in *Church Dogmatics*. The fullest treatments occur in I/2, 152; IV/1, 165, 236, and 603; IV/3.1, 442–4.

Responses to Threat Exposure: Advocacy, Alliances, Avoidance

In a study conducted with prison chaplains in the western United States, Allison M. Hicks found that while chaplains enter prisons with rehabilitative goals, i.e., ideas about the possibility of encouraging the positive transformation of incarcerated people, chaplains are quickly socialized into institutions that are more concerned with confinement and control than rehabilitation. She explains that chaplains becoming risk managers who "learn to watch out" and de-escalate threats within the institution.[7] She also notes that chaplains renegotiate their relationships to corrections officers, realizing that they cannot accomplish their goals or operate safely within the system without positive relationships with other prison staff.[8] While chaplains often come into the job believing that they have different goals than the officers in a prison, they revise those beliefs in at least two ways. They revise their calling to include ministry to officers, and they qualify the extent to which they might achieve the rehabilitation of incarcerated people. Hicks offers a nuanced and detailed assessment of the ways that chaplains change their behavior and thinking in response to the reality of prisons. In my own interviews, I found that chaplains engaged in an even wider set of identity shifts and behavioral responses to the institution. Chaplains responded to the violence of prison by becoming advocates for incarcerated people, accommodating to prison culture and forming alliances with other prison staff, and renegotiating job responsibilities to avoid risky and draining situations.

In *Rethinking Incarceration: Advocating for Justice That Restores*, Dominique DuBois Gilliard sees these same responses in prison chaplains, but he describes the behaviors as three historic roles that chaplains have played. Using historic prison chaplains as examples, Gilliard suggests that chaplains tend to operate as advocates for incarcerated people, as ministers who believe that the harsh environment of prisons can serve a positive role in rehabilitation but who have limits on what levels of state violence are acceptable, or as employees who fully embrace and "baptize" the punitive nature of prisons.[9] One leaves Gilliard's analysis with the sense that prison chaplains are either "social justice" chaplains or "pro-prison" chaplains.

When speaking about their peers, chaplains in this study gave a similar impression. One chaplain who worked hard to maintain relationships with his

---

[7] Allison M. Hicks, "Learning to watch out: Prison chaplains as risk managers," *Journal of Contemporary Ethnography* 41, no. 6 (2012): 636–67.
[8] Allison M. Hicks, "Role fusion: The occupational socialization of prison Chaplains," *Symbolic Interaction* 31, no. 4 (2008): 400–21.
[9] Dominique DuBois Gilliard, *Rethinking Incarceration: Advocating for Justice that Restores* (Downers Grove: IVP Books, 2018), 126–35.

warden and security staff lamented that too many chaplains are on the side of "inmates" to the point of having no relationship with fellow staff. On the flip side, other chaplains complained that their peers were too security-minded, never willing to challenge the prison's policies or the behavior of individual officers. Chaplains on both sides complained that some of their peers were simply "riding a desk," doing as little as possible until their state or federal pensions kicked in. Chaplains seemed habituated to assess and to classify their peers as social justice chaplains, pro-prison chaplains, or chaplains who simply rode a desk. But the stories that they told about their own navigations of prisons and their own varied responses to high levels of threat painted a much more complicated picture. There were no chaplains who were simply advocates of incarcerated people, only allies of prisons, or always avoiding the chaos to the point of riding a desk. Rather, any given chaplain engaged in multiple behaviors and identities, sometimes all at the same time.

Advocates and Allies

In many ways, Chaplain Floating was the chaplain in this study who risked the most to report prison abuses; he was a clear "social justice" chaplain. He had bravely reported on superiors and been transferred to a different facility because of it. He had gone on record about incidents that his prison system had tried to cover up. He told me stories of reporting prison abuses that cannot be shared in this study because they continue to have ongoing implications for him and the accused prison staff. He was open to saying that he loved the incarcerated men whom he served, and he described coming to the prison early, tennis shoes in hand, to walk and jog the prison track with incarcerated men before work. He also acknowledged that there were many times over his eighteen years of prison chaplaincy when he witnessed abusive treatment of incarcerated men that he did not report. Sandwiched between stories of reporting prison abuses, Chaplain Floating told me the following story of choosing not to report.

Chaplain Floating:

> At the old prison there was an officer who asked me to come down to seg.[10] And when I got down there, they said, "We got an inmate raising hell. Says we're freezing him to death. We've given him extra blankets, but he won't shut up."

> So I went back to his cell, and I'd never met this guy. I hadn't been there long. And he wanted to know who I was, and I told him I was

---

[10]Short for "segregated housing," what is commonly called solitary confinement outside of prisons.

the chaplain. And then I looked at him, and I said, "I hear you're on the verge of having hypothermia."

And he said, "What's hypothermia?"

And I said, "Well, where you get real cold, and you know, you start shivering—and I told him all about what hypothermia was—and then you just go to sleep and die." I said, "Are you close to that place?"

And he looked at me and smiled.

And I said, "Look, we both know what you're doing, but I'm gonna tell you what's going to happen: You keep this up, and these guys are gonna roll back here, and they're gonna take everything out of your cell, and they're gonna strip search you. And they're going to humiliate you every way they know how." I said, "There won't be anything I can do about it. There won't be anything you can do about it."

So I went on around through seg, and sure enough, he started up. They came. Stripped him. Spread-eagled him. Handcuffed him to the bunk.

And then they'd walk by two at a time and say little cute things about his bodily form, if you get what I mean.

And I didn't want to embarrass him any more, so I walked up part of the way to his cell, and I said, "Look. You know, *these guys have the power* down here. And you've gotta learn to play the game. You know you've got to learn."

He was a young, young guy.

So I went back to the officers, and I said guys, "Really? You know, you really think that humiliating somebody like that is going to, in the long run, do anything other than make this man angry or see the system as being awful and terrible?"

And so that's ... I didn't report them. Maybe I should have. I don't know.

But again, the rules: the carrot and the stick. I don't know how you change people doing that.

Now there's, there were officers that you know, I was responsible for two officers getting moved out of that place. And then there was the inmate who got killed ...

I don't know, Sarah.

When, when do you run to the administration, which I often found not trustworthy and not willing to do anything. Not willing to do anything. Which put me in a position where it hamstrung me to some extent.

It put me at odds with … as I used to tell my trainee: Don't take sides. Don't take sides.

Don't be part of the institution. And don't be always on the inmate's side. Don't, don't, don't do that.[11]

I didn't report them. Maybe I should have. I don't know. This is a complicated story. Chaplain Floating is an advocate for an incarcerated person, and he is not. He is a trusted member of the prison staff (officers call him to de-escalate a situation), and he also speaks a critical word to officers about their behavior. Chaplain Floating shows respect to the incarcerated man, manages to develop some rapport with him even mid-crisis (the man smiles at him), and continues to respect the man even as he is being humiliated (he stands where he cannot see the man's nakedness in order to speak further). But he also encourages the man to "learn to play the game" of prison in which officers have ultimate authority in dorms and cells, even the authority to strip, spread-eagle, cuff, and humiliate a person. Chaplain Floating ultimately withdraws from the incident before it is resolved, leaving a man cuffed naked to a bed.

In this story, Chaplain Floating is faced with an incident with a moderate level of violence, a moderate level of threat, and a high level of degradation. He advocates. He befriends the incarcerated person. He maintains positive professional relationships with the officers and does not report on them. He withdraws from the scene with the incident unresolved. He is a "social justice" chaplain, but he could easily be described as having sided with the officers in this story. He could not be described as "riding a desk," but he does retreat to his office when his efforts seem ultimately unsuccessful. On two more occasions throughout the interview, he will pause, shake his head, and say, "Maybe I should have reported those officers. I don't know." Chaplain Floating expressed a sense of regret, failure, confusion, and weary resignation that universally characterized the chaplains in this study as they reflected on their own responses in the face of prison's mundane threats, degradations, and violences. He also exemplifies the way that chaplains do not take on one characteristic identity or role in response to prison violence. Rather, chaplains deploy all of these roles and responses, sometimes in rapid succession, as they try and fail to de-escalate threat.

---

[11] Interview with the author on May 5, 2021.

Avoidance

No one in this study described themself as "riding a desk," but occasionally chaplains would admit to using avoidance strategies to cope with the stress of prison. Chaplain Levine described initially being excited to take over pastoral responsibility for the segregation unit of his prison from his supervisor. Segregation units (or seg, the hole, lock-up, "jail," H-Con, M-Con, I-Con, restrictive housing, etc.) are what the public often calls solitary confinement. People are kept in single cells, without a roommate, for 23–24 hours a day, sometimes for years. Segregation is most often used as a punishment for disciplinary infractions. Due to the negative mental health impacts of being kept in a small space in this way, solitary confinement is widely considered torture in the international community and is not permitted in prisons in many countries.[12] Rounding on a segregation unit means observing the severe degradation of human beings, but the degradation has been challenged in state and federal court and found to be legal in the United States.[13] There is nothing to report. Chaplain Levine described the impact of making twice weekly rounds in seg to me:

> It gets back to the sort of the secondary trauma part of trauma. You know, it's like I ... that just ... was really hard to sustain.
>
> I found ... I came to realize ... in a way, that in some ways, you know, it was embarrassing.
>
> Or I felt like a failure in some ways ...
>
> but it was just so hard ...
>
> To be there ...
>
> And to see people treated like that, and you know some men are in there, literally for years and just ...
>
> So I've thought about that ...
> thought about that piece a lot ... like both how unbelievably important it was to go there, and how unbelievably hard it was to go there ...
> in any consistent and sustainable way.

---

[12]David H. Cloud, Ernest Drucker, Angela Browne, and Jim Parsons, "Public health and solitary confinement in the United States," *American Journal of Public Health* 105, no. 1 (2015): 18–26.
[13]Peter Scharff Smith, "The effects of solitary confinement on prison inmates: A brief history and review of the literature," *Crime and Justice* 34, no. 1 (2006): 441–528.

Sarah Jobe:

Hmmm ... How did you sustain it?

Chaplain Levine:

Well, I'm not convinced I did. I think I ... what I ...

What I noticed in me was—because there's always plenty to do right? I mean, there's always more people to call up. It's not like, right, you kind of have to prioritize that over other things. And I found my ...

I found myself ...
I found it becoming harder and harder to prioritize that.

I could still do things that were valuable, but segregation started getting the short, the short end of the stick.

It was just—I'm just aware that for me, and you know this wouldn't be true for everybody, necessarily, but for me it just—what it, what it asked of me to prioritize, to prioritize that, and to be there was just so hard.

Some of it was the smells ... I mean it was just ... it was the whole experience I just
found so overwhelming.[14]

How unbelievably hard it was to go there ... in any consistent and sustainable way. Chaplain Levine names that repeated exposure to the conditions of solitary confinement is a form of trauma exposure. He still remembers the smells. As one can see in the transcript, his speech begins to break up even as he attempts to describe the space and its impact on him. By definition, trauma exceeds the body and brain's capacity to make sense of or assimilate what was experienced.[15] In the face of overwhelming conditions, humans are hardwired to responses of fight, flight, freeze, or tend and befriend.[16]

---

[14]Interview with the author on April 23, 2021.
[15]Bessel Van Der Kolk, *The Body Keeps the Score: Brain, Mind, and Body in the Healing of Trauma* (New York: Penguin Books, 2014), 7–21.
[16]Ibid., 51–73. For an introduction to the addition of "tend and befriend" as a women's health intervention into the previously understood responses of "fight, flight, or freeze," see Shelley E. Taylor, Laura Cousino Klein, Brian P. Lewis, Tara L. Gruenewald, Regan A.R. Gurung, and John A. Updegraff, "Biobehavioral responses to stress in females: Tend-and-befriend, not fight-or-flight," *Psychological Review* 107, no. 3 (2000): 411.

Chaplain Levine has the self-awareness to name that he fled. He spent less and less time on segregation because of the cost to him of going there. He did not "ride a desk." He simply saw the myriad people who needed to be seen on less intensive housing units. He also left the profession after two years.

Chaplain Stanford used similar avoidance strategies to keep away from other prison staff. She stopped going to the staff dining hall and simply stayed at her desk during lunch. She shared, "when I did go to the staff dining room, people were unhappy, and they were talking about, they were sort of bitching about work, and I really didn't feel like it was helpful ... and so I didn't want to participate, but I didn't have the strength to be always redirecting the conversation in a positive way. And so it was just easier to be by myself."[17] She names her experience of working in prisons as "lonely."

Chaplain Barrett named days when he would stay in his office because he could not bear to answer another request. He said, "I have bad days ... just like anybody else, I have bad days. I have bad days. And there are days when I do, I look out, and I tell them, 'I really don't care today. It really doesn't matter today.' And of course, that usually gets me cussed out worse. But sometimes you have to be honest and say, 'I can't do this today.'"[18] Chaplain Barrett admits that there are days when he simply does not have the capacity to face the needs of incarcerated people. On those days, he stays in his office. If incarcerated people come to his office, he tells them he cannot help. When chaplains see their peers using avoidance strategies to cope with prison, they critique those behaviors as "riding a desk," but chaplains were also vulnerable enough to state that sometimes they simply could not stay present to the mundane traumas of prison life.

Trauma Response as Professional Identity

Some of the chaplains who could easily be characterized as "social justice" chaplains lamented moments when their behavior seemed to indicate that the prison's culture of force was shaping them more than they were shaping it. Both Chaplains Moise and Lin described verbal altercations with incarcerated people in which they yelled back at the person in front of them, escalating violence and giving in to the prison's usual tactic of using loud threats to force submission from incarcerated people. Chaplain Moise shared that she has contacted newspapers to report abuses within her prison. She will tell stories about going on record in lawsuits against the state for inhumane treatment of incarcerated people that might satisfy the standards of "cruel and unusual punishment" in the hopes of improving living conditions in prisons. Right before she tells the story of yelling at an incarcerated person,

---

[17]Interview with the author on January 22, 2021.
[18]Interview with the author on August 30, 2021.

she has explained that she made a decision not to carry pepper spray or a radio in order to indicate to incarcerated people that she trusts them. She is committed to nonviolence, and she takes risks by not arming herself in order to communicate to incarcerated people that she believes that they are capable of interacting with one another without threat or force. And yet, in at least one moment of escalating tension, Chaplain Moise fails to uphold her own ideals.

Chaplain Moise:

We're not, in our system, chaplains are not certified staff, so we don't carry weapons. You have to go through a special training to carry pepper spray, and I decided not to go through that training. I actually don't carry a radio, although many chaplains do. So you're kind of on your own. *(laughs)* I don't, I also don't actually have an officer with me. That's all starting to sound a little rough when I name it out loud, but … yeah … so you're sort of on your own and …

I don't ….feel at risk … but …

You know, prisons are sort of like highly pressurized, combustible space and so … in … in that … you know, disagreements erupt. Fights erupt … and … as a chaplain, you will sometimes find yourself as the only person, the only staff person, around when those things happen. And so being able to de-escalate violence and tension without any form of threat to rely on or any kind of weapon … just … just who you are, and your ability to talk to people, and your ability to physically inhabit a space in a nonviolent way … that goes a long way. And it is something that you do have to learn to do. Or I, I really had to, I had to learn to do that to stay in that job.

So …

Yeah, I can remember actually one year early, early on … maybe a year or two into the job … I feel like maybe I hadn't quite learned it the way I wanted … the way I now feel that I have and feel good about learning to de-escalate conflict. And so, I can feel the tension building in the trailer. We are doing something sort of loose and free. I think it was a "Hanging of the Greens" event. So there were a lot of people getting to do a lot of freedom of movement stuff. And so it was a little bit less controlled, a little bit chaotic *(smiling)*. I was trying to give people as much freedom as possible, and one woman … you know, one woman was having a fairly normal disagreement with another woman about how to decorate part of the trailer. *(laughs)*

But, you know, their voices were starting to escalate. It was turning into an argument.

And so I kind of leaned out of my office where I was working on something and just said, you know, "Hey ladies, let's take it down a notch."

And one of them yelled back at me ...
and at the time ...
I yelled back at her, like really yelled, and said that she would be written up if she couldn't comply with my orders.

And I can remember her face just looking completely shocked that I'd said it.

And I had this sick feeling like ... this ... this is not the pastor that I want to be.

But I also didn't ... kind of like ... I didn't know what to do ... because we're all, you know, thirty people that I'm in charge of, no backup, no weapon, nothing, and this verbal altercation has broken out ... and ... you know ...

My next shift, I called her to apologize for having spoken so harshly in front of other people to her. And she also, you know, said she, she was hoping to come apologize that same day. That it was, that she shouldn't have spoken to me in front of others the way that she did.

But I haven't done that since.[19]

And I had this sick feeling like ... this is not the pastor that I want to be. But I also didn't know what to do. Seminaries do not train people in how to repeatedly experience threats, verbal altercations, and attacks against their person and continue to uphold the dignity and worth of the people posing the threat or perceived to be posing a threat. Without such training, humans revert to their pre-conditioned responses of fight, flight, freeze, or tend and befriend in the face of threat. Often even with training, humans will default to those responses. But when trauma-exposure happens on every shift, these trauma responses become roles and identities that are, quite often, in tension with the roles and identities a prison chaplain might ideally want to uphold.

---

[19]Interview with the author on January 1, 2021.

Someone who tends to respond to threat by fighting might often look like a social justice chaplain, fighting to change the system, or they might literally fight back in the moment of altercation, seeming to support the prison's usual tactics of shouting, force, and intimidation. As we see above with Chaplains Lin and Moise, they might also do both. Someone who tends to freeze or flee in crisis might become a chaplain who uses avoidance strategies to the point of "riding a desk" or simply leaves the profession altogether. People who tend toward "tend and befriend" responses might be perceived as overly allying themselves with incarcerated people or overly allying themselves with prison staff. As in Chaplain Floating's case, they might do both at once. In all of these cases, prison chaplains watch themselves doing things they do not want to do and becoming people they do not want to be. They struggle with regret and disappointment. Even as they accomplish a lot, they experience themselves as having failed. In describing her own moment of yelling at an incarcerated man, Chap Lin explained, "I think I made him feel like he was just little tiny ... his value didn't shine through, and I didn't hold that value properly. I might have been right. I prevailed, but at what cost? At what cost?"[20]

The Case of Harald Poelchau, Prison Chaplain in Nazi Germany, 1933–45

In April 1933, Harald Poelchau began work as a prison chaplain at Tegel Prison in Berlin, Germany. Poelchau was trained in psychology and social work, and he received a doctorate in theology studying under Paul Tillich, who had served as a military chaplain in the First World War in addition to his well-known work as a theologian.[21] Poelchau thought he was simply going to work at a maximum-security prison. He knew that witnessing executions once or twice a year was a part of the job; a clergy person was legally required to be present for an execution to occur in Germany at the time. But right as Poelchau began his career as a prison chaplain, Adolph Hitler rose to power and the National Socialist Party took control of the German government. The nature of Poelchau's work shifted. Tegel Prison began holding a large number of political prisoners and hosting exponentially more executions than it previously had. Ralph Kruger reports, "From 1890 to 1932, a total of thirty-six persons convicted of murder were executed with an ax in Plötzensee Prison's outdoor courtyard. From 1933–

---

[20]Interview with the author on January 6, 2021.
[21]Ralph Kruger, *Dr. Tegel Miracle Worker of Berlin: Harald Poelchau in Nazi Germany* (Mustang: Tate Publishing, 2013), 43.

1945, 2,891 persons were killed in Plötzensee."[22] Chaplain Poelchau would be the chaplain assigned to witness more than 1,000 of these executions.

I learned about Harald Poelchau when I was gifted an English translation of Freya and Helmuth James von Moltke's letters to one another in the year before Helmuth's execution while he was imprisoned at Tegel.[23] The von Moltke's had been active participants in the Kreisau Circle, one of the underground resistance movements in Nazi Germany. The introduction to their correspondence states:

> The fact that Freya and Helmuth were able to engage in this conversation at all is in itself something of a miracle. By all rights, they should not have been able to write to each other during the years of his incarceration—save for a few authorized, censored letters ... but by a stroke of incredible good fortune, Harald Poelchau was the prison chaplain at Tegel. Poelchau was a close friend of the Moltke's, a member of the Kreisau Circle who had also participated in the plenary meeting in Kreisau in the Spring of 1942 but remained undetected.[24]

Every single word in this 345-page book was carried in and out of Tegel Prison on the person of Harald Poelchau. I was impressed and intrigued. This seemed like the type of prison chaplain I would like to become, i.e., someone who knew how to play the game so well that he could operate in Berlin, in a Nazi prison, for twelve years as both a Nazi-employed prison chaplain and a member of a German resistance movement in order to facilitate human connection and advance political resistance. I was even a little excited. I told my friends and my advisor that I had found the chaplain who held the secret key to navigating carceral complicity toward the ends of life, dignity, and freedom.

As I learned more about Chaplain Poelchau, his work as a chaplain and his resistance work were more wide-ranging and riskier than I had first understood. As a prison chaplain, he smuggled food into Tegel Prison where incarcerated people were being given less than 1,000 calories per day, which was less than prisoners were being given in many concentration camps.[25] He created "religion" classes for Communist prisoners to give them a way to gather because they were barred from Christian worship by prison policy, and he built a prison garden to get people out of their cells and into the

---

[22]Kruger, *Dr. Tegel*, 68. Plötzensee was a separate facility from Tegel Prison. The condemned were transferred to Plötzensee from Tegel on the morning of their execution. Poelchau would ride in the prison van with the condemned to their death, taking down last words and holding a cigarette to their lips since their hands were secured behind their backs (Kruger, *Dr. Tegel*, 65).
[23]Freya and Helmuth James Von Moltke, *Last Letters: The Prison Correspondence 1944–1945*, trans. Shelley Frisch (New York: New York Review Books, 2019).
[24]Von Moltke, *Last Letters*, ix.
[25]Kruger, *Dr. Tegel*, 54.

sunshine for an excused purpose.²⁶ When people were notified that they would be executed the following morning, Poelchau stayed at the prison overnight to keep vigil with them and take down last words for their families. The government had no formal mechanism by which to notify family members that their loved one was executed. Rather, the government simply sent an invoice to families "charging them for the costs of the execution and disposal of the body" after the fact.²⁷ Chaplain Poelchau took it upon himself to personally notify family members of the death of a loved one immediately after witnessing executions.

Poelchau and his wife Dorothee ultimately began hiding Jewish people in their own home.²⁸ He volunteered to be the air raid captain for his block so that no one else would ever have reason to inspect his home. Poelchau began forging documents to aid Jewish people escaping Germany. He participated in the Uncle Emil Group's rescue of Christine Hartman.²⁹ He was the prison chaplain to Dietrich Bonhoeffer, Hans von Dohnanyi, Mildred Harnack, and other well-known political prisoners in their last months prior to execution.³⁰ He was not the chaplain assigned to the execution of his friend and fellow conspirator Peter Yorck, but he managed to get into both the courtroom and to the execution to act as a supporter in his friend's death and to communicate final words from his friend to his family.³¹

Both Kruger's biography of Poelchau and the commentary in the von Moltke letters marvel repeatedly at how Poelchau went undetected in these activities as he operated in a Nazi prison in the heart of Berlin from 1933 to the fall of Berlin in 1945. Kruger even speculates that perhaps it was because Poelchau, with his blond hair and blue eyes, looked more Aryan than the Aryans. Kruger notes that he dressed professionally and kept a strict boundary between his personal and professional life.³² Yet many members of resistance movements who were arrested and killed looked Aryan, were professional and well-educated, and held positions of power. Yet to me, as a prison chaplain, that Poelchau went undetected as a member of the German resistance while he served inside of a prison as a chaplain did not seem like a marvel. It seemed like he was simply doing the job of prison chaplaincy. The Nazi regime exacerbated the death-bound and death-driven aspects of Poelchau's prison work, but Poelchau did what all prison chaplains do in

---

²⁶Ibid., 56.
²⁷Ibid., 68.
²⁸Ibid., 100.
²⁹Ibid., 165–6.
³⁰Harald Poelchau, *Die letzten Stunden, Erinnerungen eines Gefängnispfarrers* (Berlin: Volk und Welt, 1949). See also Annedore Leber, *Conscience in Revolt: Sixty-four Stories of Resistance in Germany 1933–45* (London: Valentine, Mitchell & Co., 1957), 119.
³¹Kruger, *Dr. Tegel*, 154.
³²Ibid., 57.

a less extreme and perhaps less crystalized form: he worked for life while being an agent in a system purposed toward death.

Poelchau's navigation of a Nazi prison as both an employee and a resister goes much deeper than "code switching" or knowing how to hide in plain sight. Poelchau was successful in remaining undiscovered as a resister of the Nazi regime because he became an active, paid participant of that regime. He participated in more than 1,000 executions. His presence permitted those executions to be carried out. He saved people from death, and he participated in executions. He was able to save some people from death *because of* his role in participating in other people's executions. He was able to feed prisoners because he was a paid employee of a regime that refused to feed prisoners enough to live. When Dietrich Bonhoeffer was incarcerated in his prison, he was able to visit with him sometimes because he also refused to visit Bonhoeffer when it was too risky to do so.[33] Chaplain Poelchau, like all prison chaplains, learned to hold both horror and holiness within himself. Becoming horrific was the price for bringing holiness to horror. Chaplain Poelchau paid that price. Communist prisoner Edith Holzapfel said of Poelchau, "His behavior in the midst of hell was very difficult for him."[34] While Poelchau was unwilling to comment on the impacts it had on him, his wife Dorothee said that "after night or early morning executions, he was completely shattered. He suffered from nightmares and anxiety attacks."[35] He died in 1972, at age sixty-eight from heart problems after repeated hospitalizations for a variety of health problems. Chaplain Harald Poelchau was a paid employee of the National Socialist Party, and he used his position to work for life in the midst of unrelenting death. He was made sin for salvific work, and he was also made sin-sick, ultimately to the point of death via stress-related conditions.

Being Made Sin for the Sake of Salvation: Jesus as Prodigal

Early on in *Church Dogmatics,* in a section entitled "Very God and Very Man," Barth insists that Jesus did not simply become a human being; he became the worst that human beings could become. Jesus became a "sinful creature" in order to reconcile sinful creation together with the holiness of God in his own body.[36] As inconceivable as God's glory is and as inconceivable as human evil can be, Barth says the most inconceivable thing

---

[33]Wolf-Dieter Zimmerman and Ronald Gregor Smith, *I Knew Dietrich Bonhoeffer*, trans. Käthe Gregor Smith (New York: Harper & Row Publishers, 1966), 222.
[34]Kruger, *Dr. Tegel*, 127.
[35]Ibid., 66.
[36]Barth, *CD* I/2, 155–6.

is that the divine heights and the human depths, horror and holiness, have been brought together in the person of Christ:

> The Word became "flesh" in this definite sense, this consummation of God's condescension, this inconceivability which is greater than the inconceivability of the divine majesty and the inconceivability of human darkness put together: this is the revelation of the Word of God.[37]

Barth uses 2 Cor. 5:21—he who knew no sin was made sin for us—as a touchstone for explaining the mystery of horror and holiness coming together in one body. When he does, Barth doubles down on the Gospel details that depict Jesus as a sinner:

> Him who knew no sin, he hath made to be sin for us, it may even be said (2 Cor. 5:21). And what do the Evangelists fail to record of him? "He is beside himself" (Mk. 3:21). "He hath Beelzebub" (Mk. 3:22). "A man gluttonous and a wine-bibber, a friend of publicans and sinners" (Mt. 11:19). "He deceiveth the people" (Jn. 7:12). "He blasphemeth" (Mt. 9:3; cf. 26:65). They are not afraid to speak of the suspicions already attaching to His parentage (Mt. 1:19). At the beginning of His life they let Him "fulfill all righteousness," that is, take upon Himself the baptism of repentance (Mt. 3:15). They let Him be crucified between two malefactors (Mt. 27:38). He bears away the sin of the world, but He does bear it (Jn. 1:29). It can all be summarized in the terrible saying of Gal. 3:13 γενόμενος ὑπὲρ ἡμῶν κατάρα. That He was innocent of it, without sin of His own, that the whole accusation does not touch Him but us, and Him only in our stead: that is another question which will require separate treatment. But He became a curse for us. He was not a sinful man. But inwardly and outwardly His situation was that of a sinful man.[38]

Jesus was made sin. He was made a curse. He bears away the sin of the world, but he does bear it. Barth is walking a fine line. He affirms that Jesus does not sin in some active or agential sense, but he insists that "inwardly and outwardly His situation was that of a sinful man." Barth asks the reader to table the issue of Jesus' innocence as "a question which will require separate treatment," and to consider instead the fullness of the way that Jesus was made sin for us. Barth does not let the claim that Jesus is made sin occur at the level of cosmic exchange, i.e., that a divine, unblemished

---

[37]Ibid., 152.
[38]Ibid. The German here is straightforward. Barth writes, "Daß er es unschuldig wurde, ohne eigene Sünde, daß jene ganze Anklage nicht ihn trifft, sondern uns, und ihn nur an unserer Stelle, das ist eine Sache für sich, von der besonders zu reden sein wird. Aber er wurde ein Fluch für uns. Er war kein sündiger Mensch. Aber seine Situation war innerlich und äußerlich die eines sündigen Menschen" (*KD* I/2, 165–6).

Jesus is somehow "made a sin offering" on the cross. Neither will Barth concede that Jesus is somehow "made sin" but still presents as sinless. For Barth, Jesus is not made a "sin-offering" at the moment of the crucifixion, rather Jesus is "made sin" throughout his life as he draws into fellowship with sinners and becomes identified himself as a glutton, drunk, blasphemer, bastard, and liar.

Barth thinks this distinction—between being made sin and being made an unblemished sin offering—is critical. He explains that if Jesus had become a human being, but not a sin-full human being like us, he would have simply been a taunting reminder of what humans could have been if they had not fallen. Barth quotes H. Bezzel saying, "his becoming man would have been a sneer at my misery, as surely as a man in the glow of health and strength, when he is brought to a sickbed, will always be felt like a pain by the sick."[39] Barth says that if Jesus had remained untouched by sin, his incarnation would not be a "revealing or reconciling action. He would bring us nothing new."[40] But in his willingness to be made sin, Jesus "exists in the place where we are, in all the remoteness not merely of the creature from the Creator, but of the sinful creature from the Holy Creator … In the hallowing of our unholy human existence He draws supremely and helpfully near to us."[41] By embodying sin as God, Jesus hallows our hells. He makes the horrors of this world holy, but he does it by being made into those horrors himself.

Sin-sickness and Jesus as the Prodigal Son

Barth will circle back to the idea that Jesus is "made sin" repeatedly throughout *Church Dogmatics*, deepening the claims and making them more repugnant each time. The first time Barth takes up 2 Cor. 5:21 again is in CD IV/1 in his Doctrine of Reconciliation, in the section "The Way of the Son of God into the Far Country," which we began to explore in the last two chapters.[42] The section title refers to the story of the Prodigal Son in Lk. 15:11-22.[43] Jesus tells a story of two brothers. The younger asks for his inheritance before his father dies. He takes his inheritance to a "far country" and διεσκόρπισεν τὴν οὐσίαν αὐτοῦ ζῶν ἀσώτως. The phrase can be translated "squandered his wealth on wild or profligate living," and later in the story, the older brother will accuse the younger of wasting the family wealth on prostitutes (15:13, 30). The phrase might also be translated something like "scattered his own being (οὐσίαν) living abundantly or lavishly." When the

---

[39]Barth, *CD* I/2, 155.
[40]Ibid., 155.
[41]Ibid., 155-6.
[42]2 Corinthians 5:21 is cited in CD IV/1 on pages 165, 236, and 603.
[43]Kendall Walser Cox, *Prodigal Christ: A Parabolic Theology* (Waco: Baylor University Press, 2022).

son's wealth has been scattered to nothing, he tends pigs and becomes so hungry that he wishes to eat the pigs' food. At this point, fully humbled and close to death, he returns to his father's house saying, "Father, I have sinned against heaven and against you. I am no longer worthy to be called your son. Make me one of your hired hands" (15:18-19). The Father rushes to greet his son, embraces him, clothes him, and creates a feast for him saying "this son of mine was dead and is alive again; he was lost and is found" (15:24). The older son, who had always done what was right and served the Father faithfully, is angry and refuses to celebrate. The Father says to him, "my son, you are always with me, and everything I have is yours. But we must celebrate and be glad because this brother of yours was dead and is alive again, was lost and is found" (15:31-32).

Barth takes the younger son to be a type of Christ. Jesus is the one who travels away from the Father, deep into the far country, to inhabit the place of human beings at their worst.[44] The Gospel language is redolent with double meaning. Jesus "spends himself on lavish living."[45] As explained above, the phrase could mean wasting money on prostitutes and parties or it could mean wasting his very being on abundant life. Barth thinks the point is that Jesus does both simultaneously. Jesus takes both horror and holiness into himself. As the fulness of the Father, Jesus becomes not just a Son, but the Prodigal Son. Because Jesus journeys all the way to where humans are living in a pigsty and comes to live in the pigsty with them, Jesus is the one who can lead them out of squalor and back to the Father. Barth acknowledges that "the more seriously we take this, the stronger becomes the temptation to approximate to the view of a contradiction and conflict in God Himself."[46] But Barth continues to insist that Jesus does not lose his divinity when he takes on the fullness of sin. He writes, "God does not sin when in unity with the man Jesus, He mingles Himself with sinners and takes their place."[47] At the same time, even in the fullness of his divinity, "He was not immune from sin. He did not commit it, but he was not immune from it."[48] The language of immunity is evocative, suggesting the old concept of sin as sickness. Jesus becomes sin-sick, sick from sin, as he draws fully into the circumstances of the sin from which humans need saving.

---

[44] While much of *CD* IV/1 is devoted to this conception of Jesus, Barth provides a short and helpful summary of Jesus as Prodigal Son in *CD* IV/2, 23.

[45] I am translating ζῶν ἀσώτως as "lavish living" or alternately "abundant life." The basic translation of ἀσώτως is "profligate," an idea that holds within itself the idea of excess, hence lavish or abundant. Another possible translation might be "unsaved life" or "unsaveable life." ἀσώτως comes from the same root as ἀσωτία which Strong's Concordance notes is simply formed from the negative particle and the root σῴζω, "to save." Strong's Concordance thus suggests that at base, the word can be translated "unsavedness" or a state of being unsaved, thus "profligate, abandoned, or dissolute."

[46] Barth, *CD* IV/1, 185.

[47] Ibid., 185.

[48] Ibid., 216.

Being Made Sin and Sin-sick in Prison Chaplaincy

Both of these concepts—being made sin and being made sin-sick—are helpful ways of understanding what happens to chaplains as they are exposed to the conditions of prisons. As she attempts to offer incarcerated people a chance to enjoy decorating the chapel, Chaplain Moise is responsible for de-escalating conflicts. When a threat arises, she yells at an incarcerated woman. She is "not the minister I wanted to be." Chap Lin draws near enough to an incarcerated man to be able to bear his burdens, but when that encounter becomes threatening, Chap Lin makes the man feel "little tiny." Chaplain Barrett continues to go into prison past the point of his own exhaustion only to avoid incarcerated people on his worst days. He admits that prison has "made me a harder minister." Chaplain Levine avoids visiting solitary confinement. Chaplain Floating watches a naked man cuffed to a bed be humiliated by officers, and he does not report it. Perhaps one could just say that these chaplains sinned. That is certainly one true thing to say. But there is also a way in which they have been formed into people who routinely have to fight, flee, and accommodate horror by the very environments that they are committed to transform. As explained above, these are not one-time actions or choices. Because threat exposure is a routine, daily occurrence in prison, these trauma responses start to become identities and roles, not simply choices. These are not the roles the chaplains want to inhabit, and they are not the only roles that the chaplains do inhabit. These same chaplains are advocates. They treat incarcerated people with dignity and respect. They create programming that is diverse, authentic, and freeing. They accompany people in places that often feel God-forsaken. They hold horror and holiness within themselves. Chaplains are being made sin *in the process of and for the sake of* inhabiting salvation.

Chaplains, like Jesus, are also being made sin-sick. The chaplains in this study described having nightmares, heart palpitations, headaches, and insomnia. They described going to therapists, getting EMDR, and experimenting with a wide range of body-based trauma treatments in attempts to cope with the stress of prisons. In the very first interview I did for this study, a chaplain described how her children tease her that she cannot sit with her back to a room when they go to a restaurant. My children do the same. They joke that I scan a room for threats, that I hear everything, that I'm always looking over my shoulder. "What are you looking for?" they ask laughing. Until I heard another chaplain describe the exact same responses, I had worried that my inability to turn off my hyper-attentive state after shift was a sign that I was not cut out for the job and that I was not able to properly manage the stress of the job. In the course of this study, I have learned that no one is able to manage the stress of the job. Hyper-arousal is the cost of working in prison.⁴⁹ It also makes one sick.⁵⁰

The physical state of hyper-arousal created by the constant assessment of potential threats is not the only way that prisons make people sick. Chaplains talked about the sheer exhaustion of being the only chaplain for over a thousand, sometimes multiple thousands, of incarcerated people. Some talked about commuting over an hour to get to their jobs, an issue that they share in common with officers and other prison staff. Some talked about sleeping at the prisons at which they worked—in empty cells and in Winnebago's in the prison parking lot—to work multiple shifts in a row before driving hours back to their homes.⁵¹ They talked about contracting Covid on the job when the disease would hit hundreds of people in the same prison at once. One man was asked to move out of his monastic community if he wanted to continue working at the prison during Covid because his level of disease exposure was deemed a threat to those with whom he lived. Another chaplain was asked by his partner to move out of his home for the same reason. When faced with a similar choice, another chaplain chose to leave his prison work instead of risking his family during the pandemic. Even before Covid, most of the chaplains in this study shared that they could not talk about what they saw at work with their families. This created an added layer of work-related stress, even after hours.

Exposure to sinful conditions creates sickness, but there is another level at which sin-sickness operates in the work of chaplaincy. Sometimes sin-sickness is not a result of simple exposure to traumatic conditions, but rather the direct result of offering pastoral care. The work of the chaplain sometimes means taking on the burdens of another person, including a portion of the impacts of those burdens. In these cases, receiving some of another person's stress is a direct result of coming alongside another person. Sin-sickness is a side-effect of following in Jesus' salvific footsteps. Chaplain Tyrone described this as the phenomenon of stress transference. He had just been telling me about staff and resident suicides, and I asked if he thought those suicides were related to the conditions that people were exposed to in prison.

---

⁴⁹Hicks, "Learning to watch out," 654–7.
⁵⁰Jason Denis Blunt, "Hyperarousal: The critical determinant of post-trauma sequelae," PhD diss., 2016; John Briere, Natacha Godbout, and Colin Dias, "Cumulative trauma, hyperarousal, and suicidality in the general population: A path analysis," *Journal of Trauma & Dissociation* 16, no. 2 (2015): 153–69; Pierre Fossion, Christophe Leys, Chantal Kempenaers, Stephanie Braun, Paul Verbanck, and Paul Linkowski. "Beware of multiple traumas in PTSD assessment: The role of reactivation mechanism in intrusive and hyper-arousal symptoms," *Aging & Mental Health* 19, no. 3 (2015): 258–63.
⁵¹Marc Mauer, "Thinking about prison and its impact in the twenty-first century," *Ohio State Journal of Criminal Law* 2 (2004): 607.

Chaplain Tyrone:

    I think, I think they are related.
    Yeah, I think, I think they're related because …

    When you, when you're

    dealing with …
    it's almost like there's a transference of pressure
    or stress.

    A person hears that his son has just got killed,
    And you, as a father, hear the story, and you begin to worry about,
    you worry about your child.
    Then you begin to kind of worry too much.

    Or sometimes it would be kind of in the sense of
    The demand that the prison asks of you and from you …

    whether it's the pressure of dealing with an inmate that may have had a personal situation take place …

    It may not actually be your fault,
    but then it kind of just transfers over to you.

    Or vice versa, where a staff person perhaps may be having a bad day because
    they're so stressed out from being either mandated to do things,
    or they're stressed out from feeling like they're being asked to do too much,
    to do so much with very little support.
    That has a tendency to kind of make you feel as if you're being under appreciated
    and have little value.

    So I just try to navigate the best way I can to try to find the best approach.
    What can I do to make the best of the situation without it negatively impacting me later on in my life? And I try to share that same information with others.
    Sometimes it works, and unfortunately, sometimes it doesn't.

    At the same time, I just try not to carry so much guilt if something doesn't work out the way that I anticipated it to work out.

Sarah Jobe:

Do you have any strategies to offload that guilt or to offload the stress of the job?

Chaplain Tyrone:

I would, I would be dishonest if I said that I had some good ones.

>   *(both laugh)*

Yeah ... I ...
work is ...
I am really stressed.

I think perhaps maybe the only thing that I find helpful is really just having someone to talk to about it. Having a candid conversation with someone that is free to just listen and not have any bias—like, just hear my story out. Just be able to kind of, just discuss it. I used to work out, but I don't have that aspect as often because with the zoom classes I don't work out as much as I would like to. But yeah, for now, I'm fine with just having the conversation.[52]

It's almost like there's a transference of pressure or stress. Chaplain Tyrone is not talking about transference in the technical sense, in which someone projects their feelings about one person or situation onto an entirely unrelated person or situation. What Chaplain Tyrone is describing might fall under the category of countertransference or projective identification. I would classify it as "somatic empathy."[53] No matter how one technically classifies the phenomenon, Chaplain Tyrone is naming the way that a caregiver can take on the emotions of the person before them as they use active listening skills like facial and postural mirroring, nonverbal affirmations, and naming what they hear to create a safe container for a person to process negative experiences. While there are ways to interrupt the process by which emotions bleed from care-receiver to care-giver, there is also data that suggests that this sharing of emotions is a part of what builds empathy.[54] The ability of the caregiver to take on some of the emotions of the care-receiver is one of the goods offered in a one-on-one therapeutic relationship, including chaplaincy relationships. Chaplain Tyrone offers to take on part of the burden of an incarcerated man's loss of his son. He offers

---

[52]Interview with the author on March 15, 2021.
[53]For a discussion of the distinctions in these dynamics, see Rothschild, *Help for the Helper*, 12–34.
[54]Rothschild, *Help for the Helper*, 35–94.

to take on part of the burden of an officer's job stress. In doing so, he both alleviates a portion of their suffering, and he takes that suffering on himself. He is made sin-sick—in that he takes on the stress and health impacts of the burdens of others—for the sake of the salvific work of drawing alongside others in their pain and relieving some of their burden.

Reasons to Worry: Taking up the Cross, Self-Care, and Jesus as Criminal

When Barth writes about Jesus being made sin, he acknowledges that there are reasons to want to resist the claim. This chapter has primarily operated at the level of description rather than prescription. I have been describing *what is* rather than saying what *should be*. Chaplains, like Jesus, are made sin and are made sin-sick in the course of salvific work. I hope I have stopped shy of saying that chaplains (or Jesus) *should be* made sin or *should be* made sin-sick when inhabiting salvation. Even so, the above description raises at least three concerns. One is theological, one pastoral, and one ethical. Namely:

1 Wasn't Jesus made sin specifically so that humans don't have to be?
2 Chaplains being made sin and made sick sounds like an embrace of martyrdom. What about self-care?
3 When Jesus was made sin, he was made an incarcerated person, not a chaplain. Does that distinction matter?

I turn now to address these important concerns.

Concerned Question 1: Isn't Jesus Made Sin so That Humans Don't Have To Be?

Being "made sin" is a unique phrase in the New Testament, and in 2 Cor. 5:21, it is specifically "he who knew not sin" who was "made sin for us." Perhaps being "made sin," is a role that is unique to Jesus. Perhaps humans just sin, plain and simple. Are humans really "made sin" in their following of Christ, or is being "made sin" one of the things from which humans are saved? In his last citation of 2 Cor. 5:21 internal to the Doctrine of Reconciliation, Barth asks what it means to hear, see, obey, and love the one who was "made sin" for us. He writes:

> To hear Him to-day is to hear the sigh of this One judged in our place. To see Him to-day is to see the One condemned, expelled and rejected in our place. To believe in Him is necessarily to realize that His place ought to have been ours. To love Him and to hope in Him is to be required,

in remembrance of what we deserved and as a sign of fellowship with Him, to take up and bear our much smaller crosses, and not to be able to escape this requirement.[55]

Barth is clear that in being "made sin," Jesus is giving us an example. We cannot escape the "requirement" to take up and bear "our much smaller crosses" in both remembrance of what Jesus did and in ongoing fellowship with him. Barth goes on to say that as shocking as it is to receive Jesus as the Prodigal Son, we also resist the idea of horror and holiness sitting fully together in one body because we do not want to admit that this is the truth about our own selves. Barth writes, "This is why we are shocked. We are not prepared quite so easily and self-evidently to be the lost son, nor to have to be converted ... both seem absurd, the one as a miracle we cannot really expect and the other as a demand we cannot really concede."[56] Barth says that Jesus made sin and humans made sin-sick *in the pursuit of salvation* is "alien" and "repugnant," something we would "like to change but ... cannot change."[57]

The chaplains in this study do not want to be made hard, avoidant, or allied with prisons in their pursuit of life in the face of death, but they have been made those things. Having been made those things, they will sometimes make choices to act sinfully, even if they would hope to make different or better choices. In their repeated exposure to threats against themselves and others, they have, at times, become people they do not want to be and acted in ways they regret. In this chapter, I have sought to contextualize the individual "sins" of chaplains within the wider context of the harms to which they are regularly exposed on the job and the ways that those harms will inevitably malform anyone exposed to them, i.e., systemic or social sin. This description might feel like letting chaplains "off the hook" for choices that are avoidant, unkind, irresponsible, or harsh. It is not. It is, rather, an attempt to place chaplains' responsibility for their individual actions within a wider framework of corporate responsibility for the existence of and conditions within prisons. Chaplains can make better and worse, more just and less just, daily choices in navigating the complexities of prisons, but until systemic change occurs, chaplains cannot avoid the overall dynamics described in this chapter. As chaplains draw near to incarcerated people and face down systems of confinement and control, they sin; they are made sin; and they are made sin-sick. Being made sin and being made sin-sick is the cost of inhabiting salvation.

When one is the active agent of harm, especially while acting inside of a sinful system that one is trying to resist and stand against, it can feel

---

[55]Barth, *CD* IV/3.1, 442.
[56]Ibid., 444.
[57]Ibid.

like losing oneself and losing one's identity. Chaplain Moses told me he finds himself wondering, "Am I going off the deep end?" This is where Barth thinks that Jesus has a special role in the economy of salvation. Barth acknowledges that when one experiences being made sin or being made sin-sick, there is a real risk to "losing oneself." This is why Jesus, in the fullness of his divinity, takes on the horror of being fully identified and impacted by the worst of humanity: one who cannot lose himself has gone ahead of us into the far country in order to lead us home. Barth writes, "What would be the value to us of His way into the far country if in the course of it He lost Himself?"[58] Jesus is not unique in drawing so near to people who are impacted by systems of confinement and control that he is made sick and made sin by those systems. That is the call of all who follow Christ. But Jesus is unique in that he cannot lose himself and does not sin in the process, so he can be a guide and a touchstone to all who are rendered unrecognizable to themselves by the very systems of sin they seek to transform. As chaplains are made sin and act sinfully in response, Jesus' witness stands as a chastisement, a corrective, and a beacon back to life-giving behaviors and identities.

Concerned Question 2: What about Self-care?

As I collected the stories for this study and continued to work as a chaplain during Covid, I started trying to bring to speech the levels of trauma, sickness, heightened confinement, and human rights abuses that I and others were experiencing each day under state and national Covid policies in prison. In sharing these stories with friends, students, and neighbors, I was describing our shared, social response to broken laws, what we call our criminal justice system. I was not describing times when the system accidentally went wrong; I was describing the system itself. My listeners were thus implicated in the stories I was sharing, but literally, without fail, the first or second question someone would ask after hearing the stories shared in this chapter was, "What are you doing to take care of yourself?" This question treats systemic sin and its sicknesses like something that can be healed and managed at the individual level, and it cannot. One cannot pray, exercise, or healthy eat one's way out of mass incarceration and its impacts on those who live and work in prison, just as Jesus cannot yoga his way out of imperial execution.

And yet, I fell into the same rhetorical trap in the interviews for this study. Because I was using a semi-structured interview protocol, I had flexibility about when I asked the question, "What are you doing to process or cope with the impacts of prison?" More often than not, I used that question as a response to someone naming overwhelming carceral horror. As I re-read myself asking what people were doing to cope with systemic horror, I sound

---

[58]Barth, *CD* IV/1, 185.

tone-deaf, and my interlocuters sound stunned. When I asked Chaplain Levine, "How did you sustain it?" the silence stretched between us. "Well, I'm not convinced I did," he finally said.[59] Chaplain Floating's response is similarly representative of the responses as a whole:

Sarah Jobe:

The things you're describing that you carried and held and witnessed are extremely heavy. What, what kind of kept you going? What sustained you in the work?

Chaplain Floating:

Honestly?

Sarah Jobe:

Please!

Chaplain Floating:

I don't know.

Sarah Jobe:

You don't know? *(both start laughing)*
(both grow quiet)

Chaplain Floating:

18 years of my life, and I don't know. But I did it. And I didn't turn out bitter.[60]

Chaplain Tyrone responded similarly in the conversation recounted in the last section. He said he would be lying if he claimed to have good strategies to cope with the stress of the prison environment, but then he went on to say that conversations with someone who does not judge him and physical exercise helps. Every chaplain in this study had a list of "self-care" practices that they engaged. Many named that those practices had to be engaged on a daily basis in order to be able to return to prison for a next shift. Many

---

[59]Interview with the author on April 23, 2021.
[60]Interview with the author on May 5, 2021.

described realizing in the first year on the job that they needed a veritable arsenal of self-care practices to be able to stay in this profession. And yet, as Chaplain Love explains, it is never enough.

Sarah Jobe:

What kind of, like what kind of mechanisms and tactics did you use to let go of the stress?

Chaplain Love:

You know, I did several things. One is that I had a long commute. It helped me to have some distance to drive, and to kind of think about the day and do some releasing before I got home.

And then, I have a wonderful spouse who, when I, you know, I was driving from an hour away, so he would have dinner on the table. And he was, and he was, he's always been a good listener about my day. And so I would say at least enough to be able to not burden him all the time, but, but to do a little bit of releasing of what I experienced.

And I did, I have good friends, really the best of friends, and sometimes I would need to call one up and just say, "Oh, what happened today was just horrendous," and be able to name, to name it.

I also love to take hikes. And I like to also sit outside. And I like to light candles on the inside, and you know, there were a lot of different things. And sometimes I would write down what had happened, in order to kind of get it from here inside *(points to her head and heart)* out there on a piece of paper. That helped.

But, but I can also say:

None of it was enough.

    (long pause)

And I think
that everybody who works
and shows up
and lives in the prison setting
you are
you're traumatized every day in one way or another.

And you can do all the good things like I am able. I am able to do a lot. And I have far more support systems than most human beings on the planet. And I know a lot about body care and spirit care and mind care and all those things that help.

But it wasn't enough.

And I didn't know how much it wasn't enough, until I left.

And I would say that I went through a couple of years of some of the characteristics of people that have PTSD.[61]

It wasn't enough. And I didn't know how much it wasn't enough until I left. Chaplain Love engages myriad daily practices of self-care. She has a robust support system. But like Barth says of Jesus, she is "not immune" to the consequences of being exposed to sin. Self-care is not a vaccine or a cure-all. If one is simply healing up enough to go back into a traumatic environment the next day, self-care can never fully heal those mental, physical, and spiritual wounds.

I am not saying one *should be* made sin in the pursuit of salvation. I am not saying that sin-sickness is a good. I am saying that if a person is serious about engaging systemic evil through the incarnational logic of drawing near to it, being made sin or being made sin-sick is unavoidable. Followers of Jesus are not promised freedom from the negative impacts of the systems they come up against. Christians are not promised freedom from sin-sickness. They are, as I will take up in Chapter 6, promised life after sinful systems kill them.

Concerned Question 3: When Jesus Is Made Sin, Isn't He Made into a Convicted Person Rather than a Chaplain to Convicted People?

Halfway through writing the Doctrine of Reconciliation in *Church Dogmatics*, Karl Barth starts visiting Strafanstalt Schällenmätteli, or Basel Prison, in Basel, Switzerland.[62] In 1954, Chaplain Martin Schwartz invited Barth to be his relief preacher there, and over the next nine years, Barth preached twenty-seven services at Basel Prison, eighteen of which fell on liturgical holidays.[63] Barth was not only a relief preacher at Basel Prison; he

---

[61]Interview with the author on March 12, 2021.
[62]Tietz, *Karl Barth: A Life in Conflict*, 344.
[63]Schwartz, "Karl Barth in der Strafanstalt," 210.

will ultimately come to refer to himself, somewhat jokingly, as the "Vicar of Spitalstrasse," the street on which the prison was located.[64] Chaplain Schwartz documents that Barth led discussion groups at the prison on weekday evenings, did visitation with long-time prisoners during vacation seasons, and ultimately offered one-on-one pastoral care. In many ways, Barth served as a volunteer prison chaplain. Schwartz documents that Barth would write up case notes concerning his conversations with incarcerated men and pass those on to Chaplain Schwartz as the supervising chaplain. Barth was an ordained Swiss Reformed pastor who began his career in parish ministry, but for the last fifteen years of his life, he exercised his ministerial vocation primarily inside the walls of Basel Prison.[65]

Barth's sermons to the men of Basel Prison were collected, preserved, and typeset by the men incarcerated there.[66] Because the sermons are chronologically preserved in two volumes, *Deliverance to the Captives* and *Call for God,* one can compare the theological development in the prison sermons to developments in the theology of *Church Dogmatics* IV/3. One of the most pronounced transitions in Barth's thought is how he comes to describe Jesus more and more as a "criminal" in the years from 1954–9, his first five years spending time in prison. This shift in language and imagery begins in his prison preaching and is subsequently reflected in *Church Dogmatics*. In his third sermon there, Barth preaches his way into the powerful truth that the incarcerated congregation shares an identity with Jesus that is at the heart of the Christian faith. Barth proclaims:

> I live. When spoken by Jesus this means: "I live my divine life for you … Without you, I do not care to be the Son of God or to enjoy my divine life … I live my divine life by taking your place, the place that is allotted to you. I become what you are (not just some of you, but all of you), a prisoner, a convict, sentenced to death."[67]

As Barth seeks to write this incarcerated congregation into the story of God, Barth realizes that an incarcerated person is at the heart of the story already. Jesus was "a prisoner, a convict, sentenced to death." Barth will return to this theme in many of his prison sermons as he simultaneously writes the second half of *Church Dogmatics* IV.

When *CD* IV/3.1 is published in 1959, the reader finds that the "Prodigal Son" or a "man put on trial" are no longer the primary descriptors for

---

[64]Ibid., 212.
[65]Schwartz, "Karl Barth in der Strafanstalt," 213. Barth's active ministry of preaching and visiting inside of prison last for ten years. In the last five years of his life, he was too ill to visit the prison. Chaplain Schwartz documents in the above-cited report that during those last years, incarcerated men would visit Barth on their home leave passes or after their release.
[66]Schwartz, "Karl Barth in der Strafanstalt," 210.
[67]Barth, *Deliverance to the Captives*, 30.

what it means for Jesus to have taken on the worst of the human condition. Barth's imagination for human horror has been expanded by his time in prison, and Barth now depicts Jesus as a prisoner condemned to death, not simply in the past but in the present. In trying to explain how the work of Christ is efficacious today, Barth writes that Jesus is "present here today among us in all our confusion, aberration and abandonment, before all our locked prison doors, at all our sick-beds and gravesides."[68] He writes, "In what may be called both in the narrower and broader sense the almshouses and prisons and hospitals and mental homes of our collective existence, the cemeteries of our more solid and more extravagant hopes," Jesus is present there as "the presence of the Crucified."[69]

It is important to note that in both Barth's prison sermons and *Church Dogmatics IV/3*, Jesus shows up in prisons *as a prisoner*. Barth does not have Jesus showing up in zones of social abandonment—in prison, at the sick bed—as some shiny savior (or chaplain). Barth has Jesus showing up in the world's hellholes looking just like everybody else in those hellholes. Barth writes, "(Jesus) is still the Friend of publicans and sinners whose very family think that He is mad, who is accused of blasphemy and sedition, who is reckoned with malefactors and crucified with them, who is forsaken by his disciples and our God."[70] As explained in Chapter 2, through Christ's presence in zones of social abandonment, the God of the universe enacts that there is no God-forsaken place and no God-forsaken person, but this truth is accomplished by Jesus coming to fully inhabit the *most impacted* subject positions in locations of God-forsakenness. Jesus is "made sin" throughout the *Church Dogmatics*, but after Barth witnesses the reality of life in prison, Barth clarifies that Jesus is made sin by being made a criminal.

Jesus' arrest and execution come to mark the primary descriptors that Barth uses for Jesus. *CD* IV/3.1 is the volume of *Church Dogmatics* in which Jesus is called the man of Gethsemane and Golgotha, the Victor of Gethsemane and Golgotha, and the Afflicted of Gethsemane and Golgotha. Gethsemane is the site of Jesus' arrest, and Golgotha is the site of his execution. The carceral has become embedded in Barth's primary descriptors of who Jesus is. As with his previous claim about Jesus being the Prodigal Son, Barth knows that the claim is offensive, and he leans into the offense. He writes:

> Jesus encounters us in this form or not at all. We must be ready to be told by him that we shall not find God where we think we should look for him, namely in the supposed height. It means that we must be ready to be told by Him that we shall find him precisely where we do not think we should look for him, namely in direct confrontation with and at the very heart of our own reality. The lonely man of Gethsemane and Golgotha,

---

[68]Barth, *CD* IV/3.1, 395.
[69]Ibid., 394–5.
[70]Ibid., 397.

the lonely God, then comes together with lonely man isolated in his deepest need. Each of us can then say that in this place, even though he is forsaken and alone, he is not forsaken and alone ... there among the smitten and abased, among those whom we would prefer not to reckon ourselves, God has raised His throne.[71]

As I said in Chapter 1, Jesus comes to set the captives free, but he is rendered captive in the process. The chaplains in this study seem to know this truth. As I have said already, they rarely compare themselves to Jesus, but they frequently name seeing Jesus in incarcerated people. Even as she described the toll that prison takes on her as a chaplain, Chaplain Moise noted that she, as a chaplain, is not bearing the worst of the sin and sickness doled out by the carceral system.

Chaplain Moise:

> So there was a time, two years in to the job, where I really wanted to leave. I really felt like it was taking a pretty big toll on me. I felt like I was noticing myself change, becoming a more jaded person. I recently took the Secondary Trauma Symptoms Scale, and ...
>
> It's bleak ... *(laughs)*
>
> It's looking abysmal. My secondary trauma symptoms are right there between high and severe. *(laughs again)*
>
> So it does take a toll, it takes a real toll. Working in prisons takes real toll. So I was starting to notice that my second year, feeling like maybe it wasn't worth it. I was also feeling just like, I don't know, a little torn about being a part of the system. And I was praying about leaving and just heard the Lord say very clearly:
>
> Who are you to leave? No one else in your congregation has the right to leave. That prison is taking a toll on every single person in your congregation in the same way it is taking a toll on you. It's taking more of a toll on them than it's taking on you. Who are you to leave?
>
> And ever since I heard that I just haven't left. I just don't feel released to leave. And every time I think about leaving whether it's because I feel like I've just witnessed something that is awful and I don't want to be complicit in it, or whether the toll is feeling steep in terms of my own

---

[71]Ibid., 416.

mental health and physical health ... I just still don't feel released to leave.[72]

That prison is taking a toll on every single person in your congregation in the same way it is taking a toll on you. It's taking more of a toll on them than it's taking on you. When chaplains risk death, risk being made sin, or risk being made sin-sick to embody the truth that there is no God-forsaken place, they are inhabiting Christ's salvation. They are making real God's reconciliation or atonement in the world today, and they are paying a similar price to the price that Jesus paid. But at the end of the day, most chaplains are not put to death by the state. They follow the full arc of the story into the witness of carceral death, but they do not inhabit Christ for the full arc of the story. In the story of salvation, Jesus is made a condemned man. He looks more like an incarcerated person than a prison chaplain. His prophetic life work and his full presence with humanity at its worst lead him to execution. Incarcerated people, not prison chaplains, are those who most fully inhabit Christ. This is one of the mysteries entombed in carceral death to which we now turn.

---

[72]Interview with the author on January 1, 2021.

Interlude

The Crucifixion and 58 Other Carceral Deaths

(long pause)
—CHAPLAIN KING, INTERVIEW ON JANUARY 15, 2021

The following are seven stories of carceral death. In these seven stories, fifty-nine people die. I had thought that in the pages of this book I would recount every death that was told to me in this study. In *Trauma and Recovery,* Judith Herman begins with the dictum that "remembering and telling the truth about terrible events are the prerequisite both for healing the social order and for the healing of individual victims."[1] It seemed important to honor the loss of each life that the chaplains remembered and named. However, I sat down to sort through the deaths that were recollected, and I could not write them all. The data overwhelmed. I started sorting the stories into piles according to the type of death. Six types of carceral death emerged: the suicides of prison staff, the suicides of incarcerated people, murders that occurred in prison, the deaths of incarcerated people's loved ones, executions, and mass deaths from Covid. In the pages that follow, I have shared one story from each category. I have shared only one story from any given chaplain, though many chaplains told multiple death stories from multiple categories. These arbitrary boundaries have contained the horror to a level that I can hold. I hope these limits also mean that you, as reader, can bear witness to each of the lives and deaths recollected here before moving on to the chapter that follows. It took me three days just to edit the punctuation marks in these seven stories. Perhaps it will take you less time to read them, perhaps more.

The chapter after this interlude is not an attempt to make sense of these deaths. The losses described here do not make sense. They resist legibility. The chapter that follows simply places these fifty-nine carceral lives and

---

[1] Herman, *Trauma and Recovery,* 186.

deaths in near proximity to the life and death of Jesus Christ. Jesus' carceral death has always been flanked by two other executions and the suicide of a person who felt complicit in his execution. By one account, the chapter simply attempts to re-member Jesus' death in its original context of wider carceral deaths. But it might also be the case that Barth and I are gesturing toward something more significant: the intuition that re-placing Jesus' death alongside other carceral deaths is indeed where one finds anything at all salvific in how prisons kill. By that account, setting these carceral deaths alongside the carceral death of Jesus becomes a sort of "dying alongside" that Barth calls the first Christian community.[2]

---

[2] Barth, *Deliverance to the Captives*, 77–8.

Death by Covid: Thirty Incarcerated People and One Officer
Recollected by Father Michael on April 16, 2021

They introduced a bunch of prisoners from another institution who were all infected with Covid into our prison. For three months, we were doing really great. There weren't any cases, and all of a sudden, we had all these cases. It just, it was like a fire. It spread to the whole institution. There are 4,000 people in the prison—prisoners—and 3,000 of them got Covid.

Hundreds of staff people ... I got it eventually. I wasn't terribly sick, but ...

But we lost thirty prisoners, and one of the CO's died.
So it was traumatic.

And, and plus the fear, you know?

I was there for the first month or two months before Covid hit there, and these guys are stuck in these cells. They are like sitting ducks, just waiting for this to come to them.

And it was almost terror.

So ....there was a lot of stress there, and so, then leaving under the circumstances of getting Covid myself and not being able to really terminate well. A lot of the guys died who I knew. And I didn't get to say ... you know ... especially the ones on Death Row, who are older ...

So there was grief, and there was loss. The guard who died, I liked him. We got along really well. He was one of the good ones. So there was grief and loss. And then I came into a parish where things were kind of shut down with Covid and all the adjustments that come with entering a new ministry.

And so ...

it's ...

it's been a rough, rough year. And I guess I realized when I went back there at Easter how much I missed the place.

Death by Assault: One Incarcerated Person
Recollected by Chap Lin on January 6, 2021

I can remember early on we had a prisoner who was stomped to death. Sarah, I'm sorry. That's so graphic.

They only let like one or two people together in a rec cage, and these two people had a history of doing fine together. One was younger. One was older. But the younger one really felt like the older one owed him some cigarettes, and when the man said, "I'm not going to give you any cigarettes," he stomped him to death. And the officers there could not respond.

There's always two people there, but one had stepped out. I mean by policy, everything was done by the book. To do something, he has to wait for three people, and he could just yell at the guy, and not unlock the door until they got these other two.

And so I went by to check on him about a week later. And said just, you know, "I know you had a rough time … what's going on? You know, how you doing?"

"Oh, I'm fine. It's just another day," he says.

And I did something that I didn't realize at the time was important. I sat down. I didn't leave. I just sat down and said, "You got any coffee around here?"

And then after just sort of sitting there, it came out.

So there was some stress relief that could happen … but it was an accident. *(laughs)*

You know, I didn't know …

Just …

I think it's just …

    (crying)

The hardest thing is all the pain.

I said to a colleague one time, you know, it feels like mopping the floor with a Q-tip here. And he corrected me, and he said, "No, no, no, no, Chaplain. It doesn't feel that way. That's exactly what we are doing. We *are* mopping the floor with a Q tip."

Death by Suicide: One Incarcerated Person Recollected by Chaplain Dismas on July 1, 2021

There was a guy once, he was struggling with the fact that the mother of his child was out on the street. And she and the child were living in her car, and she was hooked on heroin. And so the two year old daughter, or three year old daughter, was basically in the backseat, and she was shooting up in the front seat of the car. They're living in the car.

And he's just beside himself as to what to do because he has no control, because they're not married and there's no proof. They hadn't done the DNA testing or something. There's teams that actually come and do that, you know, for child support and that type of stuff. None of that had happened, but it was his child; and we all knew that.

He, he became so distraught that he went back to the cell house, and this particular cell house has got five tiers, so it's a five-story cell. And the officer that was escorting him turns to talk to another officer. And this inmate ran all the way up the stairs to the top level and dove headfirst onto the concrete floor below him and splattered and died there.

And there was a giant pool of blood. There was brain matter that had splattered into the cells of the guys that were right there.

There was another inmate, who was a cell house worker that he splattered … it just happened …
like, he was within three feet of this guy diving right in front of him.

The officer was beyond distraught.

So I got the call from the lieutenant, you know, "All this just took place. I need you over here."

So, so I go over there.

And I literally was there, probably four hours.

And this was near the end of my, of my shift, but it didn't matter, it was so … traumatic that you just had to …

you just had to go through the situation.
That's all.
You know time, the timecard wasn't, wasn't a piece at that point.

So.

I've got inmates in the cells down below that can't take the brain matter off of themselves and off of the cells, because it's a crime scene.

um ...

So now I've got security, and they're coming down.
And they've got it,
you know, they've got the crime scene roped off.

And I'm trying to explain to them, "Look, you need to hurry up with this, because you got, you got guys that are so traumatized. They've got brain matter on them that they can't take off. I mean, how do we, what are you gonna do with this?"

You know ...

And they were just kind of terse about it, you know.
Which, these things take time.
You just have to,
you know,
write it out.

I said,

"I've been here for hours.
I've been here for hours and that pool of blood is still there.
He's laying there in that pool of blood, dead.
How much time do you need?"

So it was about another hour,
and then they finally came and took the body out,

and

they took all their pictures
got all your information,
and then they finally,
you know,
came and had an inmate mop up the blood,
the cell house worker,
that he,
that he splattered in front of.

Death by Suicide: A Prison Staff Person Every Other Year for Ten Years
Recollected by Chaplain King on January 15, 2021

Chaplain King:

Unfortunately, Sarah, we've had several, several, too many staff suicides. And that's when everything just shuts down. Now we've had, we have inmate suicides, too. And that's horrific as well. And we have memorial services for the prisoners who die. Of course, you know, their body isn't present, but the prisoners can come to the chapel.

I mean …

It's a different kind of memorial service because this person took their life … and all that they had going for them … it just leaves so many unanswered questions. So chaplains participate in those. Like I said, I normally pray. I did have to preach one. This was 2018, this particular guy committed suicide. It was so hard. I mean, he had been there for almost 20 years. Their families attend the service, and that, that was, that was the most difficult one. But ever since I started, there's been a staff suicide maybe every other year.

And so that's when the chaplains really are, quote unquote "at their finest" because we're there for the staff. We're there for the staff member's family just trying to help them to walk through this valley of the shadow of death as best as we can.

Sarah Jobe:

I'm wondering about, you know, the data does bear out that those of us who work in corrections have higher suicide rates than the general population.

Chaplain King:

That is true.

Sarah Jobe:

When staff commit suicide, does it feel like it is connected or does it raise that possibility in the mind of other staff? Do y'all talk about it openly or …

Chaplain King:

Normally I get, after a staff suicide, maybe after a memorial service, you know, I get the same theological and biblical questions. Is this person going to heaven? Are they going to hell? You know, I try not to engage in those kind of questions, but that …

But yes, you,
you,
you do see an increase,
and people just wondering, "How could this happen?"

Like I said, people, staff members, who've died from suicide …
from the outside, Sarah, it looked as if they had everything going well for them.
And so it shook everybody.

It, you know,
there are two men in particular who died …

His, his …
his memorial service was so well attended that they had the video conference from the prison to Washington, DC. That's how many people he had affected over the years …
and so that …
it just raised so many questions.

And I remember when,
when that person committed suicide,
we went around, the chaplains along with the crisis support team,
we hosted at each institution these small grieving sessions where we allowed the staff to just grieve. I mean that went on for weeks. I think that was very helpful because like I said, no one could understand.

Why would this guy take his life?

I mean, he was a
He was,

He was a model employee!
He was.
It still baffles me.

But, but yeah, you're right there. The data does show that there is a connection between working in that environment and suicide.

(long pause)

Sarah Jobe:

It's a weighty thing to hold.

Chaplain King:

Yeah.

(sighs)

The people who look the strongest sometimes,
you know, they are carrying so much.

And we always try to let the staff members know, "Hey look, we're here for you," because some staff don't feel comfortable going to the psychologist.

(sighs again)

But it does weigh on you
like, man I ...

Could I have done more?
Could I have said something?

You know ...

Am I accessible?
Do people think that they can reach out to me?

You know..

I can't hold ...
I can't carry that.

Because …

I can't.

You know that's not good for me …

But …

Death by Shooting: One Child of an Incarcerated Father
Recollected by Chaplain Camillus on September 22, 2021

One of my very first weeks there,
you know, eleven years ago,
there was the man who
the night before, you know
we're doing a service in the morning,
on Sunday.

The night before it,
his six-year-old child
has been murdered
through gang violence.

And you know the system …
there was,
there's no compassionate release.
So there's,
no one was going to let this man out
to go to his child's funeral.

And so that, you know …

Chaplains have been called to come and give him the news of his son's death, but also, you know to sit and hear what it felt like to be a father, you know.

Because he was in prison, he hadn't protected his son.
Because he was in prison, he couldn't even attend his son's funeral.

You know that's …

I think that is, to me, you know,
the important part of the work of chaplaincy
is to witness the suffering,
to just, you know, hear the pain,
to try to share
you know, a message of compassion
amidst what is, you know,
a very unreal world of prisons.

Death by Execution: Nineteen Incarcerated Men
Recollected by Chaplain Harald on May 6, 2021

Chaplain Harald:

Thank the Lord, I never had to witness an electrocution.

But at this point I've been on death watch 42 times.

I've witnessed 19 executions.

Including a botched lethal injection.

And I found out, a botched lethal injection …

is also really horrible.

And I've had to deal with that, and fortunately I've had really good advice and an excellent trauma therapist who helps me with my tune ups. Because when you … I used to describe AIDS ministry as walking into a room to meet a stranger who you're there to fall in love with so you can go through their death with them.

This is same thing, except there's a darkness to it that's even worse.

I'm there to meet a stranger, to fall in love with them, and then go through them being killed by other people, while I watch.

It's a very dark undertaking, what we do in those execution chambers.

I ended up … I couldn't do it … *(tears up)*

by myself.

It was, it was too much ….

The whole thing was just otherworldly.

My wife is my partner in ministry, and during the executions, she takes care of the family and loved ones of the condemned because they're not allowed to be present.

Sarah Jobe:

No family at all? In your state, no family is allowed at all?

Chaplain Harald:

In the morning, but six hours before the scheduled execution you have to get off the prison property. The state's greatest fear on that day is that the family of the condemned and the family of the victim will end up in the same space. And you could have another homicide. I mean the emotions are so high.

The tension is so high.

The last thing anybody wants is for these two families to cross each other's path. And so my wife would make sure they all left by 12 noon. She would make sure they got to their cars. She would meet them wherever they wanted to meet, and she would accompany the family off site. And I would be there for the family goodbyes in the morning. But then the rest of the day I would be down in the death house with the person who was going to be executed that night until it was time to go to the witness room and be there for them visually. Of course, now the US Supreme Court held they have to let the spiritual advisor in the execution chamber.

Sarah Jobe:

Mmm … not just in the viewing room?

Chaplain Harald:

Have to be in the execution chamber.

Sarah Jobe:

Wow …

Chaplain Harald:

God will give me what we need to deal with that when I get scheduled for that. I'm not going there yet.

But I knew I couldn't make the drive back to the prison for this deathwatch appointment by myself, it just … it was a bridge too far.

And so my wife went with me. And we drove together and then she stayed in the Chapel.

Well, I had my first deathwatch appointment with this man since my Chaplain in Training died, and then they proceeded toward execution. He got executed in February of that year.

Death by Execution: One Incarcerated Man
Recollected by Mark; Remembered on December 14, 2022

The room they do it in …
they call it, "The Skull."

He was offered something to dull the pain,
but he didn't take it.

        (long pause)

And they executed him.

Divided up his clothes after …
drew straws for who would get them …

It was 9am on Friday morning when they executed him.
The official charge was treason.

They executed him with two people charged with felony larceny …
all at once.

And everyone was making fun of him.
Insulting him.
Acting like if he could do such great things,
he should have saved himself from execution.
Even the chaplains and lawyers joined in.
I remember they said,
"He saved others, but he can't save himself."

Even the other people being executed with him said those things.

It was noon,
when the sky just got dark.
For three hours …
it was dark until 3pm.

And at 3pm, he cried out,
so loud,
in our native language,

"My God, my God, why have you forsaken me?"

Most of the people there didn't know what he said.
They just kept watching ...

waiting.

Someone tried to give him something to drink,
but that guy was told to step back,
told not to interfere.

Jesus screamed out his last breath.

—a paraphrase of Mark 15:22-37

5

Recollecting Death:

Dying with Jesus in Prison

The will of God was done as the will of Satan was done.
The action of God was identical with the action of Satan.
That was the frightful thing.
—KARL BARTH, CHURCH DOGMATICS IV/I, 268

There is no godforsaken place. There is always a
representative of the Holy,
even in the midst of unholy things.
—CHAP LIN, INTERVIEW ON JANUARY 6, 2021

The salvation of the cosmos happens inside of a set of carceral deaths. Jesus is executed. Jesus has allegedly claimed Jewish kingship, and the charge displayed at his execution translates to something like treason or sedition (Mt. 27:37). Two men are executed with him who have been found guilty of either robbery or rebellion. They are identified as λῃσταὶ, which can be translated "thieves" but also indicates "rebels" when used of both Jesus and Barabbas at other places in the Gospel texts (Mt. 26:55, Lk. 22:52, Jn 18:40). Judas dies by suicide. Matthew's Gospel reports that "when Judas, who had him arrested, saw that he was condemned, he was filled with regret."[1] Judas attempts to return the money he received for giving up Jesus' location. He regrets his paid participation in the arrest and execution of Jesus, and Judas hangs himself (Mt. 27:3-5).

---

[1] My translation of Mt. 27:3a, "τότε ἰδὼν Ἰούδας ὁ παραδιδοὺς αὐτὸν ὅτι κατεκρίθη μεταμεληθεὶς."

When trying to write about how the execution of Jesus might contain the "goodwill of God," Barth notes "that many have suffered grievously, most grievously, in the course of world history. It might even be suggested that many have perhaps suffered more grievously and longer and more bitterly than did this man in the limited events of a single day."[2] One might assert that some of the people in the death stories recollected above have suffered more than Jesus did. Barth notices that human death can be "deserved or undeserved, voluntary or involuntary, heroic or not heroic, important for others or not important for others."[3] Barth says that all suffering, Jesus' included, can be "shattering."[4] So why do Christians profess this one carceral death to be salvific? How does the salvation of the world happen inside of a story of three executions and a suicide born of carceral complicity? Barth gives one answer in his Doctrine of Reconciliation in *Church Dogmatics*, published in 1956.[5] He gives a slightly different answer when he preaches the death of Christ on Good Friday in 1957 inside Basel Prison.

Finding Salvation in the Execution of Jesus, Attempt I

As was explored in the previous chapter, Jesus takes up the worst of the human condition and brings the fullness of his holiness into the fullness of creaturely horror, thereby hallowing the horrific. Barth understands Jesus' death by execution to be the ultimate instantiation of Jesus' willing participation in human horror. Jesus goes all the way down with humans to the point of death. Jesus takes up the very places and experiences that separate humans from God and inhabits those *as God*. On the cross, Jesus takes up separation from God itself—what Barth calls "eternal death"—and inhabits that separation *as God*, thereby vacating even death as a site of separation from the divine.[6] Barth writes, "Here in the passion in which as Judge He lets Himself be judged, God has fulfilled this responsibility. In the place of all men, He has Himself wrestled with that which separates them from Him. He has Himself borne the consequences of that separation to bear it away."[7]

Barth takes seriously that when Jesus cries out on the cross, "My God, my God, why have you forsaken me?" that Jesus is indeed entering into a

---

[2]Barth, CD IV/1, 245.
[3]Ibid., 246.
[4]Ibid.
[5]In what follows, I will treat primarily the section on the cross that occurs in the end of the "Judged Judge" §59.2 in CD IV/1, 241–83, and the section on Christians taking up the cross in "The Christian in Affliction" in CD IV/3.2, 614–46.
[6]Barth, CD IV/1, 247.
[7]Ibid., 247.

site of God-forsakenness.[8] But having entered a site and experience of God-forsakenness with the fullness of his divinity, that site and experience will never be God-forsaken for anyone else again.[9] Jesus goes all the way down into the worst of the human condition with us—vacating death as a site of separation from God. In the words of Chap Lin, because of Jesus' presence in death, "There is no God-forsaken place, no God-forsaken person."[10] Even death is no longer God-forsaken because God has been in it. I want to highlight two points about this formulation.

First, in the economy of salvation as described in the Scriptures and amplified by Barth, state-sponsored execution is the ultimate instantiation of God-forsakenness. When God wants to be with humans in the depths of their horror and vacate that horror with God's holiness, God does that by entering into a court system that calls punishment an act of justice and killing people-found-guilty justifiable. Barth does not simply name execution as God-forsaken; he names arrest as the work of Satan, too.[11] Talking about Jesus' arrest at Gethsemane, Barth names that the frightful thing about this story is that "the will of God was done as the will of Satan was done. The action of God was identical with the action of Satan. That was the frightful thing. The coincidence of the divine and the satanic will and work and word was the problem of this hour, the darkness in which Jesus addressed God in Gethsemane."[12] According to Barth, Gethsemane is satanic, and Golgotha is God-forsaken. As I have said before, Gethsemane and Golgotha are the sites of Jesus' arrest and execution. Throughout these sections of *Church Dogmatics*, Barth calls Jesus the "Victor of Gethsemane and Golgotha" and the "Afflicted of Gethsemane and Golgotha." These bookend sites come to serve as shorthand for the whole of Jesus' criminal justice experience, often called his "passion." There is an inherent critique here of a criminal justice system that begins with arrest and receives carceral death as an acceptable end when it is pinpointed as the worst of the human condition into which God enters. God willingly becomes a victim of that system in order to "release man from a legal relationship fatal to him, from an intolerable commitment which he has accepted, from an imprisonment in which he finds himself."[13] Salvation happens internal to a set of carceral deaths

---

[8] Barth, *CD* IV/3.2, 637.
[9] Barth does not take up the issue of time here—i.e., whether Jesus vacating death as a site of God-forsakenness is efficacious both forwards and backwards in time. I will take up Barth's movement toward *apokatastasis*, the redemption of all things, in the Postlude. While there is not space to take up this question fully, I would argue on the basis of his movement toward *apokatastasis* that it is a faithful reading of Barth to understand Jesus' action here to stretch both forward and backward in a full redemption of God-forsakenness not simply to all places but to all times.
[10] Interview with the author on January 6, 2021.
[11] Barth, *CD* IV/1, 268–70.
[12] Ibid., 268.
[13] Barth, *CD* IV/1, 256.

because carceral death either is, or is at least representative of, the ultimate horror from which humans need saving. When Jesus enters carceral death, he does not condone it; he suffers the worst of it, and by his divine presence as an executed person, he both unmasks and vacates execution as a site of God-forsakenness.[14]

Second, while Jesus takes away the power of death as a site of separation from God, he does not abolish death; indeed, Christians have an inescapable mandate to "take up the cross" and follow Jesus "both into prison and to death."[15] The call to follow Jesus does not stop at the foot of the cross, but the Christian must inhabit an "unavoidable fellowship with the Crucified."[16] Barth is clear that when Christians take up the cross, it is not to make the cross efficacious, but rather to re-present what Jesus has already accomplished. He says things like "Christians suffer something corresponding in their little passions, as a reflection and likeness of His great passion."[17] They "bear the stamp of the Crucified" as an "analogy" and "reflection."[18] He sometimes even calls the Christian passions not "taking up the cross" but rather taking up "the shadow of the cross."[19] In calling the Christian inhabitation of the cross a reflection and an analogy, Barth is saying that *humans are both like Jesus and unlike Jesus* when they inhabit the part of salvation in which God dies.

Humans are like Jesus when they inhabit the cross in that they, like Jesus, cannot presume to be saved from death. Salvation from death is not promised.[20] Barth acknowledges that solidarity with other people to the point of death has some serious risks and temptations, both for Jesus and for those who would follow him. One of those temptations is to risk death with a sure knowledge that one will be saved from it. Barth sees this enacted in the final temptation of Christ in the wilderness when Satan suggests that Jesus take a headlong plunge into death to prove that God and God's angels will save him.[21] This would not be a Godly death because it presumes salvation, and Jesus refuses that death. Barth is also clear that Jesus and Christians do not *choose* death. They do not choose it with despair, nor with the sure knowledge of salvation, nor for their own religious self-glorification.[22] They do not choose it at all. Rather Christians, like Jesus, *risk* death for the sake of community with those who are most impacted by the systems of death

---

[14] For a book-length treatment of this sentence see Taylor, *The Executed God*.
[15] Barth, *CD* IV/3.2, 639.
[16] Ibid., 643.
[17] Ibid., 642.
[18] Ibid., 641.
[19] Ibid., 636–7.
[20] Barth is even explicit that we must resist the temptation to look toward the resurrection for an answer about how God's work is accomplished in execution. He writes, "the event of His resurrection lies beyond the answer" (*CD* IV/1, 268).
[21] Barth, *CD* IV/1, 262–3.
[22] Ibid., 263–4.

in this world. When they do this, salvation from death is not promised, but salvation from God-forsakenness has already been accomplished and is guaranteed.

Which brings one to how humans are *not* like Jesus in their "little passions." Humans are not like Jesus in that they are promised that even in carceral death, they will never be separated from God. Even in risking death for the sake of following Christ, the Christian must realize that after Jesus has inhabited death, no one will ever experience death as Jesus experienced it, as forsaken. After Jesus brought his Divine Life into Death, death can never be a site of separation from God again. Christians must acknowledge this difference in the description of their own passions in order to "avoid wild exaggeration" about the extent to which they can image Jesus in death.[23] The mystery of how salvation occurs in death is bound up with the fact that Jesus is both God and human being. Jesus, as both divine and human, vacates death as a site of separation from God by placing his divine life into it. Any given human cannot represent both sides of this human-and-divine, life-in-death truth simultaneously. But perhaps, though Barth does not say it, we can represent the fullness of this salvific, life-in-death, Divine-in-Godforsaken story when we enact it together in community.

I see the stories of carceral death in the interlude inhabiting salvation in this corporate way. The deaths are not salvific. They are a needless, horrific, insupportable destruction of life. But when the chaplains in this study take those carceral deaths up, when they stand in and with them, when we recollect them alongside the carceral death of Jesus Christ, perhaps we are inhabiting the arc of salvation together. The nineteen men who are executed stand as an icon to the executed Christ. Chaplain Harald stands at their executions as an embodiment of the truth that executions are not God-forsaken. The little boy who was shot is, in a very straightforward way, the Son who was killed. The Father and Chaplain grieve the loss together and re-member Him after His death. The incarcerated man who dives over the railing of the five-story cell block inhabits the full horror of human desperation. The incarcerated man who bears his splattered remains and cleans him up off the floor after death bears witness to the God who keeps living in the face of horror.

Chaplains are not always representing the divine, and incarcerated people are not always representing the human in this corporate inhabitation of salvation. As with Deacon Joe in Chapter 1, sometimes it is the chaplain's life that ends, and the condemned person's life that keeps going and bears witness to the loss of the chaplain. Even then, the roles are not cemented in place. In that story, the condemned life was ultimately executed, and Chaplain Harald, taking up the other half of the divine-human witness, stood with him as he was killed. By this reading, we can only ever represent

---

[23]Barth, *CD* IV/3.2, 637.

the divine and human Jesus at the moment of his carceral death—i.e., inhabit salvation—together, as a community. Carceral death is, at every level, more than any human body can hold alone. Some, still living, stand as witness to a God whose life draws into death and stays alive in the face of it. Some, dying in prison, stand as an embodied witness to the depths of human horror and the truth that sinful systems are always barreling toward death. No one human being can live and die simultaneously, as Jesus does when the fulness of his divinity descends to hell.

This is Barth's answer to how carceral death is salvific when he is speaking to a predominantly free audience. But when he preaches Jesus' death inside of prison, the dynamics of salvation change in a few important ways. In the last chapter, I argued that Barth's theology changes over time as he comes to understand and be changed by the realities of prison. Here, we see something a little different. The two passages that I have been exploring from *Church Dogmatics* IV/1 and IV/3.2 were written on either side of the sermon I will describe below. By the time Barth writes IV/3.2, he has been visiting and preaching in prison for multiple years. He has preached this specific sermon in prison already. The theologies are not incompatible, but they are different. I think we see here not change over time, but rather, the way that theology is shaped by its immediate context. Barth says something slightly different about the carceral death of Christ to incarcerated people than he does to non-incarcerated people.

Finding Salvation in the Execution of Jesus, Attempt II

In 1957, Barth preaches the Good Friday Service at Basel Prison.[24] At this point, he has been preaching and visiting in prison for three years. He takes as his text the passion narrative from Luke, and he titles his sermon, "*Die Übeltäter mit ihm,*" which is a direct citation of Lk. 23:33. The published English translation titles the sermon, "The Criminals With Him."[25] Barth's words serve as the precursor to a celebration of The Lord's Supper. As he introduces the text, Barth says that the story of "the suffering and death of

---

[24]Barth, "The Criminals with Him," in *Deliverance to the Captives*, 75–84.
[25]It is worth noting here that "criminals" is, perhaps, not the best translation of Übeltäter, "wrong-doers or malefactors." Part of why it is worth noting is because Barth seems to avoid using language of "criminal, offender, and inmate." Barth does not use the word *Kriminell* here, or by my accounting, ever in *Church Dogmatics* or in his sermons to the men at Basel Prison. Similarly, he rarely uses the terms *Straftäter,* "offender" or *Rechtsbrecher,* "law breaker." He uses the term *Insassen,* "inmates," twice in his sermons to men at Basel Prison. Both times he is listing positions in prisons, and "inmates" are listed with warden, officers, etc. See Karl Barth, *Predigten 1954–1967, Gesamtausg*abe (Zurich, Zurich Canton: Theologischer Verlag, 1979), 77, 282.

Jesus Christ ... contains the whole history of the world," and thus cannot be given due diligence in one sermon. In light of this, he chooses to focus on a single verse, Lk. 23:33, which reads, "They crucified him with the criminals, one on either side of him." His opening words prefigure many of the major moves of the sermon.

Chaplain Barth:

> "They crucified him *with the criminals.*" Which is more amazing, to find Jesus in such bad company, or to find the criminals in such good company? As a matter of fact, both are true! One thing is certain: here they hang all three, Jesus and the criminals, one at the right and one at the left, all three exposed to the same public abuse, to the same interminable pain, to the same slow and irrevocable death throes. Like Jesus, these two criminals had been arrested somewhere, locked up and sentenced by some judge in the course of the previous few days. And now they hang on their crosses with him and find themselves in solidarity and fellowship with him. They are linked in a common bondage never again to be broken, just as the nails that fasten them to the piece of wood would never break. It was as inescapable for them as it was for him. It was a point of no return for them as it was for him. There remained only the shameful, pain-stricken present and future of their approaching death. (Strangely enough, there are many paintings of Jesus' crucifixion where the two criminals are lost to sight. It would perhaps be more appropriate not to represent Jesus' death at all. But if it is done, then the two thieves on the right and left must not be left out. In any painting or representation where they are absent, an important, even an essential, element is missing.)
>
> *They crucified him with the criminals.* Do you know what this implies? Don't be too surprised if I tell you that this was the first Christian fellowship, the first certain, indissoluble, and indestructible Christian community.[26]

The two people executed with Jesus are *important ... even essential. They are the first certain, indissoluble, and indestructible Christian community.* Their suffering with Jesus is an indispensable part of the story of Jesus' suffering, such that Jesus' death should not be represented without their dying alongside his.

As Barth opens his sermon, he stresses that Jesus is the same as the men executed with him. He has been through the same events. He has been criminalized in the same way. His suffering is the same. Barth will take an

---

[26]Ibid., 76–7.

interlude in the center of the sermon to explain the way that Jesus' divinity made his death efficacious for others (i.e., how Jesus is different), and when he does that, he rehearses much of the same theology described above from *Church Dogmatics*. He will say at the end of that section, "He the living One took the place of us the dying ... This is reconciliation."[27] But then Barth will turn his attention back to the three men executed together for the remainder of the sermon. He will explain that in dying alongside Jesus, "No one before and no one after has witnessed so directly and so closely God's act of reconciliation, God's glory and the redemption of the world, as these two thieves."[28] As they become the first and most intimate witnesses to Jesus' work of reconciliation, these two men come to occupy a prioritized place in the kingdom of God. They outrank the disciples. If anyone wants to draw near to Jesus, they must "get in line behind" these two executed men.[29]

There are two important shifts happening here in Barth's theology: one that he names aloud and one that he does not. The first shift is that salvation is no longer about belief but about suffering alongside Jesus. Basing his claim on Rom. 6:8, Barth proclaims, "But if we have died with Christ, we believe that we shall also live with him."[30] Because both of these men died with Christ, both will ascend to heaven with him. They become the first Christian community, not through belief, but through carceral death. Barth says, "Now these two thieves have literally died with Christ, and theirs was the assurance that they would also literally live with him."[31] Barth acknowledges that only one of the men is said to have confessed the truth about Jesus. The other died alongside Jesus but remained resistant to the truth of who Jesus was.[32] Barth acknowledges this difference and insists that the promise of life extends to both executed men. Barth asks:

> Did they accept this miracle, understand it, believe it? Let us leave this question open. This much is certain, that the promise was meant for them, that they were covered by this promise, that they received and possessed it, that they were allowed to suffer and die with him. This promise is given and is valid wherever men may suffer and die as criminals with Jesus. This promise and nothing else constitutes the Christian community and makes man a Christian. These criminals were the first two who, suffering and dying with Jesus, were gathered by this promise into the Christian fold.[33]

---

[27] Barth, *Deliverance*, 80.
[28] Ibid., 81.
[29] Ibid., 78, 82, 83.
[30] Ibid., 82.
[31] Ibid.
[32] Barth is preaching the Lucan account where one of the men being executed is reported to confess belief. In Matthew and Mark, both of the men with whom Jesus is executed join the crowd, chief priests, and teachers of the law in mocking Jesus (Matt. 27:44, Mark 15:32). In those two accounts, neither is reported to confess belief.
[33] Ibid., 82.

The Christian community is constituted *only* by the fact that if one dies with Christ, one will live with him. Barth says the promise is "given and valid" at every carceral death.³⁴

While extending salvation to all who die a criminalized death is startling, perhaps more startling is the sense in the sermon that Jesus does not die alone. In the passages above from *Church Dogmatics,* the difference between Jesus and all other deaths is that Jesus enters death as a God-forsaken space and by his very presence there, renders it a place in which one is attended, through horror, by God. No one else can ever die a death like Jesus because God is now in death. But if the Jesus in this sermon is still God-forsaken in his death (and it is not clear that he is), he is not alone. Jesus is not forsaken by other executed people. Barth makes much of the fact in both *Church Dogmatics* and this sermon that Jesus' disciples did not stay with him at either Gethsemane or Golgotha. But here, Barth says that the two men executed with Jesus kept vigil with him in a way his disciples could not. Barth proclaims:

> But in this hour they could not abandon him, they could not sleep. Willingly or not, they were forced to watch with him many long hours on the cross. Nor could they escape his dangerous company. They could not very well deny him, being publicly exposed as his companions. This is how they were in fact the first certain Christian community! He and they, they and he, were bound together, were not and are not to be separated in all eternity.³⁵

He and they, they and he, were bound together, were not and are not to be separated in all eternity. Barth explains the radical and efficacious implications of bound-togetherness for the two men executed with Jesus. He does not take up the fact that the bound-togetherness might also have radical implications for Jesus himself. In *Church Dogmatics,* Jesus enters into "unshakable solidarity" with human beings in his death.³⁶ Here, these two executed men enter into unshakable solidarity with Jesus in their deaths. It is almost as if the two thieves are Jesus for Jesus. If the work of the cross is to overcome the separation of God and human beings even at the point of death and Jesus accomplishes that by bringing his Divine life into human death, these two men bring their human lives into Jesus' Divine death so

---

³⁴This is different than the sections described above from *Church Dogmatics.* In *CD* IV/1, in the sections described above, Barth explicitly says that knowledge of God and knowledge of God's action in Jesus on the cross is needed for the work of Christ to become "truth" for any given person. He writes, "It can come about individually only in the decision of faith" (*CD* IV/1, 245).
³⁵Barth, *Deliverance,* 78. The irregular capitalization of "He/he" for Jesus is original to the published text.
³⁶Barth, *CD* IV/3.1, 405.

that He too does not die alone. Embedded in the story of salvation, is the salvation of the Savior. The Savior's saviors are also arrested, tried, and executed men. They stand with Jesus to the very end in a way his disciples did not and could not. They are an enduring witness that Jesus is not alone, even in death, just as Jesus accomplishes that same work for the cosmos.

Barth does not say the above explicitly, but perhaps Jesus himself alludes to this mystery in Mt. 25:31-46. This passage is a touchstone for prison ministry and was cited by chaplains throughout this study. The story goes that when Jesus comes "in his glory" and separates people into groups— those who will enter the kingdom of God and those who will not—the measuring stick for entrance will be that some people met the physical needs of Jesus and some did not. Jesus says to those who will enter the kingdom, "For I was hungry and you gave me something to eat, I was thirsty and you gave me something to drink. I was a stranger and you invited me in, I needed clothes and you clothed me, I was sick and you looked after me, I was in prison and you came to visit me" (25:35-36). Even those who did the right actions are confused. "When did we do this?" they ask. And the Lord replies, "I tell you the truth, whatever you did for one of the least of these brothers of mine, you did for me" (25:40).

Jesus is explaining the sacrament of presence, i.e., how he shows up in other people. As we explored in Chapter 2, the real presence of Christ can be found in other people, particularly when people inhabit the same conditions that Jesus inhabited in his life. As explained in the earlier chapters of this book, Jesus says that he comes to give good news to the poor, to set captives free, to heal the blind, to release the oppressed, and to announce Jubilee economics (Lk. 4:18-19 citing Isa. 61:1-2). Jesus does these things, but as he does them, he becomes them himself. He becomes poor, incarcerated, and oppressed. In Matthew 25, Jesus explains that in the economy of salvation, people are expected to offer to Jesus exactly what Jesus offers to them. Salvation is cyclical. We experience the real presence of Christ as we alternate between occupying his subject positions—sometimes being one who is hungry and sometimes one who feeds, sometimes being one who is incarcerated and sometimes one who keeps watch with incarcerated people.

In Chapter 1, I noticed that the one thing in Lk. 4:18-19 that Jesus says he will do and does not do is to free any prisoners. Rather, he simply becomes a prisoner himself. Matthew 25 has a similar outlier. The Gospels present Jesus as a homeless prophet who relies on others for food, drink, and welcome. They also present him as a prisoner, but the Gospels do not ever present Jesus as "sick." The Greek for "I was sick, and you looked after me" is ἠσθένησα καὶ ἐπεσκέψασθέ με. "ἠσθένησα" can be translated "sick," but it can also be translated "weak" or "powerless." "ἐπεσκέψασθέ" can be translated as "visit," but it has an ocular range of meaning, thus the translations "look after" or "look in upon" or perhaps "keep watch." The phrase might also be translated, "I was powerless, and you kept watch with me." In 2 Cor. 13:4, when ἀσθενείας is used again, it is specifically used to reference the powerlessness of Jesus on the cross. 2 Cor. 13:4 says that Jesus was crucified in ἀσθενείας, weakness, vulnerability, or powerlessness. On this reading, the phrase, "I was powerless, and you kept watch with me" becomes a reference to the cross. The kingdom of God is reserved for those who have kept watch, both at Jesus' execution, and when "the least among us" are executed.

In the logic of *Church Dogmatics*, we can only ever inhabit the salvific nature of Christ's death as a community because Jesus is the only one among us who is both human and divine, and any given one of us will only ever be able to represent either horrific death or enduring life at any given time. We will always need someone alongside us to represent the other half of the mystery of salvation. But in Barth's prison preaching, we can only ever inhabit the salvific nature of Christ's death as a community because it was only ever salvific in community to begin with. Death was vacated as a site of God-forsakenness when Jesus kept watch with two incarcerated men as they kept watch with him until he screamed out his last breath.

Missing the Mockery: Mistaking Vacated Sentences for the Absolution of Carceral Systems

We are now a couple of pages away from direct testimonies of carceral death, so perhaps the horror is not as palpable as it was even a few minutes ago. But I would be remiss if I did not say that perhaps the most faithful word to speak in the face of carceral death—state-sponsored executions, the suicides of officers and incarcerated people, the murders committed inside of prisons, the mass deaths of prison-related illness—is simply, "No." No, I will not engage in this practice. No, this is not salvific. If this system can kill God, it can kill anybody. It is not simply that "Gethsemane and Golgotha" as a criminal justice system does more harm than good; it does far more harm than can be accepted. Perhaps the best response to carceral death would have been to have given no explanation at all and allow the reader to be shocked into refusing it. One would, after all, hate to tell Jesus that we are honoring his execution by replicating it.

The letter to the Colossians has a carceral setting. While the author, named as Paul, awaits his own trial, he writes about what he understands to have happened on the cross.[37] The standard English translations mask

---

[37] I do not intend to take a stance here on the dating of Colossians or on whether or not it should be considered as part of the authentic Pauline corpus. I am, however, quite concerned to retain the letter's carceral context in whatever date, location, and authorship one ascribes to it. One might accept a classic understanding of authentic authorship with a late date during Paul's Roman incarceration or follow Douglas Campbell in his argument for authentic authorship with an early date in an earlier Pauline incarceration. One might also reasonably decide that

the carceral and juridical aspects of what the author is saying as well as the scandal of his imagery. Below is Col. 2:13b-15 in Greek and in my own translation.

(2:13b) ὑμῶν συνεζωοποίησεν ὑμᾶς σὺν αὐτῷ χαρισάμενος ἡμῖν πάντα τὰπαραπτώματα (14) ἐξαλείψας τὸ καθ' ἡμῶν χειρόγραφον τοῖς δόγμασιν ὃ ἦν ὑπεναντίονἡμῖν καὶ αὐτὸ
ἦρκεν ἐκ τοῦ μέσου προσηλώσας αὐτὸ τῷ σταυρῷ (15) ἀπεκδυσάμενος τὰς ἀρχὰς καὶ τὰς ἐξουσίας ἐδειγμάτισεν ἐν παρρησίᾳθριαμβεύσας αὐτοὺς ἐν αὐτῷ

(2:13b) He made you alive with Him, having pardoned us all our offenses, (14) having smeared out the writing of the decree with all its regulations against us and hostile to us, he took it away, nailing it to the cross. (15) Having disarmed the rulers and authorities, he made a public example of them, triumphing over them through it.

The image is startling. The ancient author references here the way that the charge against a person would have been displayed at their execution, a fact we heard earlier in the recollection of Jesus' execution from Mark. In the moment of his execution, the author imagines Jesus "smearing out" the written charge, not against himself but against us, and then nailing the smeared charge to the cross anyway. A smeared-out charge remains nailed in the place where a legitimate justification for execution was previously understood to have been nailed. In that "smearing out" of the legal code, Jesus makes a spectacle of, triumphs over, or makes an example of the authorities who are supposedly making a spectacle of him. He mocks the validity of their legal code and its executions by receiving the worst of it in his own divine, and sinless (even if sin-sick) person. As he mocks the failure of arrest, conviction, and execution to produce justice and reconciliation, Jesus simultaneously redeems the God-forsakenness of carceral death.

That God can redeem the irredeemable is not license to keep creating irredeemable conditions. One legitimate response to the stories of carceral death shared in this study must be to stand in horror and start refusing to participate in a system that calls the march from Gethsemane to Golgotha a just or adequate response to human harm. If we are willing to keep watch with carceral death—like Jesus, chaplains, and incarcerated people do—we

---

the letter is not authentically Pauline but still acknowledge that the community that attributed the letter to Paul continued to remember Paul as an incarcerated person and remember details about his incarceration as relevant to his theology and legacy. See Douglas Campbell, "Chronology," in *T&T Clark Handbook to the Historical Paul*, ed. Ryan S. Schellenberg and Heidi Wendt (Edinburgh: T&T Clark, 2022), 265–86.

might find that we have to change our minds about how to right wrongs. Barth does.

After he spends time in prison, Barth changes his mind on the death penalty and engages in advocacy efforts toward de-criminalization. Right after the Second World War, Barth writes in support of the death penalty, but when he addresses a gathering of prison chaplains in 1960, someone in the audience notices that his previous support of the death penalty does not seem in line with his current remarks upholding the dignity and worth of every human life, incarcerated and not. Barth admits that he has changed his mind over the time he has spent in prison and can no longer support putting people to death.[38] Similarly, in the last year of his life, when he is so weak that Eberhard Busch has to write most of his letters for him, Barth takes precious time to go on record about legal reform toward the de-criminalization of homosexuality. In this letter he is unclear on his views about homosexuality, but he is very clear that there is no theological interpretation that could ever justify the "defamation" of people or the "(indeed irrational) juridical 'penalizing' of homosexuals."[39] Barth is clear that in the religious-political drama of criminalizing queer people, those who are in the moral and ethical wrong are the "Pharisees" that bring criminal charges against other people by "degrading (often inequitably applied) sections of the legal code, or in condemnatory whispers."[40] After he has kept watch with Jesus by keeping watch with other incarcerated people, Barth can no longer condone the processes by which people are criminalized and executed.

But perhaps the greatest argument for saying no to carceral death is the resurrection. The first time that Barth introduces in print the idea that God's Yes and God's No to the world are embodied in Jesus Christ, he makes clear that the Resurrection is God's "No" to "the whole burden of sin and the whole curse of death that still press heavily against us."[41] In other words, the Resurrection is God's ultimate and irrefutable refusal of all things that barrel toward death. In these very first pages of Barth's first published work, he already describes this cosmic refusal of death and affirmation of life in the language of the carceral. Barth writes of the resurrection:

> Precisely because the "No" of God is all-embracing, it is also His "Yes." We have therefore, in the power of God, a look-out, a door, a hope … The prisoner becomes a watchman. Bound to his post as firmly as a prisoner in his cell, he watches for the dawning of the day.[42]

---

[38]Barth, *Barth in Conversation Vol. 1*, 50.
[39]Karl Barth, "Freedom for Community," in *Theology and Sexuality: Classic and Contemporary Reading*, ed. Eugene F. Rogers, Jr. (New York: Blackwell Publishing, 2002), 114–15.
[40]Barth, "Freedom for Community," 115.
[41]Barth, *The Epistle to the Romans*, 38.
[42]Ibid., 38.

In the resurrection, *the prisoner becomes a watchman. Bound to his post as firmly as a prisoner in his cell, he watches for the dawning of the day.* In the resurrection, God says "No" to carceral death by reversing it, by raising Jesus from carceral death and releasing Jesus from his officer-guarded tomb. The Good News of Easter is that there is life after death in prison. Carceral death never gets the last word. This is the truth to which we now turn.

6

Inhabiting the Resurrection: The Work of Life after Death

He makes impossibility possible ... nothing less than the stepping from death to life, nothing less than the life which comes from death.
—KARL BARTH, *THE EPISTLE TO THE ROMANS*, 226

What if we could learn to breathe underwater? To capture those little pockets of air that are underwater that can help sustain us until we can get back up to the surface.
—CHAPLAIN MURRAY, INTERVIEW ON SEPTEMBER 27, 2021

On the Third Day

I interviewed Chaplain Maverick in January of 2021, about a year into the Covid-19 pandemic. He had just decided to leave his prison after twenty years of service. The Covid restrictions were severely limiting to his ministry. His mother lived with him, helping to take care of his son, and his level of disease exposure at the prison was simply more than he was willing to bring home. We had been talking on Zoom for over an hour when Chap Mav told me a story about a prison riot and its aftermath. I had not realized his son was home until he started to tell me about what he had survived in prison and his son joined the interview.

Chap Mav:

> One time there was a big fight, almost considered a riot, that happened between the Muslims and the Bloods gang. And it was huge. It happened in the big yard. Dozens of guys were fighting. And then it happened in little cells on different tiers.
>
>> *(I hear a child in the background. I hear a woman trying to move the child away. The child sounds young but persistent. A little boy, maybe three years old, bursts into the room.)*

Chap Mav:

>> *(Chap Mav smiles and draws the little boy to him.)*
>
> What do want to say, son?
>
>> *(The boy whispers something to him.)*
>
> You want to give me a big hug? Okay, you can give me a big hug.
>
>> *(The boy climbs onto his lap. Chap Mav gives him a big bear hug, growling.)*

The boy:

> I love you.

Chap Mav:

> I love you, too!
>
>> *(The boy laughs.)*
>
> Good. Okay. Thank you for my hug.
>
>> *(The grandmother calls for the boy to come back out of the room.)*
>
> It's good. Its good, Mom.
>
>> *(The boy lays his head on Chap Mav's chest.)*
>
> Yeah, so they have a big riot, a big fight.
>
>> *(The boy looks up and clicks his tongue at his father.)*

And they shut down the facility, no movement for five days. And it was in August. It was burning up in people's cells, no air conditioning on certain tiers. So, it's just horrible. And so I went to the tiers, and I visited them cell by cell.

(The boy is squirming and patting Chap Mav's chest.)

So I was able to get on the tiers, and I was already experienced in that. I knew how to move, how walk on the tiers, how to respectfully talk to the officers and go door to door and talk to the guys.

(The little boy points to something off screen.)

The boy:

Daddy, please have that superhero?

Chap Mav:

(Chap Mav reaches off screen and pulls back a superhero figurine.)

Why? What are you going to do with it?

The boy:

Play with it?

Chap Mav:

What are you gonna play with it? Where's he gonna go?

Boy:

He's gonna see all my superheroes.

Chap Mav:

You gonna bring him back? That's Captain Adam. I want him back.

Boy:

What he doos?

Chap Mav:

He changes things into different things.

The boy:

Cool!

Chap Mav:

He can change a penny into a shoe.

(The little boy runs out with the superhero in his fist.)

So, um ... yeah, I would ... I would say that was a real, you know, it was a disastrous time. Some of the officers even made t-shirts, "I survived the lockdown of 2008."[1] So ... you know ...

I mean that ... that riot ... I mean, really, the prison administration was afraid they were going to try and take over the prison, so many guys fighting, but they were really fighting amongst themselves. They weren't trying to take over anything.

They were just ... it was amongst each other. But it was so big you know ...

Sarah Jobe:

Were you on site, the day that it happened?

Chap Mav:

I was there. I was there.

Everybody, whenever it was an emergency code, everybody stays in their space, you know, you can't leave. I didn't know the details until much later, you know, well, the next day. I didn't know all the details, but I knew that there was a code, a big code, in the yard. They were, it took them a long time to clear the code, and then there were other codes happening in tiers. Eventually they told us, once they cleared the aftershock codes, if you will, once they cleared those, they, they made all the staff go home.

---

[1] The date has been changed to preserve anonymity.

Sarah Jobe:

So then it was like the next day that you started this ...

Chap Mav:

So the next day I learned all the details and just stayed in my office. Then the third day, an email circulated—something that said that we are gonna be on lockdown for a while, as internal affairs interviewed the people that were involved. There's not gonna be any general movement for a while. So I think it was the third day when I talked with my supervisor, and I talked with the administration, to say, you know, maybe I need to go see the guys, you know ...

Sarah Jobe:

> *(I nod.)*

Mm hmmm.

> *(Long pause.)*

Chap Mav:

You know.

> *(We sat in silence.)*

Sarah Jobe:

Yeah.

> *(More silence.)*[2]

It was the third day when I talked with my supervisor, and I talked with the administration, to say, you know, maybe I need to go see the guys, you know ... You know. What did Chaplain Maverick think I knew? Chaplain Maverick knew I was a chaplain. It was in the Consent Form for this study, and my own experience as a prison chaplain was a part of the conversations that I had with chaplains as they discerned whether or not to go on record about their experiences in prison. Eighteen chaplains with whom I spoke decided not to go on record. For the twenty that did go on record, I got the

---

[2] Interview with the author on January 25, 2021.

sense both before and during the interviews that part of their willingness to speak was predicated on the hope that because I knew what prison was like, I might be able to understand experiences that overwhelm description and explanation. Chap Mav names that on the third day after a riot, when he learns that men will be locked in their cells for an unspecified amount of time, he does the necessary advocacy to be permitted to walk cell to cell in the wake of carceral violence. In the moment, he cannot describe what the experience of walking cell to cell is like. He goes silent. He expects that I know. I say that I do. We sit in silence together. What was I affirming that I know about visiting cells in the wake of carceral death?

I know that it tastes like metal and old paint when one puts one's mouth against a door crack so that the person sealed on the other side can hear. Mounds of Styrofoam clamshells and brown paper lunch sacks will be lining the halls in clear plastic trash bags if 1,500 people are being served three meals a day on their beds. I know to breathe through my mouth instead of my nose to help with the smell of hundreds of people who last showered before the death occurred. Some people's eyes will look relieved, even happy, to see me. Some will look vacant. Some angry. But many will sit hunched in the back of their cells and not get close enough to food slots, grates, bars, or plated windows for me to see them at all. That will, to me, feel like failure. I know that only people who know me well already will reach their hand up against glass reinforced with wire mesh to wave or to mime a touch that would not be permissible even if the doors could be opened. I know the theological crisis produced when one visits on the third day only to find the bodies still in the cells, the officers still at their posts, and the stone not rolled away. What does it mean to inhabit the resurrection in the wake of carceral death when the tomb is not empty?

As I said in the preface, this book has tried to answer the questions, "How is it possible to inhabit the atonement? How do we enact Jesus' prior act of reconciling the world to God? What does it mean to live and die with Christ the salvation of the cosmos in our own bodies and lives today?" Chaplains embody the incarnation in their ministries of presence. They risk themselves to engage the "atoning" or "reconciling" work of building communities that are diverse, authentic, and free in the face of social divisions that fracture such attempts at community. They bear the cost of that work in their bodies and minds. They follow Jesus into carceral death, becoming a witness to a God who vacates God-forsakenness by God's own presence in it. But carceral death is not the end of the salvation story. Jesus is raised from the dead. Furthermore, Christians always already know the end of the story. In very real ways, one can face carceral death because one believes that it is not the end. Life after death is possible. Free life after carceral death is practiced by Jesus in his resurrection appearances. But only one of the fifty-eight people who died in the interlude of this book was resurrected. What difference does the resurrection of one person make for all those living in spaces where carceral death appears to be winning today?

The chaplains in this study did not name this question as a question of the resurrection. But they all named the conundrum of trying to keep on doing transformative work when there were few to no signs of transformation around them. Chaplain Love said:

> We really do find out what we *really* believe about forgiveness and grace and redemption and transformation and making amends. We can preach that for years, but in prison we're really up against it.
>
> We're also asked what we really, really believe about these kind of institutions and what is our work? To see change in them. In what ways can we be agents of transformation in a system that is so cruel?[3]

Chaplain Noa, who had served for forty years as a prison chaplain when I interviewed her, named that one of the hardest parts about working in prison was "trying to be creative and create things in an environment that is not designed to be creative."[4] Chaplain Watson named the anger and frustration of facing injustices that she does not have the authority to change. She said:

> The injustice that we're exposed to inside is so overwhelming, and there's just a part of me that wants to shake the, the, the roof off this messed up place. And to not be able to … to be okay in there without being, without being an advocate. I mean, I am an advocate … but to be okay with just offering spiritual care without also trying to solve problems for people that I could see were being abused … or not being abused, but were being screwed over by the system.[5]

These chaplains are frustrated, angry, and confounded by the ability of prison systems to resist and thwart positive change, and yet, they continue making rounds after carceral death. They find the cells locked and full. They find the conditions that created the deaths still intact, and they do life-after-death work anyway. Some have theologies that support their persistence in the face of death, but most are simply practicing persistent life without much explanation. As Chaplain Barrett said, "You can't just throw your hands up in the air and say, 'Well I'm done! I'm done. Prison don't work.' When you run up against the wall, you have to figure out, how do I get around it? Can I go under it? What do I do?"[6]

This chapter will explore how chaplains are practicing persistent life in the wake of carceral death, or to borrow a phrase from Christina Sharpe, this chapter will explore the "wake work" of prison chaplaincy.[7] The chapter

---

[3]Interview with the author on March 12, 2021.
[4]Interview with the author on February 27, 2021.
[5]Interview with the author on September 20, 2021.
[6]Interview with the author on August 30, 2021.
[7]Sharpe, *In the Wake: On Blackness and Being*, 1–24.

starts in the aftermath of tragedy, at the tomb with the practices of grief, physical care, individual processing, and corporate re-membering of both the dead and the living. Wake work is grief work, but care for incarcerated dead and living is also a means of challenging the logics of carceral death that insist that some people are dispensable. Wake work thus participates in persistent life; it is the forerunner and grounds of resurrection. The chapter then turns to how one learns to see persistent life emerging in the wake of carceral death. What are the afterlives of Jesus in prison? How does the miraculous come to exist in the mundane? How are chaplains and incarcerated people inhabiting persistent life and performing mundane miracles after death? Finally, I admit that sometimes one cannot see the resurrection in prison not because one needs new vision but because carceral death has won. The chapter closes with an exploration of what it looks like to dream the resurrection when it is not there to see.

Third Day Theology: Wake Work and Re-membering in Prison

When a person dies in state-custody, the body is a first concern. Families have the right to claim the body of their loved one, but many do not have the economic means to do so. If a person has served a long or life sentence, there may be no family left to claim the body. Louisiana State Penitentiary, better known as Angola Prison, has historically been a facility only for men serving life sentences. When I visited in 2016, they were on their third cemetery internal to the 18,000-acre prison, having filled two cemeteries already.[8] The Gospel of Matthew reports similar concerns about the bodily remains of Jesus after his execution. The text specifies that a man named Joseph, who was wealthy enough to afford a burial, is willing to take Jesus' body (27:57).[9] Joseph goes through a permission process to claim the body of Christ, and only after Pilate grants permission can Joseph take the body, wrap it in linen, lay it in a tomb, and roll a large stone in front of the entrance (27:58-60).

As with Chaplain Maverick's story above, in Matthew's Gospel the day after carceral death is a day for policy, protocol, investigations, and ensuring

---

[8] See also Michael Hallet, Joshua Hays, Byron Johnson, Sung Jang, and Grant Duwe, *The Angola Prison Seminary: Effects of Faith-Based Ministry on Identity Transformation, Desistance, and Rehabilitation* (New York: Routledge, 2017).

[9] For a careful treatment of the social, political, and economic dimensions of policing and incarceration in the ancient Roman world that helps to place policed biblical characters like Jesus and Paul in a wider context of the over-policing of poor and occupied peoples, see Ryan S. Schellenberg, *Abject Joy: Paul, Prison, and the Art of Making Do* (Oxford: Oxford University Press, 2021).

the order and stability of the prison. Chap Mav gathers information, receives reports, and talks to fellow staff on the second day. Those in authority decide to lock down the prison while the violence and its aftermath are assessed. In Matthew's Gospel, Pilate consults with religious leaders and decides to station a guard outside of Jesus' tomb. He sets a seal on the stone, σφραγίσαντες τὸν λίθον, in order to see if Jesus' followers have tampered with it (27:62-66). The concern is that Jesus, having already been convicted as an "imposter" (ὁ πλάνος), will have arranged a staged, posthumous resurrection. Were his disciples to succeed in claiming that the imposter was resurrected from the dead, the authorities believe that "the last deception (πλάνη) will be worse than the first" (27:64). When the tomb is found empty, the soldiers on duty are paid to say that Jesus' disciples came and took the body. They are told that if such a report falls back on them for having not interceded, the authorities will guarantee that the soldiers are kept out of trouble (28:11-15). Even after death, the bodies of the convicted remain the concern of the state that has custody over them. Particularly after executions, the choreography of burial and the reports on the death must continue to uphold the state's authority to take the lives of people who have been convicted of crimes.[10] If social order inside and outside of prisons is to be maintained, the logic that a person has been rightfully killed cannot be shaken. Persistent life in the face of carceral death threatens Pilate's control and the logic of prison.

Even before the full persistence of Jesus' life is known, there are three women who resist the logic that Jesus' life, as a condemned person, is dispensable.[11] Mark's Gospel reports that on the third day, Mary Magdalene, Mary the mother of James, and Salome bring spices to anoint the body of Jesus (16:1). These same women honored him as a leader, teacher, and healer by following him in his life (Lk. 8:2). Even after his arrest and conviction, they refused to let him die alone by keeping vigil at the foot of the cross (Mk 15:40). They weep at the loss of him (Jn 20:11). Now they come to care for his body after death. They show by their actions that Jesus is not expendable, not an imposter, not a criminal or a threat, even if that is how the authorities have characterized him to render his execution permissible. Their bodily care for Jesus tells a counter narrative about the value of human life, particularly human life marked as criminal.

---

[10]Raymond Anthony Duff, Lindsay Farmer, Sandra Marshall, and Victor Tadros, *The Trial on Trial: Volume 3: Towards a Normative Theory of the Criminal Trial* (Oxford: Bloomsbury Publishing, 2007).

[11]While I will not take up her categories in this chapter, I am thinking here of Hortense Spillers' distinction between "body" and "flesh." The body being something reduced to a thing, captive, and flay-able; flesh being that basic materiality that resists being reduced to a body, even as it is happening. See Hortense J. Spillers, "Mama's Baby, Papa's Maybe: An American Grammar Book," in *Black, White, and in Color: Essays on American Literature and Culture* (Chicago: University of Chicago Press, 2003), 203–29.

Wake Work

When the three women who go to Jesus' tomb insist on caring for a condemned body exposed to carceral death, they are doing what Christina Sharpe calls "wake work." In her book *In the Wake: On Blackness and Being,* Sharpe writes:

> I have been trying to articulate a method of encountering a past that is not past. A method along the lines of a sitting with, a gathering, and tracking of phenomena that disproportionately and devastatingly affect Black people any and everywhere we are. I've been thinking of this gathering, this collecting and reading toward a new analytic, as the wake and wake work, and I am interested in plotting, mapping, and collecting the archives of the everyday of Black immanent and imminent death, and in tracking the ways we resist, rupture, and disrupt that immanence and imminence aesthetically and materially.[12]

Wake work is grief work—literally the work of funerals, casseroles, and sitting-with—but it is more than that. Wake work is also how to live *in the wake,* in the aftermath, of carceral death. Sharpe is specifically interested in how to live in the wake of American chattel slavery, but she acknowledges that prisons are one of the afterlives of slavery that continue to render people into disposable property; in prisons people are no longer full citizens, and laws and rights are reinterpreted and limited to reflect that status. What does it mean to live inside and to live *in the wake of* such a system?

Part of why Sharpe's work is helpful is that she acknowledges that grieving "the interminable" is different than grieving the loss of a single life. She asks "How does one memorialize chattel slavery and its afterlives, which are unfolding still? How do we memorialize an event that is still ongoing?"[13] Living "in the wake" means learning to live under conditions that have made the "catastrophic" into the "quotidian."[14] She writes:

> As we go about wake work, we must think through containment, regulation, punishment, capture, and captivity and the ways the manifold representations of blackness become the symbol, par excellence, for the less-than-human being condemned to death … How might we stay in the wake with and as those whom the state positions to die ungrievable deaths and live lives meant to be unlivable?[15]

---

[12]Sharpe, *In the Wake,* 13.
[13]Ibid., 20.
[14]Ibid.
[15]Ibid., 21–2.

Sharpe is naming the difficulty of grieving any given death in prison.[16] One person or persons have died, and those deaths call forth the work of grieving. But all the structures of carceral death remain intact that contributed toward the death being grieved. Everyone grieving the loss in that prison is still barreling toward overdose, suicide, execution, heart failure, and the violent outbursts characteristic of living by force with limited resources in a place where one does not want to live. Chaplains help a prison community grieve one life, but those who live and work in prison know full well that the current loss will be followed inevitably by another and another. As important as grieving the "ungrievable death," is the work of learning to live a "life meant to be unlivable" in the wake of that death.

Sharpe names how wake work is more than grief work, but the chaplains in this study helped me to see how when one grieves people marked as expendable, the grief work itself becomes a part of the work that challenges the narratives that uphold carceral death. Like the women who stay with Jesus during his execution and continue to honor his body after death, care for the condemned challenges the state's narrative that some people are expendable. Every chaplain in this study described their care-full practices in the wake of prison deaths. They create memorial services inside of prisons for both residents and staff. They attend memorial services in the community for both residents and staff. They create memory boards in dorms, dayrooms, breakrooms, and control centers that hold the pictures and obituaries of members of the prison community who have died. They advocate for incarcerated people to be transported to private viewings of immediate family members, and they advocate for them to be able to watch memorial services remotely or by DVD when transportation away from the prison is not possible or permissible. They make rounds, sitting with the living who are grieving the dead in communities of two and three. They run grief support groups. They make a point of having good tissues in their offices, so that people do not have to use the stiff, thin prison toilet paper to wipe their faces in the wake of a loss.

By one reading, this is basic grief work that any chaplain or pastor in any setting might do. But the grief work becomes more than itself, becomes wake work, when it is done for people marked as expendable.[17] Grief work

---

[16]Sharpe's analysis of a grief that attempts to grieve interminable conditions is a social and political analysis that attends deeply to the practices of individuals, families, and local communities. For a more clinical analysis of complicated grief and how to offer care within it that attends to social and political factors see Darcy L. Harris and Tashel C. Bordere, *Handbook of Social Justice in Grief and Loss: Exploring Diversity, Equity, and Inclusion* (New York: Routledge, 2016).

[17]For an implicit example of this see Nancy Sehested's *Marked for Life* noting the way that traumatic loss frames the entirety of her treatment of prison chaplaincy, including the stories used as bookends for the book as a whole. Nancy Hastings Sehested, *Marked for Life: A Prison Chaplain's Story* (Maryknoll: Orbis Books, 2019).

after carceral death is a re-narration that a life that was placed outside of the community through incarceration is a life that persists in importance to others. Grief work in prison re-narrates the prison not as a zone of social abandonment but as a proper community in which lives are lived and loved and lost. Wake work in prison re-narrates untouchable bodies as touchable human beings deserving of care, anointing, tears, burial, and memorializing. When a community does this wake work for any one body narrated as expendable, criminal, or untouchable, they are re-narrating *every* body marked as such, including those still persistently living in the wake of the carceral. Grief work as wake work threatens the logic and claims of prison that some lives are best kept contained, untouched, and away from community. Wake work thus participates in persistent life; it is the forerunner and grounds of resurrection.

Re-membering

What Sharpe calls wake work, Chaplain Murray calls "re-membering." Chaplain Murray has worked for twenty years as a prison chaplain. She started in a juvenile facility but has spent the majority of her career in a women's close custody prison. She was the chaplain who shared with me in the most detail about both the practices of her grief care and the thinking that undergirds it. She uses the "image of remembering" to guide her work in the wake of death.

Chaplain Murray:

> By remembering, I don't mean nostalgic remembering, but I mean bringing back into membership, re-membering. Bringing people back into a place of belonging, a place of, a place of meaning, a place of community. Even if it's just a community of two, and I'm the only other member. Because for some of them, that's all we can do. But that's my job, is to re-member people who have been disconnected from membership for sometimes their whole life.[18]

As Chaplain Murray creates a safe conversational space for women to remember their losses and what they have been through in their lives, she is re-membering them into community. Her simple, physical presence with them is one part of creating that community, but she also describes three specific postures that characterize her work of re-membering. She emphasizes and celebrates survival. She embraces hurt and harm as a site at which to experience the holy. And she affirms the bravery of feeling the fullness of one's emotions, no matter what they are. One can see each of

---

[18] Interview with the author on September 27, 2021.

these principles in action in the following description of the conversations she has with women in the wake of loss.

Chaplain Murray:

> You know that the most challenging question is always, "Why evil? Why did this happen to me?" Or, "I did this horrible thing, and I'm not worthy. I deserve to be in prison for the rest of my life. I deserve it." You know, just the self-loathing, self-hatred.
>
> And I don't know why things happen. I don't know why.
> I don't have any illusion that I have any understanding of why bad things happen.
> Why, why some of us, you know, have such, just stories …
> Like I'm always …
> I'm amazed you're even upright and walking! If I had lived your life, I would be curled up in a fetal position under my desk all day long like …
> I just wouldn't be …
>
> But you're a survivor! I mean you've survived!
> Like, how the hell did you do that?
>
> So sometimes it's just drawing out their own strengths that they already have in them.
> And sometimes it's not always the healthiest ways that they've survived, but they did.
>
> I don't know it's just like, just recognizing how awesome they are.
> And some of them are awesome, but most of them are … they've got … there's some,
> there's something about ….
>
> Oh, I know a metaphor: it's a Leonard Cohen song.
> I think it's a song, and the lyrics are:
>
> "Forget your perfect offering.
> There is a crack in everything.
> That's how the light gets in."
>
> And so I have a lot of conversations about how
> of course, you're broken.
> Of course, you are.
> And that's
> sometimes that's,

that can be a good thing.
Because that, that is what's letting something new come in.
That is what's opening you up to something new and different.
If you weren't broken, you'd just keep going the way you're going.

I often do the same thing with grief.
They're like, "I just feel horrible and so overwhelmed."

And then, I'm like, "You know what, that's a good sign, because it means you're facing it, and you're not running away from it, and you're not numbing yourself out. And you're not using. I mean you could be high, right now! You wouldn't have to feel shit if you didn't want to, but you're not ... you're sitting here in my office, and you're crying, and you're feeling like shit, and that's a victory."[19]

I'm amazed you're even upright and walking! If I had lived your life, I would be curled up in a fetal position under my desk all day long. But you're a survivor! I mean, you've survived! Like, how the hell did you do that? Chaplain Murray takes the occasion of one loss to make space for a person to name all the many things that they have lost in their life.[20] She then reframes the losses as things that a person has survived. She affirms that their survival—being upright and walking around—is astounding. She also acknowledges that survival was probably complicated and involved choices and coping strategies that may have caused harm to both self and others. She then reframes these "cracks"—bad choices, coping strategies, harms committed and harms experienced—as "the way the light gets in." Chaplain Murray is pushing beyond active listening into a model of reflecting back not just what a person is able to see in themselves and their history, but what it might be possible to see in oneself and one's history if one believes oneself to be "awesome," as Chaplain Murray puts it. Chaplain Murray presses beyond the affirmation that there is no God-forsaken place and no God-forsaken person to a recognition that surviving seemingly God-forsaken conditions is a sign of an individual's astounding ability and worth. She is re-membering a person anew as she remembers their life with them differently than they have ever remembered it before. Grief work becomes the container for the wider

---

[19]Ibid.

[20]Compound grief and complex grief are both important aspects of grief care in prison. Any given loss will often bring up a wide variety of losses that a person never had the opportunity to grieve. The deaths being grieved are often traumatic, rather than death in old age or death by illness. For more on compound grief and complex grief see Chris Hendry, "Incarceration and the tasks of grief: A narrative review," *Journal of Advanced Nursing* 65, no. 2 (2009): 270–8; Raelene M. Leach, Teresa Burgess, and Chris Holmwood, "Could recidivism in prisoners be linked to traumatic grief? A review of the evidence," *International Journal of Prisoner Health* 4, no. 2 (2008): 104–19. doi: 10.1080/17449200802038249; Katie Hunt, "Bereavement behind bars: Prison and the grieving process," *Prison Service Journal* 254 (2021): 17–23.

work of repair and restoration. Death becomes the occasion for a newly-understood and differently-inhabited life.

Chaplain Murray does not only re-member women in the work of one-on-one pastoral care; she also practices re-membering in a liturgical context. She described to me her memorial service liturgy for when residents pass away.

Chaplain Murray:

> I also have a ritual for memorial services when residents pass away. I always have a memorial service for them.
>
> And I have a big bowl, and I put water in it with a candle. And then they have these rocks, and instead of preaching or anything, I open up the space for them to come and hold a rock and tell a story about the person who died. I tell them that story is going to go into that rock, and then you put the rock in the water. And the water accepts everything. The water is going to just surround it, and it holds it, and pretty soon we're going to have all these rocks in this water, and they're all going to be together. And, by the end of our service, these waters can be holy water, and you're welcome to come up and pray with it. Put it on your hands, or put it on your, you know, whatever.
>
> And then, after everyone leaves, I'm going to take it outside and put it in the grass, so it goes back to the earth. And that has become very meaningful for them.

Re-membering a person in the wake of death and traumatic life history is hard and draining work. Part of what struck me about Chaplain Murray is that she uses the same principles of re-membering that she offers to others to sustain and re-fuel herself. After sharing about her wake work practices, she talks about needing others to hold space for her to process what she experiences in prison. She relies on friends and mentors to re-member her in one-on-one conversation when the work gets to be too much, just as she offers that re-membering to incarcerated women in one-one-one pastoral care. She talks about being personally fed and encouraged by a group that she runs for women with life sentences. Lifers, more than other people in prison, have to learn to *live* in the wake of carceral death, rather than simply grieving carceral death, since their whole lives will be lived in the wake of the carceral. Chaplain Murray describes how her lifer group is more about fellowship, relaxing, laughter, movies, sharing stories, and enjoying food together than about a specific curriculum or topic. She names that she looks forward to these groups and that they sustain her as much as they sustain the other women in the group.

Chaplain Murray:

> Being with the lifers really feeds me too, in a way. Like there are times I'm like too tired for this. I can't think of what we can, what are we gonna do this Saturday? I don't know.
>
> And then I come up with something, and then I have this meeting with them. And I just get to hear them talk, and hear what's in their minds, and hear them encourage each other, and see them laugh, and you know be goofy together and ... and I always feel better after lifers. I often feel like I learned more, like I've learned more from them than they have from me. I think I have more gratitude in my life because of them ... because I see how important that is, and also how lucky I am.
>
> And at the end, we stand in a circle, and I'll say, "May all that we have experienced sink deeply, deeply into our hearts, into our bones, and to our guts and help carry us until we are together again. Amen." And then we all go.
>
> And when I go to the beach, I often write some of their names in the sand on the coast ... kind of as a prayer. The water takes it ...
>
> the ocean takes it into the ocean ...
>
> into the ocean.[21]

This is what it looks like to live in the wake of carceral death. What Chaplain Murray is describing is clearly grief work. It is grief work done very well, a standard and model for other chaplains to follow. It is life-after-death work and an example of what I am calling "persistent life" in this chapter. But is Chaplain Murray's work really "inhabiting the resurrection"? Is this work not somehow different than Jesus being raised from the dead? By one reading, wake work is not miraculous. By one reading, it does not require divine intervention or divine life. What does wake work have to do with Jesus and his life after death?

As I turn to resurrection appearances and the afterlives of Jesus in prison, I want to name that I had originally thought wake work and resurrection should be considered in two separate chapters. One is the work of human beings; one is the work of God. One is mundane and ubiquitous, done in every time and culture; one is miraculous and rarely, if ever, experienced. But as I sat with the resurrection appearances narrated in the Gospels, I realized that one only gets to see persistent life in the wake of death if one

---

[21]Interview with the author on September 27, 2021.

shows up in the wake of death to tend to the bodies, minds, and spirits of the dead and living alike. The women who come to anoint Jesus' dead body are the ones who become eyewitnesses of the resurrection. The followers who gather together two at a time to talk about and process Jesus' execution are the ones to whom Jesus appears on the road to Emmaus (Lk. 24:13-35). As Chaplain Love puts it, "God is found in the ruins."[22] A commitment to "living in the wake" is often a precondition for learning to see the resurrected body of Christ as he shows up to eat and drink, to share his wounds, to do mundane miracles, and to bring peace after carceral death. One must visit the tomb to see if it is empty.

Resurrection Appearances: Learning to See the Miracle of Persistent Life

Chaplain Levine helped me to see this connection between wake work and the mundane miracle of persistent life. He was describing to me what he understood to be the work of the chaplain in the aftermath of trauma. Specifically, he remembered his ministry after a stabbing, after a near-fatal beating, and after an escape attempt. In the first instance, he had known the man who was stabbed, and in the second, he had known the man who did the beating.

Chaplain Levine:

> There's a lot there, of course, around sort of "aftercare self-care." Like, you know, what are the signs of secondary trauma, which are very much like the signs of trauma. And you know, doing follow up, checking in. Like, how are you still carrying this? Are you sleeping? Are you eating? What are your relationships like? Like, just ... it's really a constant though because, you know, I am just so deeply aware of the impact of being an officer and the trauma of that.

> You know, I just remember, I didn't quite have the language and tools then, but there's a lot of shut down people, and I would kind of do everything I could think of to try to help people mitigate against that.

> I think we need to know how stress and trauma and violence affect us. And affect our relationships. I think that's the main thing that I wish I knew a lot more when I started.

---

[22] Interview with the author on March 12, 2021.

Sarah Jobe:

And do you mean that for kind of the ministry to staff and residents, or literally how trauma impacts the body of the chaplain?

Chaplain Levine:

Both. Both.

And the two are intimately connected.

So much so that you can't really separate them.

Actually, like what I, what I've come to believe is that all I really can offer is my nervous system to somebody whose nervous system is dysregulated.

That's really all I got to offer.

So if I'm going into a situation with an unregulated nervous system, then I'm really offering, I'm not offering much.[23]

What I've come to believe is that all I really can offer is my nervous system to somebody whose nervous system is dysregulated. Chaplain Levine was seated, but he held his hands out from his sides as he said it, bent at the elbows. His palms were up. He looked like he was presiding over communion. As my own mirror neurons reacted to his posture, I could feel my own hands outstretched in that pose, though I did not raise them physically. I could feel myself saying the words that I say when in that posture, "This is my body, broken for you." Chaplain Levine was describing the neuroscience of compassionate care, that one person's nervous system can regulate off another person's nervous system.[24] If a caregiver can maintain settled breath, a relaxed and open body posture, and a calm tone of voice in the face of panic, anger, and despair then another person's breathing can slow to match hers, their muscles can unclench to match her relaxed pose, their mind and words can slow to her pace. One person offers her nervous system to the nervous system of another. This gift and exchange are the logic and posture of the Eucharist.

While the Christian tradition often associates this self-giving with the cross, one can also see Jesus giving his body to his disciples in this way after

---

[23]Interview with the author on April 23, 2021.
[24]Gerbarg, Brown, Streeter, Katzman, and Vermani, "Breath practices for survivor and caregiver stress, depression, and post-traumatic stress disorder," 1–31.

the resurrection. Before Jesus' death, he tells his disciples that he will send them an Advocate or Holy Spirit (Jn 14:26). He describes this gift as, "Peace I leave with you; my peace I give to you" (14:27). Then, when Jesus appears to his disciples after the resurrection, he finds them living in fear in the wake of his execution. He "came and stood among them and said, 'Peace be with you.'" Then he shows them his hands and his side, and the text notes that their fear turns into joy (20:19-20). Again, Jesus says, "Peace be with you" (20:21). Jesus offers his body and his words to his disciples in the wake of carceral death, and his presence changes their fear to joy. Jesus gives them his peace through the simple act of his peaceful, i.e. regulated, physical presence.

Chaplain Levine had jumped up out of his seat. I could hear him calling to me from off-screen, "Do you know Resmaa Menakem? *My Grandmother's Hands?*" My chaplain supervisor had just gifted me Menakem's book, *My Grandmother's Hands: Racialized Trauma and the Pathway to Mending Our Hearts and Bodies*. Much of trauma-healing theorizes and practices at the level of the individual, but Menakem's work explores how trauma theory that operates at the level of the individual body can be used to address and heal wider social traumas—collective violence, systemic racism, generational poverty, and abuse. Chaplain Levine was back on screen flipping through the pages.

Chaplain Levine:

> You know, he's a trauma therapist so he's talking about ... let's see, page 152. Wait a minute ... I need better glasses on! Just briefly, I'll just read you this paragraph. I just think it's so ... I find the whole book is amazing, but ...

> Okay, well he spent like two paragraphs before talking about, "I have a Master of Social Work degree. I am certified in EMDR. I'm certified in Gottman's seven principles for happy relationships." You know, all these things that he's done.

> And he says, "Yet none of these has much to do with why clients come to me, or how our work together helps them heal. Although they don't always realize it, people visit my office to be with my settled, regulated nervous system. At first, clients come in with dysregulated nervous systems. Over time, their repeated contact with my nervous system helps their nervous systems settle. This does not happen through a process of mirroring or cognitive training or verbal communication. What takes places is energetic, chemical, biological—a syncing of vibrations and energies. My nervous system does not model the way; over time, it helps others nervous systems access the same infinite source that mine does ... Over time, I learned to access a settledness that is always and

already present. I usually call it the infinite source ... This connection to a larger source is vital to healing."[25]

So I think you know for me it's like, yeah there's things that we know cognitively ... There's words to say, that aren't unimportant. But, at the heart of it, we're offering our own connection to God, to the divine, to what he calls the infinite source. And whatever allows us to let that be in us, and flow through us, is now—I believe more and more—is sort of the point and the gift. Because that creates the conditions where someone can begin to find that in themselves, that same capacity to be connected to God and self and others in that same way.

Sarah Jobe:

So out of curiosity, do you find this language of "a regulated nervous system" to be describing the same phenomenon as "tapping into the infinite"? Like, is it just different ways of describing the same thing or ...

Chaplain Levine:

I think it's incarnational theology! *(He laughs ... then both laugh.)*

It's what happens biologically when we're in line with the Spirit. Of course, mind, body, and spirit are not separate; it's just that we've got to talk about them separately, so we can understand it a little bit. But yeah, it's the biological, incarnational component of Spirit. That's how I think of it.

This exploration and dive into trauma has helped, has been the most fruitful path for me to understand incarnational theology. It's like: How has the Divine designed us to be in communion with the Divine?

We were created for relationship with God, right? God was lonely and created this thing called human to be in relationship. And that's really, when I say, "a settled nervous system," what I'm really saying is ... There's this whole school within neuroscience now—polyvagal theory—and basically our nervous systems have to be settled, that part of our nervous system has to be settled, for us to experience connection. It's this part of the polyvagal nerve between our face and our heart.

---

[25]Resmaa Menakem, *My Grandmother's Hands: Racialized Trauma and the Pathway to Mending Our Hearts and Bodies* (LasVegas: Central Recovery Press, 2017), 152.

Literally. I mean that's how we're designed. That's how our bodies are made. They are made for connection, but we can't access that part of our biology, that part of our spirit, unless fear is not driving the bus. You know that when our nervous systems are wired around fear, which is what trauma does—I mean what's kind of the Gospel that is announced, right? Be not afraid—I mean, fear is a part of being human, and we need that alarm to wake us up a lot of times. But if we're living in fear all the time, then we're missing why we're here. We're missing this (pointing between us). We're missing our ability to connect and feel connected and to love and feel loved.

You can talk about it in neuroscience terms, which I think is kind of helpful, but when I talk about it in neuroscience terms, I'm thinking about being fearfully and wonderfully made, you know? I'm thinking how this is what God intended!

And this is what I think Christianity's primary thing is: God became this (touches his arm) because it is so unbelievably holy.[26]

How has the divine designed us to be in communion with the divine? Chaplain Levine is pointing to one of the mysteries of human flesh: our nervous systems have to be settled to experience connection, but connection is one of the things that can help to settle the nervous system. In the wake of carceral death, people are experiencing both primary and secondary trauma depending on if they were participants in the death, eyewitnesses to the death, or if they are simply experiencing the lockdowns, stories, and institutional aftershocks of the death. The work of the chaplain in his rounds after death is to help settle human beings after these shocks, inviting them out of trauma response and back into embodied community. When Chaplain Levine pays detailed attention to what kinds of words and actions heal bodies in the wake of trauma, he understands both his attention to bodies and the work of healing to be the logic and practice of the incarnation. It is also the logic and practice of the resurrection. Coming back to life after experiencing carceral death is driven by the same compelling connection to other people and to God that drives the incarnation. The practices of presence and relationality described in Chapter 2 that mean a chaplain will witness carceral death are the same practices that restore minds, bodies, and spirits in the wake of carceral death. Those practices are about the polyvagal nerve and mirror neurons, *and* they are about the connection to an infinite Source.[27] They are both of those things inextricably at the same time.

---

[26] Interview with the author on April 23, 2021.
[27] For an accessible overview of polyvagal theory, see Stephen W. Porges, *The Pocket Guide to the Polyvagal Theory: The Transformative Power of Feeling Safe* (New York: W.W. Norton & Co, 2017).

I ask if the biological connection between mind and heart is the same as connection to God. Chaplain Levine responds, "Christianity's primary thing is: God became this (touches his arm) because it is so unbelievably holy." Coming back to life and community after the psyche-fracturing experience of carceral death happens through basic practices of bodily care and attention. In other words, the resurrection happens internal to and coterminous with the mundane practices of wake work. The resurrection of Jesus after carceral death is not mundane, but one only knows the resurrection of Jesus in the mundane activities that Jesus undertakes when he visits with his disciples in the wake of his execution. He shows them his wounds. He renegotiates his relationships with them. He eats and drinks with them. Jesus is showing them his persistent life in these actions, but he is also doing the very things needed to soothe their fear and empower them to live persistently in the wake of his execution. Jesus' resurrection appearances are filled with the stuff of Chaplain Levine's rounds in the wake of carceral trauma. He appears, and he is concerned with the everyday functions that make-up the work of healing in the wake. *Are you eating? Are you sleeping? How are your relationships?* Jesus' enduring presence with his disciples after his death is a miracle, but his enduring presence is also mundane in that his presence with them looks like what it looked like before he died.

Missing Mundane Miracles

Barth affirms the mundane nature of Jesus' resurrection appearances when he preaches an Easter Sermon at Basel Prison on March 29, 1964.[28] Though he does not know it at the time, it will be the last sermon he ever preaches at the prison. Shortly after this time, Barth will have a stroke, and his health will begin to fail until he dies four years later on December 10, 1968. The major theme of this sermon is the way that the resurrected Christ comes "into the midst" of his disciples and transforms their fear into joy by a simple "hello." Barth proclaims:

> He came into the midst of his disciples. He came, then, to the very spot which in the long hours since the evening of Good Friday they could only see as empty, where they could only see nothingness: only the memory of his blood-drenched body taken down from the cross, only his grave and with it only their own past errors and illusions, on the end of all things ... The most terrible thing had taken place: the other side had won. Jesus was definitely no longer there ...
>
> To them came the risen Jesus and stepped into their midst. Why? To make himself, in the midst of God's great mercy, the head of this forlorn

---

[28] Karl Barth, "When they Saw the Lord," in *Call for God: New Sermons from Basel Prison* (London: SCM Press, 1967), 117–25.

group, of these miserable and burdened, gloomy and frightened and cowardly men—the head of this thoroughly sick body. He did that in the simplest way imaginable: "Peace be with you", he said to them and that meant in the language of those days no less, though no more, than when nowadays a person goes up to some others and says: "Good evening (or good morning), everybody". In such a human way, so much just one of themselves, he stepped into their midst.[29]

Barth is using the resurrection text from John that I addressed above. He notices that in simply "saying hello" and coming to stand in their midst, Jesus transforms their fear into joy. Jesus steps into the wake of state execution, when the memories of a "blood-drenched body" have taken captive the minds of all who witnessed it, and he stands "in their midst" in the "simplest way imaginable ... in such a human way."[30] The resurrection is the miracle of persistent life appearing in the form of the mundane. Which is, perhaps, why the resurrected Christ is so often not recognized.

There are a few misrecognitions of the resurrected Christ recounted in the Gospels, but I would like to focus for a moment on John's account of Mary Magdalene failing to recognize Jesus when she first comes to the tomb. John has already told his reader that Mary had been the first one to come to the tomb early in the morning to find the stone rolled away (20:1). What she intended to be care for the body of a condemned man is mobilized into advocacy as she runs to find Simon Peter and the disciple that Jesus loved so that they can address what she assumes has been the theft of Jesus' body (20:2). Mary returns to the tomb with them, they confirm that the tomb is empty, the disciples leave, and Mary stays to weep for Jesus (20:3-11). From corpse care to advocacy to mobilizing a community to weeping, Mary is doing wake work. She is honoring the life of a person marked for state execution in the wake of his death. As she is mid wake work, she is visited by two angels and Jesus himself. She seems to have no fear. She answers their questions straightforwardly. But she does not recognize Jesus. When Jesus asks her why she is crying, the text tells us that she mistakes him for the gardener (ὁ κηπουρός), and she accuses him of having taken the body of Christ (20:15). In an act as simple as saying hello, Jesus says her name, and she sees him for who he truly is. The art of inhabiting the resurrection starts with wake work, but it then requires that one learn to see a survivor where one was taught to see a thief. That kind of transfigured seeing shatters the logic of the carceral. Once one learns to see this way, the carceral loses some of its hold, and all sorts of transfigurations—mundane miracles—become possible in the face of death. Chaplain Watson told me how this sort of transfigured seeing shaped one of her Easter Sundays in prison.

---

[29]Ibid., 120–1.
[30]Ibid., 121.

Chaplain Watson:

There was a young, there was a woman who the whole facility decided was what they call "a headcase" because she would stand up for herself, and say, "No that's not—you know, like if somebody was doing something she'd say—no that's not correct." Like, she would quote the law. And they hated that African American girl, well young woman.

And she had allergies, and she had to have bottled water because she couldn't drink the water. The water is disgusting in, in these facilities. Literally maggots come out of the faucets. How horrific is that? You have to run the water to get the maggots out before you put your toothbrush under it.

So anyway, she had to have bottled water, and they, they treated her like, "Oh you're so special." You know, like she became sort of persecuted by the whole facility, and I watched it happen, and then they …

put her in the hole and …

They beat her up.

I went to visit her on Easter, and she had a black eye. She'd been beaten. The back of her head was all bloody from hitting her head against the wall. And so I started advocating. You know, I went to the, to the watch commander, and anyway, I … I spent eight hours on Easter that year trying to get her water back because they were like, "No, she can't have it. She's in the hole."

I was like, "She's not going to drink anything else. She's gonna end up in the hospital. Is that what you want?"

You know …

So yeah, I was using my freedom and my privilege to try to help someone who was in trouble.[31]

I went to visit her on Easter, and she had a black eye. She'd been beaten … I spent eight hours on Easter that year trying to get her water back. Where some officers see a troublemaker, or a "headcase", Chaplain Watson sees a woman with allergies who relentlessly advocates for what is right

---

[31] Interview with the author on September 20, 2021.

even at risk to herself. Because Chaplain Watson has this transfigured understanding of the woman before her, she rejects the logic that this woman deserves the treatment that she is receiving. She spends eight hours on Easter advocating for bottled water. Chaplain Watson ultimately produces water where there was no water.

That she does this on Easter Sunday amplifies the sense that Chaplain Watson and the woman in lock-up are inhabiting the resurrection together. This story reads like an afterlife or echo of the first resurrection partially because of the day on which it happened. Chaplain Watson approaches this cell like Mary approaches the tomb. She expects to find the body of one who has been beaten by state officials. She finds that the woman, like Jesus, is wounded but alive. She re-members Christ's resurrection that year by advocating for water so that the life of one condemned person might persist in the wake of carceral violence. But the story could have happened on any day of the year and the materialization of water in a space in which it had been prohibited would be a participation in the miracle of persistent life. Chaplain Watson finds herself in the wake of carceral violence—the woman has been beaten up by others and has also slammed her own head against the wall—and Chaplain Watson produces the basic means for nourishing continued life when it had not been there before. She and the incarcerated woman with her inhabit the resurrection.

Chaplain Murray enacted a similar transfiguration. She told me the story about a time that her prison had an emergency evacuation due to encroaching wildfires. While she did not travel with the incarcerated women to their new facility, she told me about her role in getting people ready to leave on the day of the evacuation.

Chaplain Murray:

> We did have an evacuation last year, last fall or last summer. We had an evacuation. We evacuated the prison because of wildfires and sent everybody like four or five hours away. I did not go with them. I was on site when they made the announcement and had everybody pack up and had to get ready. And so I went to the units, and I helped communicate with them, you know what they could take, especially the mental health unit. And they said, "You can bring this, and you can bring this, but you can't bring this." And they were supposed to only take their hygiene. And I don't know, they would say, "Can I take my bed Bible?"

> And I had to say, "It sounds like hygiene to me!"

> "My radio?"

"I think that sounds like hygiene to me!"

So yeah ... so I helped on that.[32]

They would say, "Can I take my bed Bible?" And I had to say, "It sounds like hygiene to me!" Chaplain Murray does not call this a miracle. She does not say that she is transfiguring a prohibited item into an approved one or transforming a Bible into toothpaste. She does not claim to be the superhero from Chaplain Maverick's desk who can change a penny into a shoe. Rather, she says she is "helping," just as Chaplain Watson says she is "helping." But Chaplain Murray is seeing the needs and dignity of incarcerated women. She sees that in an evacuation, with a wildfire encroaching, women might need their Bibles and radios as much as their toothpaste and deodorant. Because she can see this way, the logic of the carceral and its regulations are no longer the limit to what is possible for her inside of prison. She speaks, and in her speaking, items that were prohibited are rendered items that are permissible. By naming Bibles and radios as the basic stuff of maintaining bodily life, i.e., hygiene, she expands the possibilities and avenues for life in the face of death. I ask again, is this really a miracle? Is this really an afterlife of Jesus, an echo of his persistent life, in prison? Is this basic act of speaking things into transfigured existence an inhabitation of the resurrection? I would answer, "yes."

In the last Easter sermon that Barth preached at Basel Prison about the simplicity and humanity of Jesus' resurrected life, Barth is clear that he expects his congregation to be able to see the resurrected Christ today. He closes that sermon with the following words:

> Dear friends, we were not there when the risen Jesus, in spite of all the folly and mourning of his disciples, in spite of these doors shut from sheer terror, came into their midst. We cannot see him now as directly as they could, nor shall we be able to see him like that until he comes to judge the living and the dead at the end of all time. But in our way, indirectly, that is in the mirror of the narrative and of the witnesses, the confession, the proclamation of the first community, we too can and may see him here and now ... Without seeing the Lord nobody can be glad. Whoever sees him will become glad. Why should this not happen here to us as well, to the little Easter congregation of prisoners in Basel's Spitalstrasse with their chaplain and their organist, with all the inmates and warders of this institution and (after all, I suppose I belong here too) with the old professor who occasionally pays a visit here? All of us can see the Lord too. So all of us may become glad too. God grant that this may happen to us. Amen.[33]

---

[32]Interview with the author on September 27, 2021.
[33]Barth, *Call for God,* 124.

Jesus is not just alive and accessible in the past. Barth makes clear that the persistent life of Jesus is accessible in prison today—to prisoners, a prison chaplain, officers, an organist, and himself as one who visits in prison. But accessing Jesus in prison means learning to see life where it is easier to see death.

Three years prior in 1961, Barth also preached the Easter Sermon at Basel Prison.[34] In that sermon, he makes the claim that there is nothing that happens on Easter that has not already happened on Good Friday. Rather, "what happened on Easter Day was the explanation, the revelation, of the mystery which took place earlier on Good Friday."[35] Easter is about learning to see God in godforsakeness or learning to see persistent life in carceral death. Barth proclaims:

> What happened on Easter day was nothing new: it was simply the flaring up of the light already lit in that darkness and at first shrouded by it; it was the uttering of the great Yes which God said to us there and of the great No which he said to our godforsakeness there, which became fact and reality there.
>
> And now we may celebrate Easter. What does it mean to celebrate Easter? It means to see this light of Good Friday. It is there, it is shining, it is waiting only for our eyes to see it. We may, we must, we want to open our eyes, to see it. To celebrate Easter means: to hear the Yes and the No which God has spoken in what he did on Good Friday: the Yes to all of us and the No to our estrangement from him.[36]

On the cross, Jesus Christ brings the fullness of his divine life into a site of godforsakeness and vacates carceral death as a site of estrangement from the divine. Easter is nothing new; it is simply a "flaring up" of Jesus' persistent life that he willingly placed in communion with human lives at their most forsaken. According to Barth, there is nothing to be seen in the resurrection that cannot already be seen in the crucifixion. Easter is about learning to see life in death. Or perhaps one might say Easter is about learning to see the miraculous in the mundane, a survivor where one was taught to see a thief, a hygienic necessity where one was taught to see a Bible, a water bottle where there was none. Easter is about learning to see persistent life in conditions of bare life. The resurrection is an unveiling of the persistent life that Jesus already brought into the midst of his execution. Inhabiting the resurrection is an invitation to live as if one sees the persistence of life in death.

---

[34] Karl Barth, "The Brief Moment," in *Call for God: New Sermons from Basel Prison* (London: SCM Press, 1967), 49.
[35] Ibid., 50.
[36] Ibid., 53–4.

Life in Death: Dreaming Resurrection When It Isn't There to See

I sat on the floor with that yard of butcher paper in front of me. Lists of people who had died ungrievable deaths and were still living unlivable lives covered the page in black sharpie. I do not know how long I sat in weary stillness before that page of black. I was staring at the words "Sgt. Wilson committed suicide on Memorial Day 2022," when I remembered his wife hugging me. It felt like a fact that should be on the paper, too. I grabbed a pink highlighter off my desk and wrote, "I told his wife what he meant to the unit. She broke and hugged me." I looked at the rest of the list. Slowly, under "LaTasha died of COVID," I wrote in pink, "first woman to hug me inside." I saw the words, "That dead 4yo girl, Cassie's," and I wrote, "our memorial service for her." I saw, "The woman who died of cancer with her unset broken arm," and I wrote in pink, "her smile through the ulcers when I visited her."

Pink highlighter is hard to read. By design, a highlighter is meant to illuminate; it is not a tool with which to write explanations. Even now, six months later, when I look at that piece of butcher paper, I must squint to see the specifics of the good news. The black sharpie still dominates the page. For a third of the horrors on the list, I could not come up with anything holy or redemptive to write in pink. Maybe this is a failure to see the resurrection on my part. Maybe I can not recognize persistent life in those situations—I can only see a thief where Jesus is standing—because I believe that carceral death has won. But maybe there is no pink marker on some parts of the page because in many of those situations, carceral death did win. Resurrection after death is possible, but it is not promised in this life. Chaplain Love never talked about "redemption" in prison, but she talked a lot about "redemptive possibility."

Persistent life does not vacate the truth that some are being made to live what Giorgio Agamben calls "bare life."[37] Bare life is life that is simply being sustained—life robbed of basic rights to family, free movement, and the pursuit of happiness. For Agamben, bare life does not just happen to occur; rather, Agamben notices how the state intentionally legislates some lives into bare, stark survival. Persistent life can be seen internal to bare life, but bare life is the mode of being legislated by the policies and procedures of prisons.[38] When one talks about inhabiting the resurrection in prison,

---

[37] Giorgio Agamben, *Homo Sacer: Sovereign Sower and Bare Life* (Stanford: Stanford University Press, 1998).

[38] Bülent Diken and Carsten Bagge Laustsen, "Zones of indistinction: Security, terror, and bare life," *Space and Culture* 5, no. 3 (2002): 290–307. See also Harry Blagg and Thalia Anthony, "'Stone Walls Do Not a Prison Make': Bare Life and the Carceral Archipelago in Colonial and Postcolonial Societies," in *Human Rights and Incarceration* (London: Palgrave Macmillan, 2018), 257–83; Karen M. Morin, "Carceral space: Prisoners and animals," *Antipode* 48, no. 5

one must not make the mistake of suggesting that it can always be done. To insist that the resurrection is always possible in conditions of bare life would be a refusal to take seriously the power of the state to legislate certain people to death. Which begs a final set of questions: How does the impossible, or at least the very rare, come into our daily lives? How do we inhabit something—the bodily resurrection of Jesus Christ—that stands beyond the possible as a regulation and a limit? Easter is not only about transfigured seeing and the transfigurations of material life that come from the ability to see life in death. Sometimes Easter is about seeing truthfully that death has won, and then seeing beyond what is to what might be.

Chaplain Harald was telling me about the impact of witnessing executions on his own mind and body. He described years of waking to nightmares in which he was trapped inside of prison. He told me how his family had encouraged him to go to a therapist and how he had found a trauma therapist who specialized in EMDR, Eye Movement Desensitization and Rerocessing.[39] He explained that this treatment had transformed his nightmares into dreams.

Chaplain Harald:

> I had to get honest. You can't pretend like this isn't having a horrendous impact on you. And so we're still in the process, after three years of working through every single man that I've lost to executions during this time. Going through it and dealing with it in EMDR. I don't know how it works. I have no idea how it works. As far as I know, nobody knows how it works. But the nightmares have stopped. The waking up screaming stopped. All my dreams, for twenty years, all my dreams were inside prison. I was inside prison sixty hours a week—that's what you were talking about, the toll on corrections people.
>
> Through the help of this therapist and her prayers and my wife's prayers and a whole lot of good people, I don't dream I'm in prison anymore.
>
> I do have a dream.
>
> I'm standing in front of the gates to these two maximum security prisons, and the gates open.
>
> *(He tears up.)*

(2016): 1317–36; Jacques Ranciere, "Who is the subject of the rights of man?," *South Atlantic Quarterly* 103, no. 2–3 (2004): 297–310.

[39]Deborah L. Korn, "EMDR and the treatment of complex PTSD: A review," *Journal of EMDR Practice and Research* 3, no. 4 (2009): 264–78.

And all the people I care about,

come out …

(Crying)

walk out.

I guess for me, that's, at this point, my vision of heaven.[40]

I'm standing in front of the gates to these two maximum security prisons, and the gates open. And all the people I care about, come out … walk out. I guess for me, that's, at this point, my vision of heaven. In the resurrection, Jesus Christ is freed from carceral death and released into life after prison. We are not guaranteed that resurrection—life after carceral death or freedom from state-custody—but because Jesus has revealed that such life and freedom are God's ultimate intention for the cosmos, we can dream the resurrection even when we cannot enact it. Dreams make all the difference for the life one lives when awake. When Chaplain Harald was dreaming the reality of what he experienced each day on death row, he experienced heart palpitations, sleep disruption, exhaustion, and all of the mind and body impacts that come with those conditions. He walked into prison each day having dreamt prison as the ultimate reality. His behavior in prison was governed by that belief. When Chaplain Harald worked in prayer, through therapy, with the support of his family to heal from the hell of prison, he was freed to dream the release of all the men he loves. Chaplain Harald now walks into prison believing that the prison's way of being is not the end of the story. Because he can dream freedom, he can live abundantly in the confines of the carceral. Because he can imagine release from prison for people condemned to death, he can begin to work toward that even when there are no signs of sentence commutation or abolition on the immediate horizon. In dreaming resurrected life, Chaplain Harald experiences the mundane miracle of his own physical healing, *and* he is gifted an imagination to begin working toward that freedom for other people here and now. People being freed from the two prisons in which he works is his "vision of heaven."

When a chaplain believes in the resurrection vision that all people might follow Christ Jesus out of carceral death and be released into life on the other side of prison, the chaplain carrying that vision will not stop working in prisons, even though each day in prison will stand in stark contrast to the vision granted by the resurrection. In an ethnography of sixteen prisons in northern England, David Scott found, "that those chaplains who most

---

[40]Interview with the author on May 6, 2021.

strongly felt prisons were immoral and counter-productive places were also those who held the strongest humanitarian commitment to do what they could on the ground to ease or mitigate the inherent degradations of imprisonment."[41] When chaplains understand themselves to be inhabiting the story of Christ, they must live between the resurrection dream of freedom from carceral death and the reality that Jesus was able to offer the fullness of that vision only because he refused to get himself out of prison, even to the point of execution. Inhabiting Christ means doggedly and consistently bringing one's persistent life into sites of carceral death in the sure knowledge that those sites stand in direct contradiction to God's work and way of being in the world.

A few of the chaplains in this study described the tension of wanting to leave prison but not feeling released by God to do so as "being denied parole." When Chaplain King used this metaphor with me, he was explaining how his family, friends, and community often encourage him to leave prison. They can see the toll that it takes on him. They know that he could be better compensated elsewhere. Chaplain King responds to these concerns by saying, "I don't really think they know who they're talking to, because I'm following the Holy Spirit! And every year I go up for parole, and the Father, Son, and Holy Spirit deny my parole." The other chaplains who used this metaphor left it at that, but Chaplain King launched into a litany of why he stays in prison doing the work of chaplaincy. Chaplain King can see the toll the job takes on himself as well. He described receiving other job offers and turning them down. As he described this, I felt like I had suddenly jumped to the high point of a sermon with my desk chair turned into a pew and my computer screen turned into his pulpit. I offer Chaplain King's blessing to me as a benediction for you.

Chaplain King:

> I don't really think they know who they're talking to because I'm following the Holy Spirit!
>
> And every year I go up for parole, and the Father, Son, and Holy Spirit deny my parole.
>
> I'm a chaplain, Sarah, because God sent me.
>
> > (*Crying*)

---

[41]David Scott, "Walking Amongst the Graves of the Living: Reflections about Doing Prison Research from an Abolitionist Perspective," in *The Palgrave Handbook of Prison Ethnography*, ed. Deborah H. Drake, Rod Earle, and Jennifer Sloan (New York: Palgrave Macmillan, 2015), 44.

That's the only answer I can give you.

    (Places his head in his hand.)

That's all I can say.

He sent me,
and I can't leave until he tells me to leave.
I feel like there's too much at stake, too many lives, too many destinies.
There are too many men that I've had the privilege to meet.
I've been blessed by their presence—the Christians and non-Christians.
I mean, they've all blessed me.
The staff, they've all ... I've grown up in prison.

    (Laughs)

Sarah Jobe:

Amen.

Chaplain King:

I didn't mean to get emotional.
But, but this is emotional, because to me, this is more than just a job.

Now there are parts of the job that they have to pay me to do.

But, but to tell a man that his,
that his baby died?
You can't pay me to do that.

You know, there are no words that I can even say.

You know, to see a man fall out of his chair when you tell him his wife has died,
to see a man who had life receive compassionate release,
and they call you on the phone ...

    (Crying)

to say thank you.

To have the inmate tell you, "Hey Chaplain, my family is coming in tomorrow.

    (Crying)

Can you stop by visitation and meet them?"

(*More tears ...*)

They're taking time out of their visit with their family

to introduce me?

(*Shaking his head*)

Who am I?

To have a staff member say,
"Chaplain, I would like to you to officiate my wedding."

To have the warden come by and say,
"Chaplain, can you pray for me?"

And then when the warden leaves your office, and you, you're walking on with them,
And an officer comes over after the warden has left,
and he says, "Chaplain, I can't stand that man."

But, but that's why you're in the middle.

You don't know that this man—I don't tell them this, but—this man has asked me to pray that God would give him wisdom to help you, to lead people like you,
but yet you can't stand him?

And so I can't take sides here.

I respond and say,
"Well, I see a different side."

You know,
I see something different,

you know ...
that,
that's why I'm still there.

So the day you hear me leaving is the day you know that I've heard from the Lord. I mean *really* heard from the Lord because I believe I'm there on divine assignment. And to be there *with* and to learn *from* other colleagues, you know, the good and the bad, you know. To be a part of this great legacy of chaplaincy.

That's why we need to write about it, Sarah. We need to write about it. So much has been written about local pastors and that's wonderful. But we need to let the world know, we need to let the church know, that there's a ministry behind the walls. There's no lights. There's no camera. There's no Facebook live, no YouTube, you know, all that stuff that glitters. And sometimes I like that. I want that, to be honest with you.

Nobody knows what we're doing …

But God does.

The men and women whose lives we're impacting, they remember.

So you continue to be faithful where you are. God has got his hand on you.

Sarah Jobe:

I appreciate that word. I appreciate that word.

I think that image is going to stick with me—to come up for parole every year …

    (*Laughing*)

And you are denied!

    (*Both laughing*)

Father, Son *and* Holy Spirit deny you every year!

    (*More laughter*)

I can relate to that …. I can relate to that.[42]

---

[42] Interview with the author on January 15, 2021.

Postlude

A Practical Soteriology: Penal Atonement in Prison

I don't think they killed Jesus for being a good guy. You know, I think he pissed off the powers that be. And I don't necessarily believe that for God to love me he had to kill off his only Son. I don't get that. And I don't believe that people are going to be eternally punished. If there's anything that anybody can do to deserve grace, it is no longer grace and mercy.
—CHAPLAIN FLOATING, INTERVIEW ON APRIL 7, 2021

My friend Lauren is an Episcopal priest. For part of each year, after she consecrates the Eucharist, she holds up the body and blood of Jesus Christ and invites the congregation to come forward with the words of Saint Augustine, "Behold what you are. Become what you receive."[1] It is a weird invitation. The Eucharist remembers Jesus specifically as his body is broken in his execution. Embedded within the ritual is a remembrance of the truth that Jesus was a convicted person, executed by the state. "Behold what you are. Become what you receive," she says.

The ritual itself is wake work, an attempt each week to re-member a community in the shattering wake of God's carceral death. But the invitation is not to re-member the body by escaping the realities of prison; rather, the invitation is to "become what you receive." Saint Claire of Assisi says it

---

[1] This Eucharistic invitation is adapted from St. Augustine's Sermon 272 in which he says, "When you received the fire of the Holy Spirit, it's as though you were baked. Be what you can see, and receive what you are." John E. Rotelle, *The Works of Saint Augustine*, Sermons, Part 3, Vol. 7, trans. Edmund Hill, O.P. (Hyde Park: New City Press, 1993), 300–1.

similarly to Saint Augustine and to Vicar Lauren. She says, "We become what we love, and who we love shapes what we become."[2] Out of love for us, Jesus takes on our flesh, but out of love for Jesus, we embody his life, execution, and release from carceral death. We become like the one we love. We inhabit salvation.

When Dominique DuBois Gilliard tries to describe the work of prison chaplaincy, he uses the testimony of a man he calls Dickie who was incarcerated for sixteen years in the Indiana State Prison. When Dickie tries to describe his prison chaplain Father Dave, he says, "One thing I can say: Father Dave *is* what most Christians talk about being. For me personally, Father Dave has been salvation—not the eternal life salvation, but the everyday salvation that most of us need in here."[3] The language is striking. Father Dave does not *offer* salvation or *preach* salvation; rather, Father Dave *is* salvation, the kind of "everyday salvation" that one needs in prison. Father Dave embodies salvation as he goes in and out of prison, drawing near to sites of carceral death and the people most impacted by them, just as Jesus did in his own enactment of the salvation of the world. Father Dave inhabits the salvation that Jesus enacted.

As I have said before, chaplains do not claim to be Christ-like themselves. They do not claim to be embodying salvation. Rather, they claim to be participating in God's pre-existent work in prisons. Chaplain Harald explains, "This isn't my show. This isn't my circus. This is God's show. He's allowing me to participate, to help Him. But that doesn't make it my show, and every single person that walks in my path, He loves them as much as He loves me."[4] Chaplain Armstrong puts it even more starkly: "I really have to remind myself that I'm not the be all, do all, end all. I am not the Savior, and anybody can walk in here and do this job. Well, not really, *(laughs)* but a lot of people. I'm replaceable."[5] Chaplains are participating in a work that God has already enacted in its fullness in Jesus Christ, but as we saw with the witness of the two men being executed alongside Jesus, salvation has always had embedded in its architecture the participation of human beings who come alongside Jesus and one another to bear witness through their own presence to the truth that there is no Godforsaken place, no Godforsaken person. Chaplain Armstrong *is not* the Savior, but Father Dave *is* salvation, everyday salvation, the kind of salvation one needs in prison.

In this book, I have tried to describe what it looks like to inhabit salvation as one embodies the witness of Jesus' incarnation, his prophetic work of reconciliation, his willingness to be made sin for the sake of salvation, his drawing so close to carceral death that he is executed himself, and his

---

[2]Shannon O'Donnell, *Finding Grace Within* (Tacoma: Pilgrim Spirit Communications, 2018), ix.
[3]Gilliard, *Rethinking Incarceration*, 120.
[4]Interview with the author on May 6, 2021.
[5]Interview with the author on July 9, 2021.

persistent life and release from prison in the resurrection. I have described what it looks like to embody this arc of salvation in the daily work of prison chaplaincy. I want to close with a few suggestions for how embodying salvation in prison might change soteriology, i.e., salvation-talk, or the ways in which we speak about and describe how and why God's arrest, trial, guilty verdict, execution, and release is efficacious for any given person or for the cosmic order at large. What kind of soteriology is produced by living and dying with Jesus in prison?

Penal Atonement: Is the Good News Better than That?

Whether one espouses penal substitutionary atonement or not, there is a long Christian tradition stemming from the biblical texts themselves of speaking about salvation in juridical terms. Some of the chaplains in this study joined scholars like Jennifer Graber, Douglas Campbell, and Andrew Skotnicki in noticing that narrating salvation as a cosmic court scene often seems to have the effect of upholding the status quo of prisons.[6] Chaplain Moses went into detail about the ways that he sees penal atonement theories dovetailing with the shaming of and shameful treatment of incarcerated people. Each year he is invited to speak for one hour at a mandatory training for officers. After serving eleven years at his prison, he felt that he had built up enough relational capital to use his hour to "challenge the mindset that is within our prison system and the culture of our staff." In the passage below, he describes to me what he has learned about what might need changing in the practices of prisons and how that is related to what might need changing in Christian soteriology.

Chaplain Moses:

> I really do believe we are here to help hold these guys accountable. I support accountability. What I'm here to challenge us on is this: we aren't doing ourselves or the inmates any favors if we think shame is the best way to hold these guys accountable. Eventually, these guys are going to be released. Eventually, they will come into our neighborhoods, our communities. And if we really, you know, care about them as humans and care about the impact they're going to have on our culture, on our communities, in our society, once they get released, we should

---

[6]Douglas A. Campbell, "Mass incarceration: Pauline problems and Pauline solutions," *Interpretation* 72, no. 3 (2018): 282–92; Graber, *The Furnace of Affliction*; Andrew Skotnicki, *Conversion and the Rehabilitation of the Penal System: A Theological Rereading of Criminal Justice* (Oxford: Oxford University Press, 2019).

want to do the best we can with them while we have them in our care here at the prison.

And, you know, treating them and reminding them that they're pieces of crap isn't going to work for them or us in the long run. And so trying to find a creative, fun, non-shaming way to remind our staff of that ... to, in essence, hold *them* accountable as fellow human beings. These guys that are in our care are our fellow human beings, created in the divine image. We don't have to agree with them. We don't have to support anything they've ever done, but never should we diminish their value as a fellow human being. It is our responsibility to hold them accountable to be the best human being that they can be.

We aren't doing ourselves or the inmates any favors if we think shame is the best way to hold these guys accountable. Chaplain Moses is noticing the way that shaming practices disempower change in individuals, both staff and residents alike. He is also noticing the way that socially accepted practices of shaming—like those baked into America's prison system—run counter to a belief that all people are made in the image of God. As the interview went on, Chaplain Moses made even more explicit his concern that American penal practices too closely parallel narrations of Christian salvation as a court scene.

Chaplain Moses:

The other somewhat related issue—and this goes along with some of my personal faith convictions and the progression of it in recent years—but kind of growing up with a very strong theological emphasis on original sin and substitutionary atonement, kind of, you know:

You're born sinful. You got all this sin. You're bad, bad, bad, and you need God to forgive you of your sin so that you can actually have a relationship with God. And God paid the penalty for your sin on the cross, and so, you know that whole story. And while I see and understand that tradition and where that comes from in the Scriptures and why people were drawn to it, I've come to believe that there are other ways of looking at the Jesus story. And that I feel like the kind of original sin perspective really does so easily get entangled with the shame approach.

You know, we're all just originally sinful pieces of crap, so to speak. Well, then sure, then I can treat these inmates like piece of crap, and I can remind them that they're pieces of crap because it kind of ties in with our mindset of original sin. And they haven't found Jesus, and so therefore that's my justification for shaming them and treating them like that, you know, anyway ...

Am I saying that sin is not a reality? By no means. We all have brokenness in our lives. But is there maybe a better story in that? Focusing more on original blessing and less on original sin, and calling people out to live into their original blessing and spend less energy on reminding them of their original sin?

And so trying to think of what that looks like in combination with what seems to be a very westernized view of atonement and focusing only on this penal substitution. You got to pay the penalty for you. And one of the podcasts pointed out how ironically, that is so intertwined with our prison system. We even got the name "penitentiary" from paying penance for your sins. I mean, it's that ingrained! It's even in the root name of our system! And so it's kind of like these inmates kind of gravitate toward the fact that, you know, yeah, I am a piece of crap, and the only way I could ever get right with God is to have him you know sacrifice to make it right. All that stuff ties in so well to the prison culture mindset of what they've experienced in our judicial system and everything about it.

You know, I remember as a kid going to some drama where they, you know, God was the judge with the gavel and the big black robe. And, you know, the kid that had done the drugs was over here on the witness stand, and he was being accused of this and that. And the only way he can get off was, you know, was if the Judge's son died. And you have all this kind of intertwined theological Jesus stuff that was super connected with the judicial law, with the justice system. And so what does that say about our judicial system as well as our faith perspective? And then what does it mean for our view of Christianity and how do inmates respond to the gospel? That's all kind of intertwined.

If my goal is to bring gospel truth into the prison environment and shine some light, I'm asking myself the question, "Is the Gospel, is the Good News, better than that?"

Is what we have given them—the church in terms of the judicial system—is that really the gospel? Or is the gospel better than that? And if so, what can we do to create a better gospel for these guys?[7]

God is a judge, and the only way for a kid accused of using drugs to be forgiven is for the judge's son to die. *Is that really the Gospel? Or is*

---

[7]Interview with the author on January 23, 2021.

the Gospel better than that? Chaplain Moses notices that how Christians sometimes tell the Gospel story looks like what routinely happens to people in courts and prisons today. The criminal justice system has not been good news to those confined and controlled in prisons, nor has it been good news to those who work in prisons. Chaplain Moses rightly wonders, is this the best way to tell the Jesus story?

As I explored in Chapter 3, when narrating salvation as a court scene, Barth draws his readers' attention to the fact that the Father is not the Judge in his reading of the Gospels. Jesus is both the Judge and the judged one. Jesus judges us not in a court, but with the example his life and the words of his teachings. He then steps down in a radical act of solidarity to crowd us out of the places at which we are being judged. If there is a substitution in this penal atonement, substitution is Jesus coming to stand with humans where they are standing. As Jesus draws precisely into those spaces where humans are being judged and crushed by the harms they have done and the harms done to them, Jesus is not judged by God in their place in some cosmic exchange. Rather, Jesus is judged in a regular Roman judicial hearing, just like those he comes to stand beside are being judged in regular criminal justice systems and other human modes of judging one another. This atonement or reconciliation happens inside a penal drama, but the "substitution" of penal substitutionary atonement is troubled. When one inhabits Jesus' story in prison, one finds that Jesus is *dying with* as much as, or more than, he is *dying for* human beings. Jesus is willing to risk death to come radically near to those being most impacted by systems of death. Jesus "takes our place," but not in a substitution so much as a coming alongside. In bringing his persistent divine life into carceral death—i.e., the deaths we deal out to one another and call just—Jesus stands against the lie that those being subjected to carceral death are godforsaken or irredeemable. There never was an irredeemable person or irredeemable situation, and by stepping into carceral death with the fullness of his own holiness, Jesus has forever unmasked and vacated this condemning logic. I want to name three implications of understanding salvation to be about *living and dying with* rather than *dying for:* one pastoral, one ethical, and one theological.

A Pastoral Implication of Living and Dying with Jesus in Prison: Salvation-Talk Impacts One's Ability to Receive God's Persistent Life-in-Death

The way that we talk about God's work in the world makes a difference for people's ability to live in the face of horror. Soteriology—salvation talk— impacts whether or not any given person can receive the possibility of inhabiting life-in-the-face-of death. Human talk about how Jesus saves does not impact *that* Jesus saves, but it does impact *the degree to which* salvation is made real and efficacious in any given person's life. The chaplains in this study expect people's theology to do good work for them. They challenge theologies when those theologies are keeping people from God's nourishing and sustaining presence. Chaplain Murray told me a very concrete story about how shifts in theology made a practical difference for one woman in her prison.

Chaplain Murray:

> Once I was talking with a woman, and she had a serious history of self-harm and suicide attempts. And she was going through a particular struggle at the time and, I said, "So how does God fit in this for you?"
>
> And she said, "God is standing over there, pointing at me and laughing."
>
> And I said, "That's horrible. I don't like that God at all." And I said, "So, what if, what would it take to get God to be more supportive of you?"
>
> And so we had a conversation about that, and I had her do something—I can't remember exactly what it was—but she put something on a piece of paper and carried it with her in her pocket, and it was like she was carrying God in her pocket. And then she thought about what that was like for the next week—to carry God around in your pocket and see if anything's different.
>
> And then she came back the next week, and we talked about it. And it was different. Her experience of God had shifted, just a little bit, you know. She was like, "Yeah, I guess he's, he's not really pointing at me. He, you know, maybe, like maybe, he is maybe trying to help me out, and I'm just not letting him."[8]

He's not really pointing at me ... maybe, like maybe, he is maybe trying to help me out. Without saying it explicitly, Chaplain Murray has helped this woman move from an understanding of God as Judge, pointing a finger at her, to an understanding of God as *with her*, as near to her as her pocket. When her conception of who God is changes, she can imagine that God might be trying to help her. She is able to name that she is sometimes standing in her own way, and she is empowered to make personal changes that might let God's help materialize in her life. The debilitating shame that Chaplain Moses talked about above is lightened (God is no longer pointing at her), and the removal of shame opens the way for responsible action.[9] One of

---

[8] Interview with the author on September 27, 2021.
[9] For more on the way that feelings of shame can impede responsible moral agency, see Peter Shabad, "Owing and being owed: Shame and responsibility toward the other," *Psychoanalytic Dialogues* 32, no. 4 (2022): 389–404; Mickie L. Fisher and Julie J. Exline, "Moving toward self-forgiveness: Removing barriers related to shame, guilt, and regret," *Social and Personality Psychology Compass* 4, no. 8 (2010): 548–58.

the things that inhabiting salvation in prison teaches us is that soteriology matters in how we care for one another and in how we live. How we talk about salvation can become a help or a hindrance to the actualization of God's persistent life in any one person's life in the face of death. The Jesus story has not changed for Chaplain Murray or this woman, but how the Jesus story is understood and talked about has changed, and that change in God-imagery and God-talk has given one person a path back into the presence of God.

An Ethical Implication of Living and Dying with Jesus in Prison: Re-embedding Christ in His Carceral Context Impacts How We Treat Incarcerated People

The only incarnate God is an incarcerated one. Incarcerated people have a special intimacy with Jesus in having experienced what he experienced. This shared experience gives people who have stood before a judge, been found guilty, been sentenced (particularly sentenced to death), and been freed into new life after prison prized insight into the Jesus story, its interpretation, and its implications for today. Incarcerated people can offer this charism to the church at large, deepening Christian theology and correcting theologies when they have gotten off course through inattention to the original carceral context of Christ.

I first learned this truth on Good Friday 2016. We had spent Lent planning a Stations of the Cross Service at my prison. Individual women had volunteered to each take a moment from Jesus' passion with which they felt particular intimacy because they had endured a similar experience. Each woman worked for weeks on how to tell the congregation about Jesus' experience by using her own experience as an entry way. On the evening of Good Friday, Mandi stood up in the prison chapel and told the story of exiting a Starbuck's and being surrounded by men with guns and helmets shouting at her to get on the ground. She dropped her coffee as she was pushed face down and handcuffed. She wondered if Jesus had been as scared as she was when he was arrested. As she sat down, the whole congregation clapped and cheered for her.

We brought forward a banner depicting Jesus before a judge. Ms. Barbara stood and shared about being in court when she received her death sentence. She said the biggest difference between her and Jesus was that she *had* taken her husband's life, whereas Jesus had no blood on his hands. But like Jesus, she had been as silent as a sheep led to slaughter; no one in the courtroom knew the circumstances of what she had been through leading up to her act of self-defense because her lawyer had advised that sharing those details would have made a positive trial outcome less likely. Barbara told us how she, like Jesus, stood quiet as she was condemned to death. As she went back to her seat, the congregation rose to their feet clapping for her. Women shook their heads. "That ain't right," they said. "You've got this," and, "God's got you," filled the sanctuary.

The drama went on. A banner depicting Jesus would be marched forward, and a woman would share her story. "Jesus was stripped," Kaye said, "Stand up if you've been stripped like him this week!" I was one of very few people to remain seated. One thing that astonished me about the service was that the power in the room seemed to build with every station. I had never been at a Good Friday Service in which there was clapping and cheering. We were not watching the drama of a sacrificial victim; they were telling the story of a God who knew exactly what they had been through, and they knew what He had been through, too.

No one in the room had been executed, so early in Lent they had decided that I would stand, as the chaplain, and say a word about Jesus' death for that station. I stood up for my turn, and none of my words fit. "Jesus died so that you don't have to." I looked at the faces of women who had received death sentences, and the phrase did not feel true. "Jesus died for you," felt equally incongruent. The words stuck in my throat. Jesus did not take anyone's place here. Everyone in that congregation still had to stand at the bar and receive their sentence. Everyone there was still being cuffed and stripped each week. Jesus had not taken their place, but Jesus was one of them. Jesus was with them. Jesus was in that prison. They had each just testified to it. Each of them was a living icon of the Executed God. I did not know how to say it at the time, but I could see it. One modest proposal for how to treat people—inside of prisons and within our churches once they are released—would be to treat them as we would hope to treat Jesus, if he were, again, in their position.

Inhabiting Christ's salvation in prison does not only change how individual incarcerated people should be treated, it changes the Christian understanding of the criminal justice system at a systemic level. Politically, the idea that when Jesus as God took on flesh, he was arrested, tried, sentenced, and executed is an indictment of the criminal justice system rather than an affirmation of it. If a system that is supposedly designed for justice can find God guilty, it can find anyone guilty. If a system can kill God, it can and will kill anyone. Jesus unmasks the lie that systems designed for confinement and control—systems that start with Gethsemane and end in Golgotha—are a way to right the wrongs that we do to one another. As Jesus unmasks the lie that criminal justice systems right wrongs, he simultaneously displays another way toward reconciliation: bringing together divisions within his own body and within the communities that he calls together, both with great joy and at great cost to himself. True reconciliation is achieved when we are willing to link up our lives so closely with those we understand to be damned, irredeemable, and untouchable that we become impacted by and implicated in the very systems that create conditions of damnation. As I said in Chapter 1, salvation is enacted, made efficacious, and materialized when one is willing to hold God's Yes and God's No together in one's body and journey to the same sites of social abandonment to which Jesus journeyed until one is so impacted by death that one needs the salvation one enacts.

A Theological Implication of Living and Dying with Jesus in Prison: The Closer One Draws to Horror, the More Radical Grace Becomes

On August 1, 1955, just one year into his ministry at Basel Prison, Barth wrote a letter to Chaplain Martin Schwartz telling him about his pastoral encounter with "P." Barth wrote:

> So yesterday, Sunday morning, I went straight to P. Perhaps I met him at a particularly good hour: in any case, he greeted me with obviously sincere joy, then immediately began, not without demonstrating his knowledge of the Bible, to talk about the Lord's Supper, and then went into an extensive report, sustained by strong emotions, about the story of his life up to that shooting, and beyond that, about his experiences with X, but at the end he became really cheerful again, so that I actually did not recognize the man who acted so despairingly on Easter morning, although he explicitly came back to that incident. Maybe I actually have become something like an optimist or even a walking representation of the false doctrine of the *apokatastasis panton*, so that I have not yet been able to leave any of these men simply shaking my head and saddened, but rather I have thought that I have seen something in each of them that has encouraged and gladdened me. Am I listening to too much Mozart? But Mozart was not an optimist. Oh well, these are probably useless reflections![10]

Barth had preached the Easter Sermon at Basel Prison the same year he writes this note, and he references meeting P on Easter Sunday when P was *verzweifelt*—desperate, despairing, frustrated, or frantic.[11] Barth notes that P's demeanor had changed so radically by the August visit that Barth hardly recognized him as the same man. Barth tells Chaplain Schwarz that P shared his life story up to the point of the "shooting," *Erschießung*, i.e., a shooting that ends in death. And Barth reports that in seeing P's transformation and hearing P's story, including the way that P took the life of another person, Barth has become *eine wandelnde Darstellung*, a walking representation, of the false doctrine of *apokatastasis panton,* the restoration of all things.[12] *I have not yet been able to leave any of these men simply shaking my head*

---

[10]Schwartz, "Karl Barth in the Penitentiary," trans. Joseph Longarino.
[11]Schwartz, "Karl Barth in der Strafanstalt," 212.
[12]Ibid., 212.

and saddened, but rather I have thought that I have seen something in each of them that has encouraged and gladdened me.

The phrase *apokatastasis panton* is taken from Acts 3:21. Peter and John have healed a lame man begging at the entrance to the temple. When people start to notice the miracle, Peter asks them why they are staring, as if the healing was done by their own power (3:12). Rather, they have healed by the power of Jesus Christ, who the "God of Abraham, Isaac, and Jacob, the God of our fathers, has glorified" (3:13). Peter launches into something of a sermon, saying that even though Jesus was handed over to Pilate to be killed, Jesus, the ἀρχηγὸν τῆς ζωῆς, leader or author of life, was raised by God from the dead (3:15). It is this power of persistent life by which they now heal others. Peter says that he was an eyewitness of this power for life in Jesus' execution and resurrection. He then moves beyond what he has witnessed to make sense of the Jesus story for his listeners. Peter commands them to turn toward God so that their sins might be "smeared out," ἐξαλειφθῆναι, the same verb used in Col. 2:14 as discussed in Chapter 5 (3:19). Jesus, the one who smears out charges, will one day be sent back again, as has been appointed to do. Currently, Peter says, Jesus remains in heaven awaiting the time that God will restore everything, ἀποκαταστάσεως πάντων, just as God promised through Moses and the prophets (3:21-22). When the priests, Sadducees, and the captain of the Temple Guard hear Peter teaching that Jesus was raised from the dead after his execution, they throw Peter and John in jail. It is the first of at least three times that Peter will be arrested in the Book of Acts.[13]

Nestled between the giving of the Holy Spirit (the Paraclete, Advocate, or Lawyer) and the first of numerous arrests, imprisonments, and executions of the apostles, is the statement that we are waiting for a promised restoration of all things. The phrase, *apokatastasis panton,* has taken on meaning well beyond this biblical text and has become shorthand for a doctrine of universalism or universal salvation. Barth calls it a "false doctrine" in this letter because in 553 CE, *apokatstasis* was listed as "anathema" or condemned by the Fifth Ecumenical Council.[14] While the condemnation probably had more to do with a point about the pre-existence of souls, it has left a legacy of contention internal to the Christian tradition about whether only some people will be saved, whether all people will be saved, or even more broadly, whether all of creation in its totality will be restored

---

[13]Acts 3:11-4:4; 5:17-20; 12:1-19.

[14]Ilaria Ramelli, *The Christian Doctrine of Apokatastasis: A Critical Assessment from the New Testament to Eriugena* (Leiden: Brill, 2013). For a shorter treatment, see Ilaria Ramelli, "Christian soteriology and Christian platonism: Origen, Gregory of Nyssa, and the biblical and philosophical basis of the doctrine of apokatastasis," *Vigiliae Christianae* 61, no. 3 (2007): 313–56.

and redeemed. Barth is often counted among those who believe that Jesus' work saves all.[15]

Four years after sending the letter telling Chaplain Schwartz that the men at Basel Prison were turning him into a "walking representation" of the restoration of all things, Barth writes explicitly about the doctrine of *apokatastasis* at the end of *Church Dogmatics* IV/3.1. This is one of the volumes in The Doctrine of Reconciliation, the primary doctrine that I have treated in this book, and it is the first volume of *Church Dogmatics* that he writes after having begun prison ministry. His treatment of *apokatastasis* occurs in the last two paragraphs of the volume. In closing his account of the reconciling work of Christ, Barth asks whether or not, in the end, we can "count upon it ... that the sick man and even the sick Christian will not die and be lost rather than be raised and delivered from the dead and live?"[16] Barth makes two major points: one taken to be a warning against *apokatastasis* and one to be an endorsement of it.

First, Barth says that to assume a guaranteed reconciliation of all things is to refuse to take seriously the power of evil and our own participation in it. When we assume that God must redeem us, we have failed to see both the depth of our own participation in the horrors of this world and the radical nature of the free gift of God's grace in response. We do not deserve restoration, and we cannot presume it. But then Barth says this:

> There is no good reason why we should forbid ourselves, or be forbidden, openness to the possibility that in the reality of God and man in Jesus Christ there is contained much more than we might expect and therefore the supremely unexpected withdrawal of that final threat, i.e., that in the truth of this reality there might be contained the super-abundant promise of the final deliverance of all men. To be more explicit, there is no good reason why we should not be open to this possibility. If for a moment we accept the unfalsified truth of the reality which even now so forcibly limits the perverted human situation, does it not point plainly in the direction of the work of a truly eternal divine patience and deliverance and therefore of an *apokatastasis* or universal reconciliation? If we are certainly forbidden to count on this as though we had a claim to it, as

---

[15] I will not, in these few paragraphs, attempt to treat the long-standing debates about Barth's universalism. I will simply note here that, to my reading, those treatments do not address this letter from Barth to Schwartz about the carceral context of his growing affinity for *apokatastasis*. If anything, my work simply adds the letter from Barth to Schwartz on August 1, 1955, to the texts under consideration on this topic. For a way into the Barth and universalism debates, see Shao Kai Tseng, "Condemnation and universal salvation: Karl Barth's 'reverent agnosticism' revisited," *Scottish Journal of Theology* 71, no. 3 (2018): 324–38; Mark Koonz, "The old question of Barth's universalism: An examination with reference to Tom Greggs and TF Torrance," *Theology in Scotland* 18, no. 2 (2011).
[16] Barth, CD IV/3.1, 477.

though it were not supremely the work of God to which man can have no possible claim, we are surely commanded the more definitely to hope and pray for it, as we may do already on this side of this final possibility.[17]

As a people who have already followed Jesus in practicing the "impossible possibility" of Christian ministry in the hells of this world, we might expect the impossible possibility that God will exercise God's freedom to redeem all things. We might "expect ... the supremely unexpected." And if we are "forbidden to count on" the restoration of all things, we are even more strongly commanded "to hope and pray for it." This is what Barth writes about universal salvation after his experience in prison.

Going to prison teaches one to take seriously the radical horrors of this world. Staying in prison teaches one to take even more seriously the boundlessness of God's redemption in the face of those horrors. As I named before, Chaplain Love calls prison the place where she has learned to see the "redemptive possibility" of being "present to people in crisis."[18] Redemption in prison is not guaranteed, but it is always possible. And if horror has no limits, then grace is the limitless limit always pressing back against it. Barth names that in seeing the transformation of one man convicted of murder, he learns to see redemptive possibility in every person he meets. But I think the belief in redemptive possibility goes even deeper than that for many of the chaplains in this study, perhaps for Barth, and certainly for me. *Apokatastasis panton* is not simply the redemption of all people, but the redemption of *all*—all people, all things, all systems—*all* must be saved. If one commits to live and die with Jesus in prison, one might find oneself living an *apokatstasis* born out of the despairing and hard-won knowledge that the whole system needs saving; no one person's full restoration can be actualized inside prison until the whole godforsaken mess is vacated. When it comes to the restoration of all things, Barth and Chaplain Love cannot guarantee it. But as they follow Jesus in and out of carceral death, they hope for that restoration. They pray for it. And they become "walking representations" of it. Living and dying with Jesus in prison invites one beyond the small but sure knowledge that some will be saved into a wild and profligate belief in the redemptive possibility that all creation—every horror, prodigal child, judging or judged one, and person or place exposed to carceral death—will be restored by the God who has brought that horror into the holiness of God's own flesh.

---

[17]Ibid., 477–8.
[18]Interview with the author on March 12, 2021.

WORKS CITED

Adams, Kevin. "Defining and operationalizing chaplain presence: A review." *Journal of Religion and Health* 58, no. 4 (2019): 1246–58.
Agamben, Giorgio. *Homo Sacer: Sovereign Sower and Bare Life*. Stanford: Stanford University Press, 1998.
Alexander, Michelle. *The New Jim Crow: Mass Incarceration in the Age of Colorblindness*. New York: The New Press, 2010.
Armstrong, Gaylene S., and Marie L. Griffin. "Does the job matter? Comparing correlates of stress among treatment and correctional staff in prisons." *Journal of Criminal Justice* 32, no. 6 (2004): 577–92.
Ayete-Nyampong, Lilian. "Changing Hats: Transitioning between Practitioner and Researcher Roles." In *The Palgrave Handbook of Prison Ethnography*. Edited by Deborah H. Drake, Rod Earle, and Jennifer Sloan, 307–25. New York: Palgrave Macmillan, 2015.
Barth, Karl. *The Epistle to the Romans*. Translated by Edwyn C. Hoskyns. London: Oxford University Press, 1933.
Barth, Karl. *Die Kirchliche Dogmatik* II/1. Zollikon: Verlag der Evangelischen Buchhandlung, 1942.
Barth, Karl. *Die Kirchliche Dogmatik* IV/1. Zollikon: Evangelischer Verlag, 1953.
Barth, Karl. *Church Dogmatics* IV/1. Translated by Geoffrey W. Bromiley. Edinburgh: T&T Clark, 1956.
Barth, Karl. "The Word of God and the Task of the Ministry." In *The Word of God and the Word of Man*. Translated by Douglas Horton, 183–217. New York: Harper Torchbooks, 1957.
Barth, Karl. *Church Dogmatics* IV/3.1. Translated by Geoffrey W. Bromiley. Edinburgh: T&T Clark, 1961.
Barth, Karl. *Church Dogmatics* IV.3.2: *The Doctrine of Reconciliation*. Edited by Geoffrey W. Bromiley and Thomas F. Torrance. Edinburgh: T&T Clark, 1962.
Barth, Karl. *Call for God: New Sermons from Basel Prison*. London: SCM Press, 1967.
Barth, Karl. *Church Dogmatics* IV/4. Translated by Geoffrey W. Bromiley. Edinburgh: T&T Clark, 1969.
Barth, Karl. *Deliverance to the Captives*. Eugene: Wipf & Stock Publishers, 1978.
Barth, Karl. "Die Übeltäter mit ihm, Lukas 23,33 (1957)." In *Predigten 1954–1967, Gesamtausgabe*. Edited by Hinrich Stoevesandt, 84–93. Zurich, Zurich Canton: Theologischer Verlag, 1979.
Barth, Karl. "Ich lebe, und ihr werdet leben, Johannes 14,19 (1955)." In *Predigten 1954–1967, Gesamtausgabe*. Edited by Hinrich Stoevesandt, 23–30. Zurich, Zurich Canton: Theologischer Verlag, 1979.
Barth, Karl. *Letters: 1961–1968*. Edited by Jurgen Fangmeier and Hinrich Stoevesandt. Translated by Geoffrey A. Bromiley. Grand Rapids: William B. Eerdmans Publishing, 1981.

Barth, Karl. "Freedom for Community." In *Theology and Sexuality: Classic and Contemporary Reading*. Edited by Eugene F. Rogers, Jr., 114–15. New York: Blackwell Publishing, 2002.
Barth, Karl. *Barth in Conversation: Volume 1, 1959–1962*. Edited by Eberhard Busch. Louisville: Westminster John Knox Press, 2017.
Barton, Susan. *Internment in Switzerland during the First World War*. London: Bloomsbury Academic, 2019.
Bennett, Jamie. "Insider Ethnography or the Tale of the Prison Governor's New Clothes." In *The Palgrave Handbook of Prison Ethnography*. Edited by Deborah H. Drake, Rod Earle, and Jennifer Sloan, 289–306. New York: Palgrave Macmillan, 2015.
Berger, Dan. *Captive Nation: Black Prison Organizing in the Civil Rights Era*. Chapel Hill: University of North Carolina Press, 2014.
Bibi Khan, Khatija. "Erykah Badu and the teachings of the nation of Gods and Earths." *Muziki* 9, no. 2 (2012): 80–9.
Biehl, João. *Vita: Life in a Zone of Social Abandonment*. Berkeley: University of California Press, 2005.
Blagg, Harry, and Thalia Anthony. "'Stone Walls do not a Prison make': Bare Life and the Carceral Archipelago in Colonial and Postcolonial Societies." In *Human Rights and Incarceration*. Edited by Elizabeth Stanley, 257–83. London: Palgrave MacMillan, 2018.
Bloch, Stefano, and Enrique Alan Olivares-Pelayo. "Carceral geographies from inside prison gates: The micro-politics of everyday racialisation." *Antipode* 53, no. 5 (2021): 1319–38.
Blunt, Jason Denis. "Hyperarousal: The critical determinant of post-trauma sequelae." PhD dissertation, 2016.
Boomershire, Amelia C. *A Breath of Fresh Air: Biblical Storytelling with Prisoners*. Eugene: Cascade Books, 2017.
Braman, Donald. *Doing Time on the Outside: Incarceration and Family Life in Urban America*. Ann Arbor: University of Michigan Press, 2007.
Bretherton, Luke. *A Primer in Christian Ethics: Christ and the Struggle to Live Well*. Cambridge: Cambridge University Press, 2023.
Briere, John, Natacha Godbout, and Colin Dias. "Cumulative trauma, hyperarousal, and suicidality in the general population: A path analysis." *Journal of Trauma & Dissociation* 16, no. 2 (2015): 153–69.
Buden, Jennifer C., Alicia G. Dugan, Sara Namazi, Tania B. Huedo Medina, Martin G. Cherniack, and Pouran D. Faghri. "Work characteristics as predictors of correctional supervisors' health outcomes." *Journal of Occupational and Environmental Medicine/American College of Occupational and Environmental Medicine* 58, no. 9 (2016): 325–34.
Bureau of Justice Assistance. "Prison Rape Elimination Act (PREA)—An Overview." Accessed on January 27, 2023. https://bja.ojp.gov/program/prea/overview.
Busch, Eberhard. *Karl Barth: His Life from Letters and Autobiographical Texts*. Translated by John Bowden. Eugene: Wipf & Stock Publishers, 1976.
Cadge, Wendy. *Paging God: Religion in the Halls of Medicine*. Chicago: University of Chicago Press, 2012.
Campbell, Douglas. "Chronology." In *T&T Clark Handbook to the Historical Paul*. Edited by Ryan S. Schellenberg and Heidi Wendt. Edinburgh: T&T Clark, 2022.
Campbell, Douglas A. "Mass incarceration: Pauline problems and pauline solutions." *Interpretation* 72, no. 3 (2018): 282–92.

WORKS CITED

Carson, E. Ann, PhD and Rich Kluckow, DSW. "Correctional populations in the United States, 2021—statistical tables." February 2023. NCJ 305542. *Bureau of Justice Statistics*: Washington, DC (2023).

Cloud, David H., Ernest Drucker, Angela Browne, and Jim Parsons. "Public health and solitary confinement in the United States." *American Journal of Public Health* 105, no. 1 (2015): 18–26.

Conover, Ted. *Newjack: Guarding Sing Sing*. New York: Vintage Books, 2000.

Cooperstein, M. Allan. "Correction officers: The forgotten police force." *Pennsylvania Psychology Quarterly* 61, no. 5 (2001): 7–23.

Cox, Kendall Walser. *Prodigal Christ: A Parabolic Theology*. Waco: Baylor University Press, 2022.

Creswell, John W., and J. David Creswell. *Research Design: Qualitative, Quantitative, and Mixed Methods Approaches, Fifth Edition*. London: Sage Publications, 2018.

Curran, Dean. "The organized irresponsibility principle and risk arbitrage." *Critical Criminology* 26 (4) (2018): 595–10.

Davis, Angela. *Are Prisons Obsolete?* New York: Seven Stories Press, 2003.

DeAmicis, Albert. "A real tragedy: Suicide by correctional officer." *American Jails* 30, no. 1 (March/April 2016): 26–30.

DeCou, Jessica. "The First Community: Barth's American Prison Tour." In *Karl Barth and the Making of Evangelical Theology: A Fifty-Year Perspective*. Edited by Clifford B. Anderson and Bruce L. McCormack, 67–90. Grand Rapids: William B. Eerdmans, 2015.

Diken, Bülent, and Carsten Bagge Laustsen. "Zones of indistinction: Security, terror, and bare life." *Space and Culture* 5, no. 3 (2002): 290–307.

Doty, Madeline Z. *Society's Misfits*. New York: Century Co, 1916.

Drake, Deborah H., Rod Earle, and Jennifer Sloan, eds. *The Palgrave Handbook of Prison Ethnography*. New York: Palgrave Macmillan, 2015.

Driskill, Gerald W.C., Alexandra Arjannikova, and John Meyer. "A dialectic analysis of a community forum on faith: The 'most segregated' or separated hour?" *Journal of Applied Communication Research* 42, no. 4 (2014): 477–96.

Dubler, Joshua. *Religious Life in an American Prison*. New York: Farrar, Strauss, and Giroux, 2013.

Dubler, Joshua, and Vincent W. Lloyd. *Break Every Yoke: Religion, Justice, and the Abolition of Prisons*. Oxford: Oxford University Press, 2020.

Duff, Raymond Anthony, Lindsay Farmer, Sandra Marshall, and Victor Tadros. *The Trial on Trial: Volume 3: Towards a Normative Theory of the Criminal Trial*. Oxford: Bloomsbury Publishing, 2007.

Erzen, Tanya. *God in Captivity: The Rise of Faith-Based Prison Ministries in the Age of Mass Incarceration*. Boston: Beacon Press, 2017.

Fiddes, Paul S. "Salvation." In *Oxford Handbook of Systematic Theology*. Edited by John B. Webster, Kathryn Tanner, and Iain Torrance, 176–96. Oxford: Oxford University Press, 2007.

Finn, Peter. "Correctional officer stress-a cause for concern and additional help." *Federal Probation* 62 (1998): 65.

Finney, Caitlin, Erene Stergiopoulos, Jennifer Hensel, Sarah Bonato, and Carolyn S. Dewa. "Organizational stressors associated with job stress and burnout in correctional officers: A systematic review." *BMC Public Health* 13 (2013): 1–13.

Fisher, Mickie L., and Julie J. Exline. "Moving toward self-forgiveness: Removing barriers related to shame, guilt, and regret." *Social and Personality Psychology Compass* 4, no. 8 (2010): 548–58.

Fong, Edmund. *Obedience from First to Last: The Obedience of Jesus Christ in Karl Barth's Doctrine of Reconciliation*. Eugene: Pickwick Publications, 2020.

Fossion, Pierre, Christophe Leys, Chantal Kempenaers, Stephanie Braun, Paul Verbanck, and Paul Linkowski. "Beware of multiple traumas in PTSD assessment: The role of reactivation mechanism in intrusive and hyper-arousal symptoms." *Aging & Mental Health* 19, no. 3 (2015): 258–63.

Foucault, Michel. *Discipline and Punish: The Birth of Prisons*. Translated by Alan Sheridan. New York: Vintage Books, 1977.

Freedman, David Noel. "Divine commitment and human obligation: The covenant theme." *Interpretation* 18, no. 4 (1964): 419–31.

Frevert, Ute. *The Politics of Humiliation: A Modern History*. Oxford: Oxford University Press, 2020.

Fritz, Charlotte, Leslie B. Hammer, Frankie Guros, Brittnie R. Shepherd, and David Meier. "On guard: The costs of work-related hypervigilance in the correctional setting." *Occupational Health Science* 2, no. 1 (2018): 67–82.

Gardell, Mattias. "White Racist Religions in the United States: From Christian Identity to Wolf Age Pagans." In *Controversial New Religions*, 1st edn. Edited by James R. Lewis, and Jesper Aagaard Petersen, 387–422. New York, 2004; online edn, Oxford Academic, May 1, 2006. https://doi.org/10.1093/019515682X.003.0018, accessed April 13, 2025.

Gerbarg, Patricia, Richard Brown, Chris Streeter, Martin Katzman, and Monica Vermani. "Breath practices for survivor and caregiver stress, depression, and post-traumatic stress disorder: Connection, co-regulation, compassion." *OBM Integrative and Complementary Medicine* 4, no. 3 (2019): 1–31.

Gilliard, Dominique DuBois. *Rethinking Incarceration: Advocating for Justice That Restores*. Downers Grove: IVP Books, 2018.

Gilmore, Ruth Wilson. *Golden Gulag: Prisons, Surplus, Crisis, and Opposition in Globalizing California*. Berkeley: University of California Press, 2007.

Goffman, Alice. *On the Run*. Chicago: University of Chicago Press, 2014.

Graber, Jennifer. *The Furnace of Affliction: Prisons & Religion in Antebellum America*. Chapel Hill: University of North Carolina Press, 2011.

Guido, Maria Grazia. "Trauma-Narrative Analysis at the Level of Text Structure." In *English as a Lingua Franca in Migrants' Trauma Narratives*, 85–112. London: Palgrave Macmillan, 2018.

Guild, Sonny. "The ministry of presence: A biblical view." *Leaven* 2, no. 2 (1992): 4–7.

Haley, Sarah. *No Mercy Here: Gender, Punishment, and the Making of Jim Crow Modernity*. Chapel Hill: University of North Carolina Press, 2016.

Hall, Stephen T. "A working theology of prison ministry." *Journal of Pastoral Care & Counseling* 58, no. 3 (2004): 169–78.

Hallet, Michael, Joshua Hays, Byron Johnson, Sung Jang, and Grant Duwe. *The Angola Prison Seminary: Effects of Faith-Based Ministry on Identity Transformation, Desistance, and Rehabilitation*. New York: Routledge, 2017.

Hanson, Rick with Richard Mendius. *Buddha's Brain: The Practical Neuroscience of Happiness, Love, and Wisdom*. Oakland: New Harbinger Publications, 2009.

Hargaden, Kevin. "Prison chaplaincy in the age of Covid-19." *Theology* 123, no. 5 (2020): 337–45.

Harris, Darcy L., and Tashel C. Bordere. *Handbook of Social Justice in Grief and Loss: Exploring Diversity, Equity, and Inclusion*. New York: Routledge, 2016.

Hendry, Chris. "Incarceration and the tasks of grief: A narrative review." *Journal of Advanced Nursing* 65, no. 2 (2009): 270–8.

Herman, Judith. *Trauma and Recovery: The Aftermath of Violence—From Domestic Abuse to Political Terror*. New York: Basic Books, 1992.

Hicks, Allison M. "Role fusion: The occupational socialization of prison chaplains." *Symbolic Interaction* 31, no. 4 (2008): 400–21.

Hicks, Allison M. "Learning to watch out: Prison chaplains as risk managers." *Journal of Contemporary Ethnography* 41, no. 6 (2012): 636–67.

Hinton, Elizabeth. *From the War on Poverty to the War on Crime: The Making of Mass Incarceration in America*. Cambridge: Harvard University Press, 2016.

Holm, Neil. "Practising the ministry of presence in chaplaincy." *Journal of Christian Education* 3 (2009): 29–42.

Hubbard Jr, Robert L. "Chaplaincy: Incarnation in action." *The Covenant Quarterly* 73, no. 3–4 (2015): 3–13.

Hunt, Katie. "Bereavement behind bars: Prison and the grieving process." *Prison Service Journal* 254 (2021): 17–23.

Jablonksi, Scott. "Making Christ Present: Ministry of presence calls us to bring God to the lives of others." *The Priest* (December 2018): 11–15.

Jernigan, Homer L. "Clinical pastoral education: Reflections on the past and future of a movement." *Journal of Pastoral Care & Counseling* 56, no. 4 (2002): 377–92.

Jobe, Sarah. "The monstrosity of God made flesh." *Journal of Reformed Theology* 13, no. 3–4 (2019): 238–56.

Johnson, Keith L. *The Essential Karl Barth: A Reader and Commentary*. Grand Rapids: Baker Academic, 2019.

Jones, Ashby. "The 'Perp Walk' debate: Prejudicial or legit?" *The Wall Street Journal*, June 19, 2008.

Jueckstock, Joel A., and Klye J. Vlach. "Claiming a substantive view of presence: The significance of the pastor's self." *The Covenant Quarterly* 73, no. 3–4 (2015): 30–9.

Kerman, Piper. *Orange Is the New Black: My Year in a Women's Prison*. New York: Spiegel and Grau, 2016.

Kimble, Matthew, Mariam Boxwala, Whitney Bean, Kristin Maletsky, Jessica Halper, Kaleigh Spollen, and Kevin Fleming. "The impact of hypervigilance: Evidence for a forward feedback loop." *Journal of Anxiety Disorders* 28, no. 2 (2014): 241–5.

Koonz, Mark. "The old question of Barth's universalism: An examination with reference to Tom Greggs and TF Torrance." *Theology in Scotland* 18, no. 2 (2011): 33–46.

Korn, Deborah L. "EMDR and the treatment of complex PTSD: A review." *Journal of EMDR Practice and Research* 3, no. 4 (2009): 264–78.

Larsson, Göran. "The five percenters: Islam, Hip Hop and the gods of New York by Michael Muhammad Knight." *Alternative Spirituality and Religion Review* 1, no. 1 (2010): 91–3.

Lassiter, Luke Eric. *The Chicago Guide to Collaborative Ethnography*. Chicago: The University of Chicago Press, 2005.

Leach, Raelene M., Teresa Burgess, and Chris Holmwood. "Could recidivism in prisoners be linked to traumatic grief? A review of the evidence." *International Journal of Prisoner Health* 4, no. 2 (2008): 104–19.

Leber, Annedore. *Conscience in Revolt: Sixty-Four Stories of Resistance in Germany 1933–45*. London: Valentine, Mitchell & Co., 1957.

Lee, Jin, Robert Henning, and Martin Cherniack. "Correction workers' burnout and outcomes: A bayesian network approach." *International Journal of Environmental Research and Public Health* 16, no. 2 (2019): 282.

Lee, Junsoo, Paul Pecorino, and Anne-Charlotte Souto. "A comparison of the female and male racial disparities in imprisonment." *Journal of Economics, Race, and Policy* 6, no. 2 (2023): 102–25.

Lee, Simon J. Craddock. "In a secular spirit: Strategies of clinical pastoral education." *Health Care Analysis* 10 (December 2002): 339–56.

Levad, Amy. *Redeeming a Prison Society: A Liturgical and Sacramental Response to Mass Incarceration*. Minneapolis: Fortress Press, 2014.

Levine, Peter A. *In an Unspoken Voice: How the Body Releases Trauma and Restores Goodness*. Berkeley: North Atlantic Books, 2010.

Lofstrom, Magnus, Brandon Martin, and Steven Raphael. "Effect of sentencing reform on racial and ethnic disparities in involvement with the criminal justice system: The case of California's proposition 47." *Criminology & Public Policy* 19, no. 4 (2020): 1165–207.

Logan, James Samuel. *God Punishment? Christian Moral Practice and U.S. Imprisonment*. Grand Rapids: William B. Eerdmans Publishing, 2008.

Mauer, Marc. "Thinking about prison and its impact in the twenty-first century." *Ohio St. J. Crim. L.* 2 (2004): 607.

McCorkel, Jill. *Breaking Women: Gender, Race, and the New Politics of Imprisonment*. New York: New York University Press, 2013.

McLennan, Rebecca M. *The Crisis of Imprisonment: Protest, Politics, and the Making of the American Penal State, 1776–1941*. Cambridge: Cambridge University Press, 2008.

Menakem, Resmaa. *My Grandmother's Hands: Racialized Trauma and the Pathway to Mending Our Hearts and Bodies*. Las Vegas: Central Recovery Press, 2017.

Miller, Reuben Jonathan. *Halfway Home: Race, Punishment, and the Afterlife of Mass Incarceration*. Boston: Little, Brown, 2021.

Miller-mclemore, Bonnie J. "Revisiting the living human web: Theological education and the role of clinical pastoral education." *Journal of Pastoral Care & Counseling* 62, no. 1–2 (2008): 3–18.

Mobley, Aaron W. *Fear No Evil: A Guide for Prison Chaplaincy*. Manchester: Aaron W. Mobley, 2017.

Mogul, Joey L., Andrea J. Ritchie, and Kay Whitlock. *Queer (In)Justice: The Criminalization of LGBT People in the United States*. Boston: Beacon Press, 2012.

Moore, Robert. "Reinventing ethnopoetics." *Journal of Folklore Research: An International Journal of Folklore and Ethnomusicology* 50, no. 1–3 (2013): 13–39.

Morin, Karen M. "Carceral space: Prisoners and animals." *Antipode* 48, no. 5 (2016): 1317–36.

Myers Jr, Samuel L., William J. Sabol, and Man Xu. *The Determinants of Declining Racial Disparities in Female Incarceration Rates, 2000–2015*. 2018. Working paper available at: https://www.prisonpolicy.org/scans/thedeterminantsofdecliningracialdisparities.pdf.

National Institute of Justice, Justice Department. "Correctional Officer Safety and Wellness Literature Synthesis". *Government. Justice Department*, December 31, 2016. https://www.govinfo.gov/app/details/GOVPUB-J28-PURL-gpo84572.

Nuruddin, Yusuf. "The five percenters: A teenage nation of gods and earths." In *Muslim Communities in North America*. Edited by Yvonne Yazbeck Haddad and Jane Idleman Smith, 109–32. Albany, NY: State University of New York Press, 1994.

O'Donnell, Shannon. *Finding Grace Within*. Tacoma: Pilgrim Spirit Communications, 2018.

Oshinksy, David M. *Worse than Death: Parchman Farm and the Ordeal of Jim Crow Justice*. New York: Free Press Paperbacks, 1997.

Paget, Naomi K., and Janet R. McCormack. *The Work of the Chaplain*. Valley Forge: Judson Press, 2006.

Pennel Jr., Joe E. *The Gift of Presence: A Guide to Helping Those Who Suffer*. New York City: Abingdon Press, 2010.

Pew Research Center. "Religion in prisons—A 50 state survey of prison chaplains." March 2, 2012. https://www.pewresearch.org/religion/2012/03/22/prison-chaplains-exec/.

Philip, M. NourbeSe. *Zong!* Middletown: Wesleyan University Press, 2008.

Poelchau, Harald. *Die letzen Stunden, Erinnerungen des Gefängnispfarrers*. Berlin: Volk und Welt, 1949.

Pollard, John. "Skinhead culture: The ideologies, mythologies, religions and conspiracy theories of racist skinheads." *Patterns of Prejudice* 50, no. 4–5 (2016): 398–419.

Porges, Stephen W. *The Pocket Guide to the Polyvagal Theory: The Transformative Power of Feeling Safe*. New York: W.W. Norton, 2017.

Press, Eyal. *Dirty Work: Essential Jobs and the Hidden Toll of Inequality in America*. New York: Farrar, Straus and Giroux, 2021.

Price, Joshua. *Prisons and Social Death*. New Brunswick: Rutgers University Press, 2015.

Quashie, Kevin. *The Sovereignty of Quiet: Beyond Resistance in Black Culture*. Piscataway: Rutgers University Press, 2012.

Ramelli, Ilaria. "Christian soteriology and christian platonism: Origen, gregory of nyssa, and the biblical and philosophical basis of the doctrine of apokatastasis." *Vigiliae Christianae* 61, no. 3 (2007): 313–56.

Ramelli, Ilaria. *The Christian Doctrine of Apokatastasis: A Critical Assessment from the New Testament to Eriugena*. Leiden: Brill, 2013.

Ranciere, Jacques. "Who is the subject of the rights of man?" *South Atlantic Quarterly* 103, no. 2–3 (2004): 297–310.

Richie, Beth E. *Arrested Justice: Black Women, Violence and America's Prison Nation*. New York: NYU Press, 2012.

Rittel, Horst W.J., and Melvin M. Webber. "Dilemmas in a general theory of planning." *Policy Sciences* 4, no. 2 (1973): 155–69.

Rittel, Horst W.J., and Melvin M. Webber. "Wicked problems." *Man-Made Futures* 26, no. 1 (1974): 272–80.

Roehrkasse, Alexander F., and Christopher Wildeman. "Lifetime risk of imprisonment in the United States remains high and starkly unequal." *Science Advances* 8, no. 48 (2022): eabo3395.

Rotelle, John E. *The Works of Saint Augustine*, Sermons, Part 3, Vol. 7. Translated by Edmund Hill, O.P. Hyde Park: New City Press, 1993.

Rothman, David J. *Conscience and Convenience: The Asylum and Its Alternatives in Progressive America*. Boston: Little Brown, 1980.

Rothschild, Babette with Marjorie L. Rand. *Help for the Helper: The Psychophysiology of Compassion Fatigue and Vicarious Trauma*. New York: W.W. Norton, 2006.

Schellenberg, Ryan S. *Abject Joy: Paul, Prison, and the Art of Making Do*. Oxford: Oxford University Press, 2021.

Schwartz, Martin. "Karl Barth in the penitentiary." Translated by Joseph Longarino. 1968. Available at https://barth.ptsem.edu/preaching-in-the-basel-prison/.

Schwartz, Martin. "Karl Barth in der Strafanstalt." *Kirchenblatt für die reformierte Schweiz* 125 (1969): 210–13.

Scott, David. "Walking amongst the Graves of the Living: Reflections about Doing Prison Research from an Abolitionist Perspective." In *The Palgrave Handbook of Prison Ethnography*. Edited by Deborah H. Drake, Rod Earle, and Jennifer Sloan, 40–58. New York: Palgrave Macmillan, 2015.

Sehested, Nancy Hastings. *Marked for Life: A Prison Chaplain's Story*. Maryknoll: Orbis Books, 2019.

Shabad, Peter. "Owing and being owed: Shame and responsibility toward the other." *Psychoanalytic Dialogues* 32, no. 4 (2022): 389–404.

Sharpe, Christina. *In the Wake: On Blackness and Being*. Durham: Duke University Press, 2016.

Skarbek, David. *The Social Order of the Underworld: How Prison Gangs Govern the American Penal System*. Oxford: Oxford University Press, 2014.

Skotnicki, Andrew. *Religion and the Development of the American Penal System*. Lanham: University Press of America, 2000.

Skotnicki, Andrew. *Conversion and the Rehabilitation of the Penal System: A Theological Re-Reading of Criminal Justice*. Oxford: Oxford University Press, 2019.

Smith, Peter Scharff. "The effects of solitary confinement on prison inmates: A brief history and review of the literature." *Crime and Justice* 34, no. 1 (2006): 441–528.

Soering, Jens. *The Convict Christ: What the Gospel Says about Criminal Justice*. Maryknoll: Orbis Books, 2006.

Sommer, Benjamin D. *The Bodies of God and the World of Ancient Israel*. Cambridge: Cambridge University Press, 2009.

Sossin, K. Mark, and Jan Charone-Sossin. "Embedding: Co-regulation within therapeutic process: Lessons from development: Response to 'Co-regulated interactions: Implications for Psychotherapy: Paper by Stanley Greenspan.'" *Journal of Infant, Child, and Adolescent Psychotherapy* 6, no. 3 (2007): 259–79.

Spillers, Hortense J. *Black, White, and in Color: Essays on American Literature and Culture*. Chicago: University of Chicago Press, 2003.

Stack, Steven J., and Olga Tsoudis. "Suicide risk among correctional officers: A logistic regression analysis." *Archives of Suicide Research* 3, no. 3 (1997): 183–6.

Stahl, Ronit Y. *Enlisting Faith: How the Military Chaplaincy Shaped Religion and State in Modern America*. Cambridge: Harvard University Press, 2017.

Stevenson, Bryan. *Just Mercy: A Story of Justice and Redemption*. New York: Spiegel and Grau, 2014.

Stokes, Janet. "Ministry of presence and presence of the spirit in pastoral visitation." *Journal of Pastoral Care* 53, no. 2 (1999): 191–9.

Stout, Taylor G. "The costs of religious accommodation in prisons." *Virginia Law Review* 96, no. 5 (2010): 1201–39.

Sullivan, Winnifred Fallers. *Prison Religion: Faith-Based Reform and the Constitution*. Princeton: Princeton University Press, 2009.

Sullivan, Winnifred Fallers. *A Ministry of Presence: Chaplaincy, Spiritual Care, and the Law*. Chicago: University of Chicago Press, 2014.

Sundt, Jody L., Harry R. Dammer, and Francis T. Cullen. "The role of the prison chaplain in rehabilitation." *Journal of Offender Rehabilitation* 35 (2002): 59–86.

Sweeney, Megan. *Reading Is My Window: Books and the Art of Reading in Women's Prisons*. Chapel Hill: University of North Carolina Press, 2010.

Tavernise, Sabrina. "White Americans are dying younger as drug and alcohol abuse rises." *New York Times*, April 20, 2016, A11.

Taylor, Mark Lewis. *The Executed God: The Way of the Cross in Lockdown America, Second Edition*. Minneapolis: Fortress Press, 2015.

Taylor, Shelley E., Laura Cousino Klein, Brian P. Lewis, Tara L. Gruenewald, Regan A.R. Gurung, and John A. Updegraff. "Biobehavioral responses to stress in females: Tend-and-befriend, not fight-or-flight." *Psychological Review* 107, no. 3 (2000): 411.

Thomas, Jim, and Barbara H. Zaitzow. "Conning or conversion? The role of religion in prison coping." *The Prison Journal* 86, no. 2 (2006): 242–59.

Tietz, Christiane. *Karl Barth: A Life in Conflict*. Oxford: Oxford University Press, 2021.

Tolgensbakk, Ida. "'More or less word for Word' Barbro Klein and transcription as analytical craft." *Western Folklore* 79, no. 4 (2020): 453–68.

Tseng, Shao Kai. "Condemnation and universal salvation: Karl Barth's 'reverent agnosticism' revisited." *Scottish Journal of Theology* 71, no. 3 (2018): 324–38.

Van Der Kolk, Bessel. *The Body Keeps the Score: Brain, Mind, and Body in the Healing of Trauma*. New York: Penguin Books, 2014.

Von Moltke, Freya, and Helmuth James. *Last Letters: The Prison Correspondence 1944–1945*. Translated by Shelley Frisch. New York: New York Review Books, 2019.

Wakefield, Sara, and Christopher Wildeman. *Children of the Prison Boom: Mass Incarceration and the Future of American Inequality*. Oxford: Oxford University Press, 2013.

Western, Bruce. *Punishment and Inequality in America*. New York: Russell Sage Foundation, 2006.

Whipp, Margaret. "Embedding Chaplaincy: Integrity and Presence." In *A Christian Theology of Chaplaincy*. Edited by John Caperon, Andrew Todd, and James Walters, 101–18. London: Jessica Kingsley Publishers, 2018.

Zimmerman, Wolf-Dieter, and Ronald Gregor Smith. *I Knew Dietrich Bonhoeffer*. Translated by Käthe Gregor Smith. New York: Harper & Row Publishers, 1966.

INDEX OF SUBJECTS, AUTHORS, AND BIBLICAL TEXTS

abyss 31, 39, 104
Advocate, the 51, 53, 191, 217
advocating 64, 113–14, 116, 129, 179, 183
Agamben, Giorgio, *Homo Sacer* 200
apokatastasis panton 161, 216–19
atonement 13, 41, 73, 92, 178
    penal substitutionary 97, 209, 212

Barth, Karl 13, 30–6, 73–4, 160
    and Eberhard Busch 32, 99, 171
    as prisoners of war 32–6
    Call for God 99–100, 139, 194, 198–9
    Church Dogmatics IV/1 13, 73, 107, 127, 159–60, 164, 167
    Church Dogmatics IV/3.1 36, 139–40, 164, 218
    Church Dogmatics IV/3.2 5, 31, 160, 164
    "courage of despair" 61
    "Criminals with Him, The" 35, 164
    Easter Sermon at Basel Prison 194, 198–9, 216
    Epistle to the Romans 33, 43, 60, 63–4, 171, 173
    first Christian community 42, 144, 166
    Good Friday sermon 1957 35, 160, 164
    in the German carceral context 32–6, 98–100
    in the Swiss carceral context 33, 59–61, 138–40
    see also reconciliation, Doctrine of
Basel Prison 32, 34–6, 99, 138–9, 164, 194, 198–9, 216, 218
Bible
    Genesis
        15:4–6 105
        15:7 105
    Isaiah
        7:14 48
        61:1–3 38, 54, 72, 94, 168
    Matthew
        1:19 126
        1:23 46
        3:15 126
        9:3 126
        11:19 126
        12:10 96
        25:26 37
        25:31–46 53, 168
        26:55 159
        26:65 126
        27:3–5 159
        27:37 159
        27:38 126
        27:51 94
        27:57–60 180
        27:62–66 181
        28:11–15 181
    Mark
        3:1–6 96
        3:21–22 126
        5:1–20 38
        15:22–37 104, 157–8
        15:40 181
        16:1 181
    Luke
        4:9–10 96
        4:14–30 38, 54, 94–5, 168
        7:1–10 86, 95
        8:2 181
        8:26–40 38, 96
        10:25–37 95
        14:1–33 111
        15:11–24 127–8

15:30–32 127
19:1–10 38
19:45–48 97
20:19 97
22:52 159
23:33 164–5
24:13–35 189
John
  1:1–18 46
  1:29 126
  4:1–42 95
  5:1–18 96
  6 96
  7:12 126
  7:32 39, 96
  8:1–11 49–50
  8:59 38
  9:1–6 38
  10:10 54
  10:31 38
  11:57 39
  14:26–27 191
  18:36 39
  18:40 159
  20:1–11 181, 195
  20:15 195
  20:19–21 191
Acts
  3:12–13 217
  3:15 217
  3:21–22 217
Romans
  6:8 36, 166
2 Corinthians
  5:21 126–7, 133
  13:4 168–9
Galatians
  3:13 126
Colossians
  2:13b-15 170, 217
Biehl, João, *Vita: Life in a Zone of Social Abandonment* 39
burial (handling of bodies after death) 8, 71, 181–2, 189, 195
Busch, Eberhard, *Karl Barth* 32, 59, 98–100, 171

Cadge, Wendy, *Paging God: Religion in the Halls of Medicine* 8

Campbell, Douglas, "Mass Incarceration" 209
carceral death 12, 143–4, 169–72, 182–4, 194, 200, 219
  assault 110–11, 146
  and the death of loved ones 153
  and prison chaplaincy 54, 59, 142, 178–81, 193, 203, 208
  and salvation 159, 161–4, 199
  Covid-19, 145, 173
  criminals executed with Jesus 166
  execution 154–60
  in serving a life sentence 187–8
  of Jesus 39–42, 142, 159, 191, 202, 212
  suicide 147–52, 159–60
chaplaincy
  carceral complicity 14, 17, 23, 64–5, 123, 160
  crisis response in 50, 113
  history of 14–17
  "middle way" 86, 91, 102
  ministry of presence 39–41, 44–6, 49, 52, 54, 68–71, 104
  navigating policy 27–8, 45, 65–71, 89, 109–11, 123, 146
  relating to prison staff 45–6, 54, 62, 84, 109, 113–14, 116, 119, 122
  risk management 113
  risks of 9, 12–13, 38, 41, 45, 59, 65, 71–2, 90–1, 106, 111–14, 130, 135, 142
  self-care 112, 133, 136–8, 189
Chaplains
  Chap Lin 52–4, 66–7, 85–6, 94–5, 104–6, 122, 129, 146, 159, 161
  Chaplain Armstrong 109–11, 208
  Chaplain Barrett 119, 129, 179
  Chaplain Camillus 78–9, 153
  Chaplain Dismas 50–1, 53, 147
  Chaplain Floating 44, 114, 116, 122, 129, 136, 207
  Chaplain Harald 9, 107, 109, 125, 154–5, 163, 201–2, 208
  Chaplain King 37, 73, 91, 102, 143, 149–51, 203–4

INDEX OF SUBJECTS, AUTHORS, AND BIBLICAL TEXTS 231

Chaplain Levine 43, 81–2, 103, 117–19, 129, 189–94
Chaplain Love 6, 48, 54, 57–9, 61, 103, 137–8, 179, 189, 200, 219
Chaplain Maverick 45–6, 75–6, 85, 88–9, 102, 173–8, 180–1, 198
Chaplain Moise 48, 76–7, 119–20, 129, 141
Chaplain Moses 68–9, 107, 135, 209–10, 212
Chaplain Murray 69, 173, 184–8, 197–8, 213–14
Chaplain Noa 67–9, 77–8, 81, 83–4, 97, 179
Chaplain Schwartz *see under* Schwartz, Martin
Chaplain Stanford 119
Chaplain Tyrone 48, 62, 87–8, 130–2, 136
Deacon Joe 9–11, 13, 40, 163
Father Katy 64, 70–1, 76
Father Michael 37, 47–8, 53, 61–2, 86–90, 96–7, 145
Poelchau, Harald 122–5
congregation, free 164, 207
congregation, incarcerated 30, 82, 99, 139, 141–2, 198, 214–15
criminal justice system 32, 34, 161, 169, 211–12, 215

death work 7–9, 12–14, 40
de-criminalization 171
dialectics 39, 53, 91, 171. *see also* God's yes and God's no
Dubler, Joshua, *Down in the Chapel* 15–16, 75
Dubler, Joshua, and Vincent W. Lloyd, *Break Every Yoke* 16, 57, 75

Easter 145, 172, 194–9, 201, 216. *see also* Barth, Easter Sermons at Basel Prison
Erzen, Tanya, *God in Captivity* 14
ethnography 18
    collaborative 24, 28
    ethnopoetics 5, 7, 11, 18–20
    participant-observation 24–7, 30

prison ethnographies 24–5, 202–3
scholar-practitioner 26
Eucharist (Communion) 47, 52, 70–1, 190, 192–3, 207

First Amendment *(US Constitution)* 12, 43
Foucault, Michel, *Discipline and Punish* 15

gangs
    presence in prison worship 80, 83–4, 89–90
    race and 18, 87, 89, 174
    violence 153
gender *see under* prison, women in
Gethsemane and Golgotha 36, 140, 161, 167, 169–70, 215
Gilliard, Dominique DuBois, *Rethinking Incarceration* 113, 208
God-forsaken 13, 52, 104, 129, 140, 160–3, 167, 169–70, 178, 186
God's Judgement 61, 63–5, 70–2, 92–4, 97
God's Yes and God's No 39–40, 71, 93, 97, 216. *see also* dialectics
Good Friday 194, 199, 214–15. *see also* Barth Good Friday sermon 1957
Graber, Jennifer, *The Furnace of Affliction* 14, 209
grief (grief work) 6–8, 145, 180, 182–4, 186, 188

Herman, Judith, *Trauma and Recovery* 18, 57, 143
holy (in unholy things) 104, 160–1, 219
hypervigilance 31, 41, 109. *see also* trauma

"impossible possibility" 45, 72, 102, 219
interfaith ministry 12, 23–4, 44, 74–5, 78, 80, 101

Jesus Christ 13, 102, 165, 199, 217
    as incarcerated Christ 34, 36, 41, 93, 96, 98, 140

as Judged Judge 32, 74, 92–4, 99, 102, 106, 160
as Prodigal Son 112, 127–8, 134, 140
as sin-offering (made sin) 41, 112, 127, 129, 133–5, 138, 140
crucifixion of 127, 160, 162, 165, 181, 194, 199
incarnation of 41, 44–6, 52, 93, 127, 138, 192–3, 208
resurrection of 42, 60, 171–3, 188, 191, 194–5, 197–8, 201–2, 209

krisis (crisis) 41, 59–61, 63–4, 100

Lassiter, Luke Eric, *The Chicago Guide to Collaborative Ethnography* 24
Levine, Peter A., *In an Unspoken Voice* 57

Malinowski, Bronislaw 26
Menakem, Resmaa, *My Grandmother's Hands* 191
metabolizing violence 209
"mini-wars" 64–5

nervous system 9, 49, 190–3

penal substitutionary atonement *see under* atonement
persistent life 42, 179–81, 188–9, 194–5, 197–200, 212, 217
post-traumatic stress disorder 41, 138
Press, Eyal, *Dirty Work* 30
prison 14–18
    administration 14–15, 17, 176
    industrial complex 14, 16, 58
    ministry 21, 168, 218
    policy 59, 68, 70, 109, 146, 200
    preaching in 85, 164, 187
    riot 173–8
    women in 15, 22, 25–6, 28–30
    worship services 68–9, 75–6, 78–85, 123, 183

racism 22, 79–80, 85, 87, 89, 104, 191
reconciliation 93, 102–6, 166, 170, 215

of divisions 41, 74, 112
Doctrine of 2, 34, 73, 91–2, 98, 127, 133, 138, 160, 166, 218
resurrection 172, 178–80, 197, 200–3. *see also* Jesus Christ, resurrection of
risking death 38, 41, 106, 112, 163

sacrament of presence 168
salvation (soteriology) 13, 125, 159–69, 208–10, 212, 214–19
    as lifework 72, 106, 112
    inhabiting 41, 112, 129, 133–4, 163, 214
    life-after-death 13, 24, 40–2, 188
    practical (carceral) soteriology 1–4, 35–41, 207, 209
    see also atonement
    see also reconciliation
Schellenberg, Ryan S., *Abject Joy* 180
Schwartz, Martin 32, 138–9, 216, 218
Sharpe, Christina, *In the Wake* 42, 179, 182–4
sin 63. *see also* Jesus Christ, as sin-offering
sin-sick 41, 112, 127–30, 133–5, 138, 142, 170
Soering, Jens, *The Convict Christ* 39, 50
solitary confinement 56, 117–18, 129
Stevenson, Bryan, *Just Mercy* 15
Sullivan, Winnifred Fallers, *A Ministry of Presence* 12

Taylor, Mark Lewis, *The Executed God* 98, 162
transfiguration 195, 197, 201
trauma 18, 57, 79, 103, 121, 147–8, 191–2
    avoidance 112–13, 117, 119, 122
    effect on the body 23, 118, 190
    effect on sleep 31, 130

recovery 12, 18, 129, 154
secondary 117, 141, 154, 189
transference 130–2
see also hypervigilance

Van Der Kolk, Bessel, *The Body Keeps the Score* 118

wake work 42, 179–84, 187–9, 194–5, 207
wicked problems 74, 80–1, 90, 94, 101–4
worship *see under* prison, worship services
zones of social abandonment 39, 140

INDEX OF STORIES AND TRANSCRIPTS

acting in the opposite spirit 50
Angola Prison's three cemeteries 180

backlog of grief 6
Barth's testimony on being in court 99
Barth's visit with P. and gladness instead of sadness 216
"Behold what you are. Become what you receive" 207
Black radicalism in the Nation of Gods and Earth 90
breaking policy to deliver sacramental wine 70
breaking policy to greet at the chapel door 68
breaking policy to hug a person in grief 69
breaking policy to touch a dying man 66
breaking policy to touch a grieving person 67

Chap Mav on navigating CO's 85
Chap Mav telling the story of a riot, being interrupted by his son 173
Chaplain Harald is gassed 107
Chaplain Love on "doing something big" 58
Chaplain Love and the SWAT Team 54
Chaplain Moses on shame 209
Chaplain Murray on "why did this happen to me?" and a Leonard Cohen lyric 185
Chaplain Murray's "image of remembering" 184
Chaplain Murray's rituals: memorials, meeting with lifers, writing in the sand 187
Chaplain Watson and bottled water miracle 195
connecting incarnational theology with neuroscience 191

Deacon Joe's heart attack 9
Death by Assault: One Incarcerated Person 146
Death by COVID: Thirty Incarcerated Persons and One Officer 145
Death by Execution: Nineteen Incarcerated Men 154
Death by Execution: One Incarcerated Man 157
Death by Shooting: One Child of an Incarcerated Father 153
Death by Suicide: One Incarcerated Person 147
Death by Suicide: A Prison Staff Person Every Other Year for Ten Years 149
diversity and prison choirs 81

early prison ethnographers get arrested 25
escaping prison through imagination 78
expanding the definition of hygiene in an evacuation 197

Father Michael on reporting abuse 62

"God is standing over there, pointing at me and laughing" 213

INDEX OF STORIES AND TRANSCRIPTS

"God with a gavel and a big, black robe" 211
Good Friday 2016, Stations of the Cross through the eyes of incarcerated women 214

Harald Poelechau in Nazi Germany 122

Jesus Christ 13, 102, 165, 199, 217
Jesus Christ beyond color 75
Jesus Christ kicking the money changers out of the temple 83
Jesus Christ on the cross in the middle 91

locking up scissors 110

Mary Magdalene doesn't recognize Jesus at the tomb 195
Ministry through a cell door 47
Minister together as if Jesus himself were physically present 37
Music and freedom 78

nightmares transformed into dreams 201
not knowing how he coped 136

not leaving even when prison takes its toll 142
not managing transference in pastoral care 137
not reporting prison abuse 115

practical (carceral) soteriology 1–4, 36–41, 207, 209
prison chapels and church in the free world 77

rounds on solitary confinement 117

"Sgt. Wilson's suicide" 5
Standing between divided sacrifices 105

The middle way is exhausting 103
there is no godforsaken place 52

welcoming officers like Jesus healed the centurion's slave 86
white nationalism and Odinism 88
woman caught in the act of adultery 49
writing carceral deaths and good news on a sheet of butcher paper 200

yelling at "Hanging of the Greens" 120